Theodoric the Goth

STATUE OF THEODORIC IN THE CHURCH
OF THE FRANCISCANS AT INNSBRUCK
(TOMB OF MAXIMILIAN).

Theodoric the Goth

King of the Ostrogoths, Regent of the Visigoths
& Viceroy of the Eastern Roman Empire,
in the 4th Century A.D.

Thomas Hodgkin

LEONAUR

Theodoric the Goth
King of the Ostrogoths, Regent of the Visigoths & Viceroy
of the Eastern Roman Empire, in the 4th Century A.D.
by Thomas Hodgkin

First published under the title
Theodoric the Goth

Leonaur is an imprint of Oakpast Ltd

Copyright in this form © 2011 Oakpast Ltd

ISBN: 978-0-85706-735-7 (hardcover)
ISBN: 978-0-85706-736-4 (softcover)

http://www.leonaur.com

Publisher's Notes

Contents

Preface

In the following pages I have endeavoured to portray the life and character of one of the most striking figures in the history of the Early Middle Ages, Theodoric the Ostrogoth. The plan of the series, for which this volume has been prepared, does not admit of minute discussion of the authorities on which the history rests. In my case the omission is of the less consequence, as I have treated the subject more fully in my larger work, *Italy and her Invaders*, and as also the chief authorities are fully enumerated in that book which is or ought to be in the library of every educated Englishman and American, Gibbon's *History of the Decline and Fall of the Roman Empire*.

The fifth and sixth centuries do not supply us with many materials for pictorial illustrations, and I do not know where to look for authentic and contemporary representations of the civil or military life of Theodoric and his subjects. We have, however, a large and interesting store of nearly contemporary works of art at Ravenna, illustrating the ecclesiastical life of the period, and of these the engraver has made considerable use. The statue of Theodoric at Innsbruck, a representation of which is included with the illustrations, possesses, of course, no historical value, but is interesting as showing how deeply the memory of Theodoric's great deeds had impressed itself on the mind of the Middle Ages.

And here I will venture on a word of personal reminiscence. The figure of Theodoric the Ostrogoth has been an interesting and attractive one to me from the days of my boyhood. I well remember walking with a friend on a little hill (then silent and lonely, now covered with houses), looking down on London, and discussing European politics with the earnest interest which young debaters bring to such a theme. The time was in those dark days which followed the revolutions of 1848, when it seemed as if the life of the European nations would be crushed out under the heel of returned and triumphant despotism. For Italy especially, after the defeat of Novara, there seemed no hope. We talked of Mazzini, Cavour, Garibaldi, and discussed the possibility—which then seemed so infinitely remote—that there might one day be a free and united Italy. We both agreed that the vision was a beautiful one, but was there any hope of it ever becoming a reality? My friend thought there was not, and argued from the fact of Italy's divided condition in the past, that she must always be divided in the future. I, who was on the side of hope, felt the weakness of my position, and was driven backward through the centuries, till at length I took refuge in the reign of Theodoric. Surely, under the Ostrogothic king, Italy had been united, strong, and prosperous. My precedent was a remote one, but it was admitted, and it did a little help my cause.

Since that conversation more than forty years have passed. The beautiful land is now united, free, and mighty; and a new generation has arisen, which, though aware of the fact that she was not always thus, has but a faint conception how much blood and how many tears, what thousands of broken hearts and broken lives went to the winning of Italy's freedom. I, too, with fuller knowledge of her early history, am bound to confess that her unity even under Theodoric was not so complete as I then imagined it. But still, as I have more than once stated in the following pages, I look upon his reign as a time full of seeds of promise for Italy and the world, if only these seeds might have had time to germinate and ripen into harvest. Closer study has only confirmed me in the opinion that the Ostrogothic kingdom was one of the great "Might-have-beens" of History.

Thomas Hodgkin.

Newcastle-On-Tyne,
January 25, 1891.

Introduction

Theodoric the Ostrogoth is one of those men who did great deeds and filled a large space in the eyes of their contemporaries, but who, not through their own fault, but from the fact that the stage of the world was not yet ready for their appearance, have failed to occupy the very first rank among the founders of empires and the moulders of the fortunes of the human race.

He was born into the world at the time when the Roman Empire in the West was staggering blindly to ruin, under the crushing blows inflicted upon it by two generations of barbarian conquerors. That Empire had been for more than six centuries indisputably the strongest power in Europe, and had gathered into its bosom all that was best in the civilisation of the nations that were settled round the Mediterranean Sea. Rome had given her laws to all these peoples, had, at any rate in the West, made their roads, fostered the growth of their cities, taught them her language, administered justice, kept back the barbarians of the frontier, and for great spaces of time preserved "the Roman peace" throughout their habitations.

Doubtless there was another side to this picture: heavy taxation, corrupt judges, national aspirations repressed, free peasants sinking down into hopeless bondage. Still it cannot be denied that during a considerable part of its existence the Roman Empire brought, at least to the western half of Europe, material prosperity and enjoyment of life which it had not known before, and which it often looked back to with vain regrets when the great Empire had fallen into ruins. But now, in the middle of the fifth century, when Theodoric was born amid the rude splendour of an Ostrogothic palace, the unquestioned ascendancy of Rome over the nations of Europe was a thing of the past.

There were still two men, one at the Old Rome by the Tiber, and

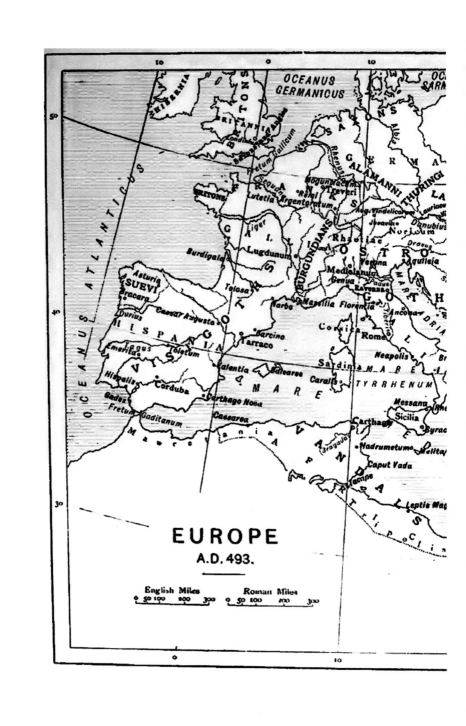

EUROPE

A.D. 493.

English Miles
0 50 100   200   300

Roman Miles
0 50 100   200   300

the other at the New Rome by the Bosphorus, who called themselves August, Pious, and Happy, who wore the diadem and the purple shoes of Diocletian, and professed to be joint lords of the universe. Before the Eastern Augustus and his successors there did in truth lie a long future of dominion, and once or twice they were to recover no inconsiderable portion of the broad lands which had formerly been the heritage of the Roman people.

But the Roman Empire at Rome was stricken with an incurable malady. The three sieges and the final sack of Rome by Alaric (410) revealed to the world that she was no longer "*Roma Invicta*," and from that time forward every chief of Teutonic or Sclavonic barbarians who wandered with his tribe over the wasted plains between the Danube and the Adriatic, might cherish the secret hope that he, too, would one day be drawn in triumph up the Capitolian Hill, through the cowed ranks of the slavish citizens of Rome, and that he might be lodged on the Palatine in one of the sumptuous palaces which had been built long ago for "the lords of the world."

Thus there was everywhere unrest and, as it were, a prolonged moral earthquake. The old order of things was destroyed, and none could forecast the shape of the new order of things that would succeed to it. Something similar has been the state of Europe ever since the great French Revolution; only that her barbarians threaten her now from within, not from without. The social state which had been in existence for centuries, and which had come to be accepted as if it were one of the great ordinances of nature, is either menaced or is actually broken up, and how the new democracy will rearrange itself in the seats of the old civilisation the wisest statesman cannot foretell.

But to any "shepherd of his people," barbarian or Roman, who looked with foreseeing eye and understanding heart over the Europe of the fifth century, the duty of the hour was manifest. The great fabric of the Roman Empire must not be allowed to go to pieces in hopeless ruin. If not under Roman *Augusti*, under barbarian kings bearing one title or another, the organisation of the Empire must be preserved. The barbarians who had entered it, often it must be confessed merely for plunder, were remaining in it to rule, and they could not rule by their own unguided instincts. Their institutions, which had answered well enough for a half-civilised people, leading their simple, primitive life in the clearings of the forest of Germany, were quite unfitted for the complicated relations of the urban and social life of the Mediterranean lands.

There is one passage[1] which has been quoted almost to weariness, but which it seems necessary to quote again, in order to show how an enlightened barbarian chief looked upon the problem with which he found himself confronted, as an invader of the Empire. Ataulfus, brother-in-law and successor of Alaric, the first capturer of Rome, "was intimate with a certain citizen of Narbonne, a grave, wise, and religious person who had served with distinction under Theodosius, and often remarked to him that in the first ardour of his youth he had longed to obliterate the Roman name and turn all the Roman lands into an Empire which should be, and should be called, the Empire of the Goths, so that what used to be commonly known as Romania should now be 'Gothia,' and that he, Ataulfus, should be in the world what Cæsar Augustus had been. But now that he had proved by long experience that the Goths, on account of their unbridled barbarism, could not be induced to obey the laws, and yet that, on the other hand, there must be laws, since without them the Commonwealth would cease to be a Commonwealth, he had chosen, for his part at any rate, that he would seek the glory of renewing and increasing the Roman name by the arms of his Gothic followers, and would be remembered by posterity as the restorer of Rome, since he could not be its changer."

This conversation will be found to express the thoughts of Theodoric the Ostrogoth, as well as those of Ataulfus the Visigoth, Theodoric also, in his hot youth, was the enemy of the Roman name and did his best to overturn the Roman State. But he, too, saw that a nobler career was open to him as the preserver of the priceless blessings of Roman civilisation, and he spent his life in the endeavour to induce the Goths to copy those laws, without which a Commonwealth ceases to be a Commonwealth. In this great and noble design he failed, as has been already said, because the times were not ripe for it, because a continuation of adverse events, which we should call persistent ill-luck if we did not believe in an overruling Providence, blighted and blasted his infant state before it had time to root itself firmly in the soil. None the less, however, does Theodoric deserve credit for having seen what was the need of Europe, and pre-eminently of Italy, and for having done his best to supply that need.

The great work in which he failed was accomplished three centuries later by Charles the Frank, who has won for himself that place in the first rank of world-moulders which Theodoric has missed. But we

---

1. Orosius *Histor.*, vii., 43.

may fairly say that Theodoric's designs were as noble and as statesman-like as those of the great Emperor Charles, and that if they had been crowned with the success which they deserved, three centuries of needless barbarism and misery would have been spared to Europe.

CHAPTER 1

Theodoric's Ancestors

Towards the end of the second century of the Christian Era a great confederacy of Teutonic nations occupied those vast plains in the south of Russia which are now, and have been for more than a thousand years, the homes of Sclavonic peoples. These nations were the Ostrogoths, the Visigoths, and the Gepidæ. Approximately we may say that the Ostrogoths (or East Goths) dwelt from the Don to the Dnieper, the Visigoths (or West Goths) from the Dnieper to the Pruth, and the Gepidæ to the north of both, in the district which has since been known as Little Russia. These three nations were, as has been said, Teutons, and they belonged to that division of the Teutonic race which is called Low-German; that is to say, that they were more nearly allied to the Frisians, the Dutch, and to our own Saxon forefathers than they were to the ancestors of the modern Swabian, Bavarian, and Austrian.

They worshipped Odin and Thunnor; they wrote the scanty records of their race in Runic characters; they were probably chiefly a pastoral folk, but may have begun to practise agriculture in the rich cornlands of the Ukraine. They were essentially a monarchic people, following their kings, whom they believed to be sprung from the seed of gods, loyally to the field, and shedding their blood with readiness at their command; but their monarchy was of the early Teutonic type, always more or less limited by the deliberations of the great armed assembly of the nation, which (in some tribes at least) was called the Folc-mote or the Folc-thing; and there were no strict rules of hereditary succession, the crown being elective but limited in practice to the members of one ruling and heaven-descended family.

This family, sprung from the seed of gods, but ruling by the popular will over the Ostrogothic people, was known as the family of the

Amals. It is true that the divine and exclusive prerogatives of the family have been somewhat magnified by the minstrels who sang in the courts of their descendants, for there are manifest traces of kings ruling over the Ostrogothic people, who are not included in the Amal genealogy. Still, as far as we can peer through the obscurity of the early history of the people, we may safely say that there was no other family of higher position than the Amals, and that gradually all that consciousness of national life and determination to cherish national unity, which among the Germanic peoples was inseparably connected with the institution of royalty, centred round the race of the divine Amala.

The following is the pedigree of this royal clan, as given by the historian of the Goths,[1] and with those epithets which the secretary of Theodoric[2] attached to the names of some of the ancestors of his lord. (The names of those who wore the crown are marked in italics.)

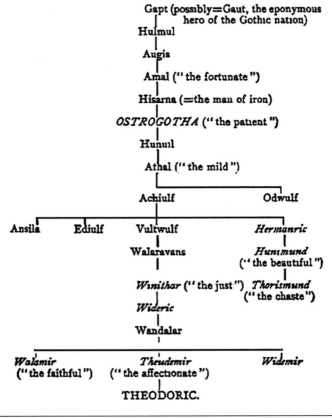

Gapt (possibly = Gaut, the eponymous hero of the Gothic nation)
|
Hulmul
|
Augis
|
Amal ("the fortunate")
|
Hisarna (= the man of iron)
|
OSTROGOTHA ("the patient")
|
Hunuil
|
Athal ("the mild")
|
Achiulf — Odwulf
|
Ansila — Ediulf — Vultwulf — *Hermanric*
|
Walaravans — *Hunimund* ("the beautiful")
|
Winithar ("the just") *Thorismund* ("the chaste")
|
Wideric
|
Wandalar
|
Walamir ("the faithful") — *Theudemir* ("the affectionate") — *Widemir*
|
THEODORIC.

2. Jordanes.
3. Cassiodorus.

These fifteen generations, which should carry back the Amal ancestry four hundred and fifty years, or almost precisely to the Christian Era, seem to have marked the utmost limit to which the memory of the Gothic heralds, aided by the songs of the Gothic minstrels, could reach. The forms of many of the names, the initial "Wala" and "Theude," the terminal "wulf," "mir," and "mund" will be at once recognised as purely Teutonic, recalling many similar names in the royal lines of the Franks, the Visigoths and the Vandals, and the West Saxons.

In the great, loosely knit confederacy which has been described as filling the regions of Southern Russia in the third and fourth centuries of our era, the predominant power seems to have been held by the Ostrogothic nation. In the third century, when a succession of weak ephemeral emperors ruled and all but ruined the Roman State, the Goths swarmed forth in their myriads, both by sea and land, to ravage the coast of the Euxine and the Ægean, to cross the passes of the Balkans, to make their desolating presence felt at Ephesus and at Athens. Two great Emperors of Illyrian origin, Claudius and Aurelian, succeeded, at a fearful cost of life, in repelling the invasion and driving back the human torrent.

But it was impossible to recover from the barbarians Trajan's province of Dacia, which they had overrun, and the emperors wisely compromised the dispute by abandoning to the Goths and their allies all the territory north of the Danube. This abandoned province was chiefly occupied by the Visigoths, the Western members of the confederacy, who for the century from 275 to 375 were the neighbours, generally the allies, by fitful impulses the enemies, of Rome. With Constantine the Great especially the Visigoths came powerfully in contact, first as invaders and then as allies (*fœderati*) bound to furnish a certain number of auxiliaries to serve under the eagles of the Empire.

Meanwhile the Ostrogoths, with their faces turned for the time northward instead of southward, were battling daily with the nations of Finnish or Sclavonic stock that dwelt by the upper waters of the Dnieper, the Don, and the Volga, and were extending their dominion over the greater part of what we now call Russia-in-Europe. The lord of this wide but most loosely compacted kingdom, in the middle of the fourth century, was a certain Hermanric, whom his flatterers, with some slight knowledge of the names held in highest repute among their Southern neighbours, likened to Alexander the Great for the magnitude of his conquests. However shadowy some of these conquests may appear in the light of modern criticism, there can be little doubt that the Visigoths owned his over-lordship, and that when Constantius and Julian were reigning in Constantinople, the greatest name over a wide extent of territory north of the Black Sea was that of Hermanric the Ostrogoth.

When this warrior was in extreme old age, a terrible disaster befell his nation and himself. It was probably about the year 374 that a horde of Asiatic savages made their appearance in the south-eastern corner of his dominions, having, so it is said, crossed the Sea of Azof in its shallowest part by a ford. These men rode upon little ponies of great speed and endurance, each of which seemed to be incorporated with its rider, so perfect was the understanding between the horseman, who spent his days and nights in the saddle, and the steed which he bestrode. Little black restless eyes gleamed beneath their low foreheads and matted hair; no beard or whisker adorned their uncouth yellow faces; the Turanian type in its ugliest form was displayed by these Mongolian sons of the wilderness. They bore a name destined to be of disastrous and yet also indirectly of most beneficent import in the history of the world; for these are the true shatterers of the Roman Empire. They were the terrible Huns.

Before the impact of this new and strange enemy the Empire of Hermanric—an Empire which rested probably rather on the reputation of warlike prowess than on any great inherent strength, military or political—went down with a terrible crash. Dissimilar as are the times and the circumstances, we are reminded of the collapse of the military systems of Austria and Prussia under the onset of the ragged Jacobins of France, shivering and shoeless, but full of demonic energy, when we read of the humiliating discomfiture of this stately Ostrogothic monarchy—doubtless possessing an ordered hierarchy of nobles, free warriors, and slaves—by the squalid, hard-faring and, so to say, democratic savages from Asia.

The death of Hermanric, which was evidently due to the Hunnish victory, is assigned by the Gothic historian to a cause less humiliating to the national vanity. The king of the Rosomones, "a perfidious nation," had taken the opportunity of the appearance of the savage invaders to renounce his allegiance, perhaps to desert his master treacherously on the field of battle. The enraged Hermanric, unable to vent his fury on the king himself, caused his wife, Swanhilda, to be torn asunder by wild horses to whom she was tied by the hands and feet. Her brothers, Sarus and Ammius, avenged her cruel death by a spear-thrust, which wounded the aged monarch, but did not kill him outright. Then came the crisis of the invasion of the Huns under their King Balamber. The Visigoths, who had some cause of complaint against Hermanric, left him to fight his battle without their aid; and the old king, in sore pain with his wound and deeply mortified by the incursion of the Huns, breathed out his life in the one hundred and tenth year of his age. All of which is probably a judicious veiling of the fact,[4] that the great Hermanric was defeated by the Hunnish invaders, and in his despair laid violent hands on himself.

The huge and savage horde rolled on over the wide plains of Russia. The Ostrogothic resistance was at an end; and soon the invaders were on the banks of the Dniester threatening the kindred nation of the Visigoths. Athanaric, "Judge" (as he was called) of the Visigoths, a brave, old soldier, but not a very skilful general, was soon out-manœuvred by these wild nomads from the desert, who crossed the rivers by unexpected fords, and by rapid night-marches turned the flank of his most carefully chosen positions. The line of the Dniester was abandoned; the line of the Pruth was lost. It was plain that the Visigoths, like their Eastern brethren, if they remained in the land, must bow their heads beneath the Hunnish yoke. To avoid so degrading a necessity, and if they must lose their independence, to lose it to the stately Emperors of Rome rather than to the chief of a filthy Tartar horde, the great majority of the Visigothic nation flocked southward through the region which is now called Wallachia, and, standing on the northern shore of the Danube, prayed for admission within the province of Mœsia and the Empire of Rome.

In 376 an evil hour for himself Valens, the then reigning Emperor of the East, granted this petition and received into his dominions the Visigothic fugitives, a great and warlike nation, without taking any proper precautions, on the one hand, that they should be disarmed, on the other, that they should be supplied with food for their present necessities and enabled for the future to become peaceful cultivators of the soil. The inevitable result followed. Before many months had elapsed the Visigoths were in arms against the Empire, and under the leadership of their hereditary chiefs were wandering up and down through the provinces of Mœsia and Thrace, wresting from the terror-stricken provincials not only the food which the parsimony of Valens had failed to supply them with, but the treasures which centuries of peace had stored up in villa and unwalled town.

---

4. Mentioned by Ammianus Marcellinus.

In 378 they achieved a brilliant, and perhaps unexpected, triumph, defeating a large army commanded by the Roman Emperor Valens in person, in a pitched battle near Adrianople. Valens himself perished on the field of battle, and his unburied corpse disappeared among the embers of a Thracian hut which had been set fire to by the barbarians. That fatal day (August 9, 378) was admitted to be more disastrous for Rome than any which had befallen her since the terrible defeat of Cannæ, and from it we may fitly date the beginning of that long process of dissolution, lasting, in a certain sense, more than a thousand years, which we call the Fall of the Roman Empire.

In this long tragedy the part of chief actor fell, during the first act, to the *Visigothic nation*. With their doings we have here no special concern. It is enough to say that for one generation they remained in the lands south of the Danube, first warring against Rome, then, by the wise policy of their conqueror, Theodosius, incorporated in her armies under the title of *fœderati* and serving her in the main with zeal and fidelity. In 395[5] a Visigothic chief, Alaric by name, of the god-descended seed of Balthæ, was raised upon the shield by the warriors of his tribe and hailed as their king. His elevation seems to have been understood as a defiance to the Empire and a re-assertion of the old national freedom which had prevailed on the other side of the Danube.

At any rate the rest of his life was spent either in hostility to the Empire or in a pretence of friendship almost more menacing than hostility. He began by invading Greece and penetrated far south into the Peloponnesus. He then took up a position in the province of Illyricum—probably in the countries now known as Bosnia and Servia—from which he could threaten the Eastern or Western Empire at pleasure. Finally, with the beginning of the fifth century after Christ, he descended into Italy, and though at first successful only in ravage, in the second invasion he penetrated to the very heart of the Empire. His three sieges of Rome, ending in the awful event of the capture and sack of the Eternal City in 410, are events in the history of the world with which every student is familiar. Only it may be remarked that the word awful, which is here used designedly, is not meant to imply that the loss of life was unusually large or the cruelty of the captors outrageous; in both respects Alaric and his Goths would compare favourably with some generals and some armies making much higher pretensions to civilisation.

Nor is it meant that the destruction of the public buildings of the city was extensive. There can be little doubt that Paris, on the day after the suppression of the "Commune" in 1871, presented a far greater appearance of desolation and ruin than Rome in 410, when she lay trembling in the hand of Alaric. But the bare fact that Rome herself, the Roma Æterna, the Roma Invicta of a thousand coins of a hundred emperors,—Rome, whose name for centuries on the shores of the Mediterranean had been synonymous with worldwide dominion,— should herself be taken, sacked, dishonoured by the presence of a flaxen-haired barbarian conqueror from the north, was one of those events apparently so contrary to the very course of Nature itself, that the nations which heard the tidings, many of them old and bitter enemies of Rome, now her subjects and her friends, held their breath with awe at the terrible recital.

Alaric died shortly after his sack of Rome, and after a few years of aimless fighting his nation quitted Italy, disappearing over the northwestern Alpine boundary to win for themselves new settlements by the banks of the Garonne and the Ebro. Their leader was that Ataulfus whose truly statesmanlike reflections on the unwisdom of destroying the Roman Empire and the necessity of incorporating the barbarians with its polity have been already quoted. There, in the south-western corner of Gaul and the northern regions of Spain, we must for the present leave the Western branch of the great Gothic nationality, while our narrative returns to its Eastern representatives.

---

5. Probably. Some historians put the date in 382, others in 400.

The Might of Attila

For eighty years the power of the Ostrogoths suffered eclipse under the shadow of Hunnish barbarism. As to this period we have little historical information that is of any value. We hear of resistance to the Hunnish supremacy vainly attempted and sullenly abandoned. The son and the grandson of Hermanric figure as the shadowy heroes of this vain resistance. After the death of the latter (King Thorismund) a strange story is told us of the nation mourning his decease for forty years, during all which time they refused to elect any other king to replace him whom they had lost. There can be little doubt that this legend veils the prosaic fact that the nation, depressed and dispirited under the yoke of the conquering Huns, had not energy or patriotism enough to choose a king; since almost invariably among the Teutons of that age, kingship and national unity flourished or faded together.

At length, towards the middle of the fifth century after Christ, the darkness is partially dispelled, and we find the Ostrogothic nation owning the sovereignty of three brothers sprung from the Amal race, but not direct descendants of Hermanric, whose names are Walamir, Theudemir, and Widemir. "Beautiful it was," says the Gothic historian, "to behold the mutual affection of these three brothers, when the admirable Theudemir served like a common soldier under the orders of Walamir; when Walamir adorned him with the crown at the same time that he conveyed to him his orders; when Widemir gladly rendered his services to both of his brothers."[1] Theudemir, the second in this royal brotherhood, was the father of our hero, Theodoric.

The three Ostrogothic brethren, kings towards their own countrymen, were subjects—almost, we might say, servants—of the wide-rul-

---

1. This is a partly paraphrastic and conjectural translation of a very obscure sentence of Jordanes.

ing king of the Huns, who was now no longer one of those forgotten chiefs by whom the conquering tribe had been first led into Europe, but ATTILA, a name of fear to his contemporaries and long remembered in the Roman world. He, with his brother Bleda, mounted the barbarian throne in the year 433, and after twelve years the death of Bleda (who was perhaps murdered by order of his brother) left Attila sole wielder of the forces which made him the terror of the world. He dwelt in rude magnificence in a village not far from the Danube, and his own special dominions seem to have pretty nearly corresponded with the modern kingdom of Hungary.

But he held in leash a vast confederacy of nations—Teutonic, Sclavonic, and what we now call Turanian,—whose territories stretched from the Rhine to the Caucasus, and he is said to have made "the isles of the Ocean," which expression probably denotes the islands and peninsulas of Scandinavia, subject to his sway. Neither, however, over the Ostrogoths nor over any of the other subject nations included in this vast dominion are we to think of Attila's rule as an organised, all-permeating, assimilating influence, such as was the rule of a Roman Emperor. It was rather the influence of one great robber-chief over his freebooting companions. The kings of the Ostrogoths and Gepidæ came at certain times to share the revelries of their lord in his great log-palace on the Danubian plain; they received his orders to put their subjects in array when he would ride forth to war, and woe was unto them if they failed to stand by his side on the day of battle; but these things being done, they probably ruled their own peoples with little interference from their over-lord.

The Teutonic members of the confederacy, notably the Ostrogoths and the kindred tribe of Gepidæ seem to have exercised upon the court and the councils of Attila an influence not unlike that wielded by German statesmen at the court of Russia during the last century. The Huns, during their eighty years of contact with Europe, had lost a little of that utter savageness which they brought with them from the Tartar deserts. If they were not yet in any sense civilised, they could in some degree appreciate the higher civilisation of their Teutonic subjects. A Pagan himself, with scarcely any religion except some rude cult of the sword of the war-god, Attila seems never to have interfered in the slightest degree with the religious practices of the Gepidæ or the Ostrogoths, the large majority of whom were by this time Christians, holding the Arian form of faith.

And not only did he not discourage the finer civilisation which he saw prevailing among these German subjects of his, but he seems to have had statesmanship enough to value and respect a culture which he did not share, and especially to have prized the temperate wisdom of their chiefs, when they helped him to array his great host of barbarians for war against the Empire.

From his position in Central Europe, Attila, like Alaric before him, was able to threaten either the Eastern or the Western Empire at pleasure. For almost ten years (440-450) he seemed to be bent on picking a quarrel with Theodosius II., the feeble and unwarlike prince who reigned at Constantinople. He laid waste the provinces south of the Danube with his desolating raids; he worried the Imperial Court with incessant embassies, each more exacting and greedy than the last (for the favour of the rude Hunnish envoy had to be purchased by large gifts from the Imperial Treasury); he himself insisted on the payment of yearly *stipendia* by the Emperor; he constantly demanded that these payments should be doubled; he openly stated that they were nothing else than tribute, and that the Roman Augustus who paid them was his slave.

These practices were continued until, in the year 450 the gentle Theodosius died. He was succeeded by his sister Pulcheria and her husband Marcian, who soon gave a manlier tone to the counsels of the Eastern Empire. Attila marked the change and turned his harassing attentions to the western state, with which he had always a sufficient number of pretexts for war ready for use. In fact he had made up his mind for war, and no concessions, however humiliating, on the part of Valentinian III., the then Emperor of the West, would have availed to stay his progress. Not Italy however, to some extent protected by the barrier of the Alps, but the rich cities and comparatively unwasted plains of Gaul attracted the royal freebooter. Having summoned his vast and heterogeneous army from every quarter of central and north-eastern Europe, and surrounded himself by a crowd of subject kings, the captains of his host, he set forward in the spring of 451 for the lands of the Rhine.

The trees which his soldiers felled in the great Hercynian forest of central Germany were fashioned into rude rafts or canoes, on which they crossed the Rhine; and soon the terrible Hun and his "horde of many-nationed spoilers" were passing over the regions which we now call Belgium and Lorraine in a desolating stream. The Huns, not only barbarians, but heathens, seem in this invasion to have been animated by an especial hatred to Christianity. Many a fair church of

Gallia Belgica was laid in ashes: many a priest was slain before the altar, whose sanctity was vain for his protection. The real cruelties thus committed are wildly exaggerated by the mythical fancy of the Middle Ages, and upon the slenderest foundations of historical fact arose stately edifices of fable, like the story of the Cornish Princess Ursula, who with her eleven thousand virgin companions was fabled to have suffered death at the hands of the Huns in the city of Cologne.

The barbarian tide was at length arrested by the strong walls of Orleans, whose stubborn defence saved all that part of Gaul which lies within the protecting curve of the Loire from the horrors of their invasion. At midsummer Attila and his host were retiring from the untaken city, and beginning their retreat towards the Rhine, a retreat which they were not to accomplish unhindered. The extremity of the danger from these utterly savage foes had welded together the old Empire and the new Gothic kingdom, the civilised and the half-civilised power, in one great confederacy, for the defence of all that was worth saving in human society.

The tidings of the approach of the Gothic king had hastened the departure of Attila from the environs of Orleans, and, perhaps about a fortnight later, the allied armies of Romans and Goths came up with the retreating Huns in "the Catalaunian plains" not far from the city of Troyes. The general of the Imperial army was Aëtius; the general and king of the Visigoths was Theodoric, a namesake of our hero. Both were capable and valiant soldiers. On the other side, conspicuous among the subject kings who formed the staff of Attila, were the three Ostrogothic brethren, and Ardaric, king of the Gepidæ. The loyalty of Walamir, the firm grasp with which he kept his master's secrets, and Ardaric's resourcefulness in counsel were especially prized by Attila.

And truly he had need of all their help, for, though it is difficult to ascertain with any degree of accuracy the numbers actually engaged (162,000 are said to have fallen on both sides), it is clear that this was a collision of nations rather than of armies, and that it required greater skill than any that the rude Hunnish leader possessed, to win the victory for his enormous host. After "a battle ruthless, manifold, gigantic, obstinate, such as antiquity never described when she told of warlike deeds, such as no man who missed the sight of that marvel might ever hope to have another chance of beholding,"[2] night fell upon the virtually defeated Huns. The Gothic king had lost his life, but Attila had lost the victory.

---

2. These are the words of the Gothic historian, Jordanes.

All night long the Huns kept up a barbarous dissonance to prevent the enemy from attacking them, but their king's thoughts were of suicide. He had prepared a huge funeral pyre, on which, if the enemy next day successfully attacked his camp, he was determined to slay himself amid the kindled flames, in order that neither living nor dead the mighty Attila might fall into the hands of his enemies. These desperate expedients, however, were not required. The death of Theodoric, the caution of Aëtius, some jealousy perhaps between the Roman and the Goth, some anxiety on the part of the eldest Gothic prince as to the succession to his father's throne,—all these causes combined to procure for Attila a safe but closely watched return into his own land.

The Battle of the Catalaunian plains (usually but not quite correctly called the Battle of Châlons) was a memorable event in the history of the Gothic race, of Europe, and of the world. It was a sad necessity which on this one occasion arrayed the two great branches of the Gothic people, the Visigoths under Theodoric, and the Ostrogoths under Walamir, in fratricidal strife against each other. For Europe the alliance between Roman and Goth, between the grandson of Theodosius, Emperor of Rome, and the successor of Alaric, the besieger of Rome, was of priceless value and showed that the great and statesmanlike thought of Ataulfus was ripening in the minds of those who came after him.

For the world, yes even for us in the nineteenth century, and for the great undiscovered continents beyond the sea, the repulse of the squalid and unprogressive Turanian from the seats of the old historic civilisation, was essential to the preservation of whatever makes human life worth living. Had Attila conquered on the Catalaunian plains, an endless succession of Jenghiz Khans and Tamerlanes would probably have swept over the desolated plains of Europe; Paris and Florence would have been even as Khiva and Bokhara, and the island of Britain would not have yet attained to the degree of civilisation reached by the peninsula of Corea.

In the year after the fruitless invasion of Gaul, Attila crossed the Julian Alps and entered Italy, intending (452) doubtless to rival the fame of Alaric by his capture of Rome, an operation which would have been attended with infinitely greater ruin to

the seven-hilled city's pride,

than any which she had sustained at the hands of the Visigothic leader. But the Huns, unskilful in siege work, were long detained before the walls of Aquileia, that great and flourishing frontier city, hitherto deemed impregnable, which gathered in the wealth of the Venetian province, and guarded the north-eastern approaches to Italy. At length by a sudden assault they made themselves masters of the city, which they destroyed with utter destruction, putting all the inhabitants to the sword, and then wrapping in fire and smoke the stately palaces, the wharves, the mint, the forum, the theatres of the fourth city of Italy.

The terror of this brutal destruction took from the other cities of Venetia all heart for resistance to the terrible invader. From Concordia, Altino, Padua, crowds of trembling fugitives walked, waded, or sailed with their hastily gathered and most precious possessions to the islands, surrounded by shallow lagoons, which fringed the Adriatic coast, near the mouths of the Brenta and Adige. There at Torcello, Burano, Rialto, Malamocco, and their sister islets, they laid the humble foundations of that which was one day to be the gorgeous and wide-ruling Republic of Venice.

Attila meanwhile marched on through the valley of the Po ravaging and plundering, but a little slackening in the work of mere destruction, as the remembrance of the stubborn defence of Aquileia faded from his memory. Entering Milan as a conqueror, and seeing there a picture representing the emperors of the Romans sitting on golden thrones, and the Scythian barbarians crouching at their feet, he sought out a Milanese painter, and bade the trembling artist represent him, Attila, sitting on the throne, and the two Roman Emperors staggering under sacks full of gold coin, which they bore upon their shoulders, and pouring out their precious contents at his feet.

This little incident helps us to understand the next strange act in the drama of Attila's invasion. To enjoy the luxury of humbling the great Empire, and of trampling on the pride of her statesmen, seems to have been the sweetest pleasure of his life. This mere gratification of his pride, the pride of an upstart barbarian, at the expense of the inheritors of a mighty name and the representatives of venerable traditions, was the object which took him into Italy, rather than any carefully prepared scheme of worldwide conquest.

Accordingly when that august body, the Senate of Rome, sent a consul, a *prefect*, and more than all a pope, the majestic and fitly-named Leo, to plead humbly in the name of the Roman people for peace, and to promise acquiescence at some future day in the most unreasonable of his demands, Attila granted the ambassadors an interview by the banks of the Mincio, listened with haughty tranquillity to their petition, allowed himself to be soothed and, as it were, magnetised by the words and gestures of the venerable pontiff, accepted the rich presents which were doubtless laid at his feet, and turning his face homewards recrossed the Julian Alps, leaving the Apennines untraversed and Rome unvisited.

Even in the act of granting peace Attila used words which showed that it would be only a truce, and that (452) if there were any failure to abide by any one of his conditions, he would return and work yet greater mischief to Italy than any which she had yet suffered at his hands. But he had missed the fateful moment, and the delight of standing on the conquered Palatine, and seeing the smoke ascend from the ruined City of the World, was never to be his. In the year after his invasion of Italy he died suddenly at night, apparently the victim of the drunken debauch with which the polygamous barbarian had celebrated the latest addition to the numerous company of his wives.

With Attila's death the might of the Hunnish Empire was broken. The great robber-camp needed the ascendancy of one strong chief-robber to hold it together, and that ascendancy no one of the multitudinous sons who emerged from the chambers of his *harem* was able to exert. Unable to agree as to the succession of the throne, they talked of dividing the Hunnish dominions between them, and in the discussions which ensued they showed too plainly that they looked upon the subject nations as their slaves, to be partitioned as a large household of such domestics would be partitioned among the heirs of their dead master.

The pride of the Teutons was touched, and they determined to strike a blow for the recovery of their lost freedom. Ardaric, king of the Gepidæ, so long the trusty counsellor of Attila, was prime mover in the revolt against his sons. A battle was fought by the banks of the river Nedao[3] between the Huns (with those subject allies who still remained faithful to them) and the revolted nations.

Among these revolted nations there can be but little doubt that the Ostrogoths held a high place, though the matter is not so clearly stated as we should have expected, by the Gothic historian, and even on his showing the glory of the struggle for independence was mainly Ardaric's. After a terrible battle the Gepidæ were victorious, and Ellak,

3. Situation unknown, except that it was in Pannonia, that is, probably in Hungary, somewhere between the Save and the Danube.

eldest son of Attila, with, it is said, thirty thousand of his soldiers, lay dead upon the field. "He had wrought a great slaughter of his enemies, and so glorious was his end," says Jordanes, "that his father might well have envied him his manner of dying."

The Battle of Nedao, whatever may have been the share of the Ostrogoths in the actual fighting, certainly brought them freedom. From this time the great Hunnish Empire was at an end, and there was a general resettlement of territory among the nations which had been subject to its yoke. While the Huns themselves, abandoning their former habitations, moved, for the most part, down the Danube, and became the humble servants of the Eastern Empire, the Gepidæ, perhaps marching southward occupied the great Hungarian plains on the left bank of the Danube, which had been the home of Attila and his Huns; and the Ostrogoths going westwards (perhaps with some dim notion of following their Visigothic kindred) took up their abode in that which had once been the Roman province of Pannonia, now doubtless known to be hopelessly lost to the Empire.

Pannonia, the new home of the Ostrogoths, was the name of a region, rectangular in shape, about two hundred miles from north to south and one hundred and sixty miles from east to west, whose northern and eastern sides were washed by the River Danube, and whose north-eastern corner was formed by the sudden bend to the south which that river makes, a little above Buda-Pest. This region includes Vienna and the eastern part of the Archduchy of Austria, Grätz, and the eastern part of the Duchy of Styria, but it is chiefly composed of the great corn-growing plain of Western Hungary, and contains the two considerable lakes of Balaton and Neusiedler See. Here then the three Ostrogothic brethren took up their abode, and of this province they made a kind of rude partition between them, while still treating it as one kingdom, of which Walamir was the head.

The precise details of this division of territory cannot now be recovered,[4] nor are they of much importance, as the settlement was of short duration. We can only say that Walamir and Theudemir occupied the two ends of the territory, and Widemir dwelt between them. What is most interesting to us is the fact that Theudemir's territory included Lake Balaton (or Platten See), and that his palace may very possibly have stood upon the shores of that noble piece of water,

---

4. Jordanes (Getica) says: "Valamer inter Scarniungam et Aquam Nigram fluvios, Thiudimer juxta lacum Pelsois, Vidimer inter utrosque manebat." It seems to be hopeless to determine what rivers are denoted by Scarniunga and Aqua Nigra.

which is forty-seven miles in length and varies from three to nine miles in width. To the neighbourhood of this lake, in the absence of more precise information, we may with some probability assign the birthplace and the childish home of Theodoric.[5]

5. Of course the location of Theudemir's palace on the actual shore of Lake Balaton can only be treated as a conjecture, but the pointed way in which Jordanes, in the passage last quoted, speaks of him as "*juxta lacuna Pelsois*," seems to make the conjecture a probable one. Some geographers have identified Pelso Lacus with the Neusiedler See, but apparently on insufficient grounds.

CHAPTER 3

Theodoric's Boyhood

The Ostrogoths had yet one or two battles to fight before they were quite rid of their old masters. The sons of Attila still talked of them as deserters and fugitive slaves, and a day came when Walamir found himself compelled to face a sudden inroad of the Huns. He had few men with him, and being taken unawares, he had no time to summon his brethren to his aid.

But he held his own bravely: the warriors of his nation had time to gather round him; and at last, after he had long wearied the enemy with his defensive tactics, he made a sudden onset, destroyed the greater part of the Hunnish army, and sent the rest scattered in hopeless flight far into the deserts of Scythia.[1]

Walamir at once sent tidings of the victory to his brother Theudemir. The messenger arrived at an opportune moment, for on that very day Erelieva, the unwedded wife of Theudemir, had given birth to a man-child. This infant, born on such an auspicious day and looked upon as a pledge of happy fortunes for the Ostrogothic nation, was named Thiuda-reiks (the people-ruler), a name which Latin historians, influenced perhaps by the analogy of Theodosius, changed into Theodoricus, and which will here be spoken of under the well-

---

1. Jordanes (cap. iii) says that the fugitive Huns "sought those parts of Scythia past which flow the streams of the river Dnieper which the Huns in their own tongue call '*Var*' (the river)." If this is correctly stated it is almost certain that it must describe some battle which happened *before* the great Western migration of the Ostrogoths, which was mentioned in the last chapter, for it would be impossible, if the Gepidæ were in Trans-danubian Hungary and the Ostrogoths in Pannonia that the Ostrogoths should have driven the Huns into the countries watered by the Dnieper. I am rather inclined to believe that this reference of the battle to an earlier period may be the correct explanation. But Danapri (Dnieper) may be only a blunder of Jordanes, who is often hopelessly wrong in his geography.

known form THEODORIC.[2]

It will be observed that I have spoken of Erelieva as the unwedded wife of Theudemir. The Gothic historian calls her his concubine,[3] but this word of reproach hardly does justice to her position. In many of the Teutonic nations, as among the Norsemen of a later century, there seems to have been a certain laxity as to the marriage rite, which was nevertheless coincident with a high and pure morality. It has been suggested that the severe conditions imposed by the Church on divorces may have had something to do with the peculiar marital usages of the Teutonic and Norse chieftains. Reasons of state might require Theudemir the Ostrogoth, or William Longsword the Norman, to ally himself some day with a powerful king's daughter, and therefore he would not go through the marriage rite with the woman, really and truly his wife, but generally his inferior in social position, who meanwhile governed his house and bore him children.

If the separation never came, and the powerful king's daughter never had to be wooed, she who was wife in all but name, retained her position unquestioned till her death, and her children succeeded without dispute to the inheritance of their father. The nearest approach to an illustration which the social usages of modern Europe afford, is probably furnished by the "morganatic marriages" of modern German royalties and serenities: and we might say that Theodoric was the offspring of such an union. Notwithstanding the want of strict legitimacy in his position, I do not remember any occasion on which the taunt of bastard birth was thrown in his teeth, even by the bitterest of his foes.

It would be satisfactory if we could fix with exactness the great Ostrogoth's birth-year, but though several circumstances point to 454 as a probable date, we are not able to define it with greater precision.[4]

The next event of which we are informed in the history of the

---

2. Jordanes wavers between Theodericus and Theodoricus. The Greek historians generally use the form θευδερίχος. German scholars seem to prefer Theoderich. As it is useless now to try to revert to the philologically correct Thiuda-reiks, I use that form of the name with which I suppose English readers to be most familiar—namely, Theodoric.

3. "*Ipso siquidem die Theodoricus ejus filius quamvis de Erelieva concubina, bonæ tamen spei natus est*" (Jordanes: Getica, 52.)

4. If there be any truth in the suggestion made above, that the Hunnish attack on Walamir was made before the Ostrogothic migration into Pannonia, the birth-year must be moved up to 452.

Ostrogothic nation, a war with the Eastern Empire, was one destined to exert a most important influence on the life of the kingly child, The Ostrogoths settling in Pannonia, one of the provinces of the Roman Empire, were in theory allies and auxiliary soldiers[5] of the emperor. Similar arrangements had been made with the Visigoths in Spain, with the Vandals in that very province of Pannonia, probably with many other barbarian tribes in many other provinces. There was sometimes more, sometimes less, actual truth in the theoretical relations thus established, and it was one which in the nature of things was not likely long to endure: but for the time, so long as the Imperial treasury was tolerably full and the barbarian allies tolerably amenable to control, the arrangement suited both parties.

In the case before us the position of the Ostrogoths in Pannonia was legalised by the alliance, and such portions of the political machinery of the Empire as might still remain were thereby placed at their disposal. The emperor, on the other hand, was able to boast of a province recovered for the Empire, which was now guarded by the broadswords of his loyal Ostrogoths against the more savage nations outside, who were ever trying to enter the charmed circle of the Roman State. But as the Ostrogothic *fœderati* were his soldiers, there was evidently a necessity that he must send them pay, and this pay, which was called wages when the Empire was strong, and tribute when it was weak, consisted, partly at any rate, of heavy chests of Imperial *aurei*,[6] sent as *strenae*[7] or New Year's presents, to the barbarian king and his chief nobles.

Now, about the year 461, the Emperor Leo (successor of the brave soldier Marcian), whether from a special emptiness in the Imperial treasury or from some other cause, omitted to send the accustomed *strenae* to the Ostrogothic brother-kings. Much disturbed at the failure of the *aurei* to appear, they sent envoys to Constantinople, who returned with tidings which filled the three palaces of Pannonia with the clamour of angry men. Not only were the *strenae* withheld, and likely to be still withheld, but there was another Goth, a low-born pretender, not of Amal blood, who was boasting of the title of *fœderatus* of the Empire, and enjoying the *strenae* which ought to come only to Amal kings and their nobles.

---

5. *Fœderati.*

6. The *solidus aureus*, the chief Imperial coin of this time, was worth about twelve shillings of our money.

7. The same word as the French *Étrennes*.

This man, who was destined to cross the path of our Theodoric through many weary years, was named like him Theodoric, and was surnamed Strabo (the squinter) from his devious vision, and son of Triarius, from his parentage. He was brother-in-law, or nephew, of a certain Aspar, a successful barbarian, who had mounted high in the Imperial service and had placed two emperors on the throne. It was doubtless through his kinsman's influence that the squinting adventurer had obtained a position in the court of the Roman Augustus so disproportioned to his birth, and so outrageous to every loyal Ostrogoth.

When the news of these insults to the lineage of the Amals reached Pannonia, the three brothers in fury snatched up their arms and laid waste almost the whole province of Illyricum. Then the emperor changed his mind, and desired to renew the old friendship. He sent an embassy bearing the arrears of the past-due *strenae*, those which were then again falling due, and a promise that all future *strenae* should be punctually paid. Only, as a hostage for the observance of peace he desired that Theudemir's little son, Theodoric, then just entering his eighth year, should be sent to Constantinople. The fact that this request or demand was made by the ostensibly beaten side, may make us doubt whether the humiliation of the Empire was so complete as the preceding sentences (translated from the words of the Gothic historian) would lead us to suppose.

Theudemir was reluctant to part with his first-born son, even to the great Roman Emperor. But his brother Walamir earnestly besought him not to interpose any hindrance to the establishment of a firm peace between the Romans and Goths. He yielded therefore, and the little lad, carried by the returning ambassadors to Constantinople, soon earned the favour of the emperor by his handsome face and his winning ways.[8]

Thus was the young Ostrogoth brought from his home in Pannonia, by the banks of lonely Lake Balaton, to the New Rome, the busy and stately city by the Bosphorus, the city which was now, more truly than her worn and faded mother by the Tiber, the "Lady of Kingdoms" the "Mistress of the World." Of the Constantinople which the boyish eyes of Theodoric beheld, scarcely a vestige now remains for the traveller to gaze upon. Let us try, therefore, to find a contemporary description. These are the words in which the visit of the Gothic chief

---

8. An expansion of the words of Jordanes, "*et quia puerulus elegans erat meruit gratiam imperialem habere.*"

Athanaric to that city about eighty years previously is described by Jordanes:

> Entering the royal city, and marvelling thereat, 'Lo! now I behold,' said he, 'what I often heard of without believing, the glory of so great a city.' Then turning his eyes this way and that, beholding the situation of the city and the concourse of ships, now he marvels at the long perspective of lofty walls, then he sees the multitudes of various nations like the wave gushing forth from one fountain which has been fed by divers springs, then he beholds the marshalled ranks of the soldiery. 'A God,' said he, 'without doubt a God upon Earth is the emperor of this realm, and whoso lifts his hand against him, that man's blood be on his own head.

Still can we behold "the situation of the city," that unrivalled situation which no map can adequately explain, but which the traveller gazes upon from the deck of his vessel as he rounds Seraglio Point, and the sight of which seems to bind together in one, two continents of space and twenty-five centuries of time. On his right hand Asia with her camels, on his left Europe with her railroads. Behind him are the Sea of Marmora and the Dardanelles, with their memories of Lysander and Ægospotami, of Hero, Leander, and Byron, with the throne of Xerxes and the tomb of Achilles, and farther back still the island-studded Archipelago, the true cradle of the Greek nation. Immediately in front of him is the Golden Horn, now bridged and with populous cities on both its banks, but the farther shore of which, where Pera and Galata now stand, was probably covered with fields and gardens when Theodoric beheld it. There also in front of him, but a little to the right, comes rushing down the impetuous Bosphorus, that river which is also an arm of the sea.

Lined now with the marble palaces of bankrupt *Sultans*, it was once a lonely and desolate strait, on whose farther shore the hapless Io, transformed into a heifer, sought a refuge from her heaven-sent tormentor. Up through its difficult windings pressed the adventurous mariners of Miletus in those early voyages which opened up the Euxine to the Greeks, as the voyage of Columbus opened up the Atlantic to the Spaniards. It is impossible now to survey the beautiful panorama without thinking of that great inland sea which, as we all know, begins but a few miles to the north of the place where we are standing, and whose cloudy shores are perhaps concealing in their recesses the future lords of Constantinople. We look towards that point of the compass, and think of Sebastopol. The great lords of Theudemir's court, who brought the young Theodoric to his new patron, may have looked northwards too, remembering the sagas about the mighty Hermanric, who dwelt where now the Russians dwell, and the fateful march of the terrible Huns across the shallows of the Sea of Azof.

The great physical features of the scene are of course unchanged, but almost everything else, how changed by four centuries and a half of Ottoman domination! The first view of Stamboul, with its mosques, its minarets, its latticed houses, its stream of manifold life both civilised and barbarous, flowing through the streets, is delightful to the traveller; but if he be more of an archaeologist than an artist, and seeks to reproduce before his mind's eye something of the Constantinople of the Cæsars rather than the Stamboul of the Sultans, he will experience a bitter disappointment in finding how little of the former is left.

He may still see indeed the landward walls of the city, and a most interesting historical relic they are.[9] They stretch for about four miles, from the Sea of Marmora to the Golden Horn. It is still, comparatively speaking, all city inside of them, all country on the outside. There is a double line of walls with towers at frequent intervals, some square, some octagonal, and deep fosses running along beside the walls, now in spring often bright green with growing corn. These walls and towers, seen stretching up hill and down dale, are a very notable feature in the landscape, and ruinous and dismantled as they are after fourteen centuries of siege, of earthquake, and of neglect, they still help us vividly to imagine what they must have looked like when the young Theodoric beheld them little more than ten years after their erection.[10]

Of the gates, some six or seven in number, two are especially interesting to us. The first is the Tep-Kapou (Cannon Gate), or Porta Sancti Romani. This was the weakest part of the fortifications of Con-

---

9. For the fact that these walls are still visible we have to thank the good offices of a recent British ambassador, I believe Lord Stratford de Redcliffe. The *Sultana Validé* (*Sultan's* mother) had obtained from her son an order to pull down the walls, and sell the materials for the benefit of her privy purse. The ambassador, however, protested against this act of Ottomanism (rather than Vandalism), and the walls were saved.

10. The walls of Constantinople were first built in 412, but having been much injured by an earthquake were rebuilt (we are told in the short space of sixty days) by the *Prefect* of the City, Constantine, at the command of Theodosius II. This rebuilding, which was partly due to the terror caused by Attila, took place in the year 447.

stantinople, the "heel of Achilles," as it has been well called,[11] and here the last Roman Emperor of the East, Constantine Palaeologus, died bravely in the breach for the cause of Christianity and civilisation, The other gate is the Porta Aurea, a fine triple gateway, the centre arch of which rests on two Corinthian pilasters. Through this gateway—the nearest representative of the Capitoline Hill at Rome—the Eastern Emperors rode in triumphant procession when a new Augustus had to be proclaimed, or when an enemy of the Republic had been defeated.

It is possible that Theodoric may have seen Anthemius, the Emperor whom Constantinople gave to Rome, ride forth through this gate (467) to take possession of the Western throne: possible too that the great but unsuccessful expedition planned by the joint forces of the East and West against the Vandals of Africa may have had its ignominious failure hidden from the people for a time by a triumphal procession through the Golden Gate in the following year (468). This gate is now walled up, and tradition says that the order for its closure was given by Mohammed, the Conqueror, immediately after his entry into the city, through fear of an old Turkish prophecy, which declared that through this gate the next conquerors should enter Constantinople.

Of the palace of the emperor, into which the young Goth was ushered by the eunuch-chamberlain, no vestige probably now remains. The Seraglio has replaced the Palation, and is itself now abandoned to loneliness and decay, being only the recipient of one annual visit from the *Sultan*, when he goes in state to kiss the cloak of Mohammed. The great mosque of St. Sophia on the right is a genuine and a glorious monument of Imperial Constantinople, but not of Constantinople as Theodoric saw it. The *basilica*, in which he probably listened with childish bewilderment to many a sermon for or against the decrees of the council of Chalcedon, was burnt down sixty years after his visit in the great insurrection of the "Nika," and the noble edifice in which ten thousand Mussulmans now assemble to listen to the reading of the *Koran*, while above them the Arabic names of the companions of the Prophet replace the mosaics of the Evangelists, is itself the work of the great Emperor Justinian, the destroyer of the state which Theodoric founded.

But almost between the Church of St. Sophia and the Imperial Palace lay in old times the Great Hippodrome, centre of the popular

11. By Dr. Dethier. *Bosphore et Constantinople*, p. 51.

life of the capital, where the excited multitudes cheered with rapture, or howled in execration, at the victory of the Blue or the Green charioteer; where many a time the elevation or the deposition of an emperor was accomplished by the acclamations of the same roaring throng. Of this hippodrome we have still a most interesting memorial in the Atmeidan (the Place of Horses), which, though with diminished area, still preserves something of the form of the old racecourse. And here to this day, (as at time of first publication), are two monuments on which the young hostage may have often gazed, wondering at their form and meaning. The obelisk of Thothmes I., already two thousand years old when Constantinople was founded, was reared in the hippodrome, by order of the great Emperor Theodosius, and some of the *bas-reliefs* on its pedestal still explain to us the mechanical devices by which it was lifted into position, while in others Theodosius, his wife, his sons, and his colleague sit in solemn state, but, alas! with grievously mutilated countenances.

Near it is a spiral column of bronze which, almost till our own day, bore three serpents twined together, whose heads long ago supported a golden tripod. This bronze monument is none other than the votive offering to the temple of Apollo at Delphi, presented by the confederated states of Greece, to celebrate the victory of Platæa. The golden tripod was melted down at the time of Philip of Macedon, but the twisted serpents, brought by Constantine to adorn and hallow his new capital by the Bosphorus, bore and still bear the names, written in archaic characters, of all the Hellenic states which took part in that great deliverance.

All these monuments are on the first of the seven hills on which Constantinople is built. On the second hill stands a strange and blackened pillar, which once stood in the middle of the *forum* of Constantine; and this too was there in the days of Theodoric. It is called the Burnt Column, because it has been more than once struck by lightning, and is blackened with the smoke of the frequent fires which have consumed the wooden shanties at its base. But

> *there it stands, as stands a lofty mind,*
> *Worn, but unstooping to the baser crowd.*

It was once 150 feet high, but is now 115, and it consists of six huge cylinders of porphyry, one above another, whose junction is veiled by sculptured laurel wreaths. On its summit stood the statue of Constantine with the garb and attributes of the Grecian Sun-God, but

The Burnt Column—Constantinople.

having his head surrounded with the nails of the True Cross, brought from Jerusalem to serve instead of the golden rays of far-darting Apollo. Underneath the column was placed (and remains probably to this day) the Palladium, that mysterious image of Minerva, which Æneas carried from Troy to Alba Longa, which his descendants removed to Rome, and which was now brought by Constantine to his new capital, so near to its first legendary home, to be the pledge of abiding security to the city by the Bosphorus.

These are the chief relics of Constantinople in the fifth century which are still visible to the traveller. I have described with some little detail the outward appearance of the city and its monuments, because these would naturally be the objects which would most attract the attention of a child brought from such far different scenes into the midst of so stately a city. But during the ten or eleven years that Theodoric remained in honourable captivity at the court of Leo, while he was growing up from childhood to manhood, it cannot be doubted that he gradually learned the deeper lessons which lay below the glory and the glitter of the great city's life, and that the knowledge thus acquired in those years which are so powerful in moulding character, had a mighty influence on all his subsequent career.

He saw here for the first time, and by degrees he apprehended, the results of that state of *civilitas* which in after years he was to be constantly recommending to his people. Sprung from a race of hunters and shepherds, having slowly learned the arts of agriculture, and then perhaps partly unlearned them under the over-lordship of the nomad Huns, the Ostrogoths at this time knew nothing of a city life. A city was probably in their eyes little else than a hindrance to their freebooting raids, a lair of enemies, a place behind whose sheltering walls, so hard to batter down, cowards lurked in order to sally forth at a favourable moment and attack brave men in their rear. At best it was a treasure-house, which valiant Goths, if Fortune favoured them, might sack and plunder: but Fortune seldom did favour the children of Gaut in their assaults upon the fenced cities of the Empire.

Now, however, the lad Theodoric began to perceive, as the man Ataulfus had perceived before him, that the city life upon which all the proverbs and the songs of his countrymen poured contempt, had its advantages. To the New Rome came the incessant ships of Alexandria, bringing corn for the sustenance of her citizens. Long caravans journeyed over the highlands of Asia Minor loaded with the spices and jewels of India and the silks of China. Men of every conceivable

Asiatic country were drawn by the irresistible attraction of hoped-for profit to the quays and the *fora* of Byzantium. The scattered home-steads of the Ostrogothic farmers had no such wonderful power of drawing men over thousands of miles of land and sea to visit them. Then the bright and varied life of the Imperial City could not fail to fill the boy's soul with pleasure and admiration.

The thrill of excitement in the hippodrome as the two charioteers, Green and Blue, rounded the *spina*, neck and neck, the tragedies acted in the theatre amid rapturous applause, the strange beasts from every part of the Roman world that roared and fought in the amphitheatre, the delicious idleness of the baths, the chatter and bargaining and banter of the *forum*,—all this made a day in beautiful Constantinople very unlike a day in the solemn and somewhat rude palace by Lake Balaton.

As the boy grew to manhood, the deep underlying cause of this difference perhaps became clearer to his mind. He could see more or less plainly that the soul which held all this marvellous body of civilisation together was reverence for law. He visited perhaps some of the courts of law; he may have seen the Illustrious *Prætorian Prefect*, clothed in Imperial purple, move majestically to the judgment-seat, amid the obsequious salutations of the dignified officials,[12] who in their various ranks and orders surrounded the hall. The costly golden reed-case, the massive silver inkstand, the silver bowl for the petitions of suitors, all emblems of his office, were placed solemnly before him, and the pleadings began. Practised advocates arose to plead the cause of plaintiff or defendant; busy short-hand writers took notes of the proceedings; at length in calm and measured words the *prefect* gave his judgement; a judgment which was necessarily based on law, which had to take account of the sayings of *jurisconsults*, of the stored-up wisdom of twenty generations of men; a judgment which, notwith-standing the venality which was the curse of the Empire, was in most instances in accordance with truth and justice.

How different, must Theodoric often have thought, in after years, when he had returned to Gothland,—how different was this settled and orderly procedure from the usage of the barbarians. With them the "blood-feud," the "wild justice of revenge," often prolonged from generation to generation, had been long the chief righter of wrongs done; and if this was now slowly giving place to judicial trial, that trial was probably a coarse and almost lawless proceeding, in which the head man of the district, with a hundred assessors, as ignorant

41

Obelisk of Theodosius in the Hippodrome at Constantinople.

as himself, amid the wild cries of the opposed parties, roughly fixed the amount of blood-money to be paid by a murderer, or decided at hap-hazard, often with an obvious reference to the superior force at the command of one or other of the litigants, some obscure dispute as to the ownership of a slave or the right to succeed to a dead man's inheritance.

Law carefully thought out, systematised, and in the main softened and liberalised, from generation to generation, was the great gift of the Roman Empire to the world, and by her strong, and uniform, and, in the main, just administration of this law, that Empire had kept, and in the days of Theodoric was still keeping, her hold upon a hundred jarring nationalities. What hope was there that the German intruders into the lands of the Mediterranean could ever vie with this great achievement? Yet if they could not, if it was out of their power to reform and reinvigorate the shattered state, if they could only destroy and not rebuild, they would exert no abiding influence on the destinies of Europe.

I do not say that all these thoughts passed at this time through the mind of Theodoric, but I have no doubt that the germs of them were sown by his residence in Constantinople. When he returned, a young man of eighteen years and of noble presence to the palace of his father, he had certainly some conception of what the Greeks meant when he heard them talking about *politeia*, some foreshadowing of what he himself would mean when in after days he should speak alike to his Goth and Roman subjects of the blessings of *civilitas*.

12. *Officium*, or *Militia Literata*.

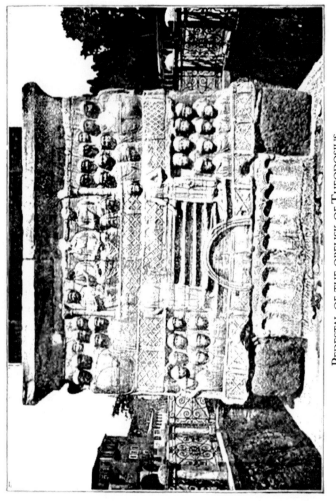

PEDESTAL OF THE OBELISK OF THEODOSIUS.

CHAPTER 4

The Southward Migration

The young Theodoric, who was now in his nineteenth year, was sent back by Leo to his father with large presents, and both the recovered son and the tokens of Imperial favour brought joy to the heart of the father. There had been some changes in the Ostrogothic kingdom during the boy's absence. There had been vague and purposeless wars with the savage nations around them,—Swabians, Sarmatians, Scyri— besides one final encounter with their old lords, the Huns. These last, we are told, they had driven forth so hopelessly beaten from their territory, that for a century from that time all that was left of the Hunnish nation trembled at the very name of the Goths. But in a battle with another people of far less renown, the barbarous Scyri beyond the Danube, Walamir, while cheering on his men to the combat, was thrown from his horse and being pierced by the lances of the enemy was left dead on the field. His death, it is said, was avenged most ruthlessly on the Scyri, and Theudemir, the brother who was next him in age, became chief king of the Ostrogoths.

Scarcely had Theodoric returned to his home when, without communicating his purpose to his father, he distinguished himself by a gallant deed of arms. On the south-east of the Ostrogothic kingdom, in the country which we now call Servia, there reigned at this time a Sclavonic chief called Babai, who was full of pride and self-importance because of a victory which he had lately gained over the forces of the Empire. Theodoric had probably heard at Constantinople the other side of this story: on his journey to the north-west he had passed through those regions, and marked the pride of the insolent barbarian. Sympathy with the humiliated Empire, but, far more, the young warrior's desire at once to find "a foeman worthy of his steel," and to win laurels for himself wherewith he might surprise his father, drove him into his new enterprise.

Having collected some of his father's guardsmen, and those of his people with whom he was personally popular, or who were dependent upon him, he thus mustered a little army of six thousand men, with whom he crossed the Danube.[1] Falling suddenly upon King Babai, he defeated and slew him, took his family prisoners, and returned with large booty in slaves and the rude wealth of the barbarian to his surprised but joyful father. The result of this expedition was the capture of the important frontier city of Singidunum (whose site is now occupied by Belgrade), a city which Babai had wrested from the Empire, but which Theodoric, whatever may have been his inclination to favour Constantinople, did not deem it necessary to restore to his late host.

This incident of the early manhood of Theodoric is a good illustration of the Teutonic custom which Tacitus describes to us under the name of the *comitatus*, a custom which was therefore at least four centuries old (probably far older) in the days of Theodoric, and which, lasting on for several centuries longer, undoubtedly influenced if it did not actually create the chivalry of the Middle Ages. The custom was so important that it will be better to translate the very words of Tacitus concerning it, though they occur in one of the best-known passages of the *Germania*.

> The Germans transact no business either of a public or private nature except with arms in their hands. But it is not the practice for anyone to begin the wearing of arms until the state has approved his ability to wield them. When that is done, in the great council of the nation one of the chiefs, perhaps the father or some near relation of the candidate, equips the youth with shield and spear. This is with them like the *toga virilis* with us, the first dignity bestowed on the young man.
>
> Before this he was looked upon as part of his father's household—now he is a member of the state. Eminently noble birth, or great merit on the part of their fathers, assigns the dignity of a chief[2] even to very young men. They are admitted to the fellowship of other youths stronger than themselves, and already

---

1. The words of Jordanes (which are important on account of their bearing on the passage of Tacitus quoted below) are: "*Ascitis certis ex satellitibus patris et ex populo amatores sibi clientesque consocians pæne sex mille viros cum quibus inscio patre emenso Danubio super Babai Sarmatarum regem discurrit*" (Getica, lv.).

2. *Dignationem principis*; the true rendering of this sentence is very doubtful.

tried in war, nor do they blush to be seen among the hench-men.[3]

There is a gradation in rank among the henchmen, determined by the judgement of him whom they follow, and there is a great emulation among the henchmen, who shall have the highest place under the chief, and among the chiefs who shall have the most numerous and the bravest henchmen. This is their dignity, this their strength, to be ever surrounded by a band of chosen youths, an honour in peace, a defence in battle. And not only in his own nation, but among the surrounding states also, each chief's name and glory are spread abroad according to the emi-nence of his 'train of henchmen'[4] in number and valour. Chiefs thus distinguished are in request for embassies, are enriched with costly presents, and often they decide a war by the mere terror of their name.

When they stand on the battlefield, it is held a disgraceful thing for the chief to be surpassed in bravery by his henchmen, for the henchmen not to equal the valour of their chief. Now too it will mark a man as infamous, and a target for the scorn of men for all the rest of his life, if he escapes alive from the battle-field where his chief needed his help. To defend *him*, the chief; to guard *his* person; to reckon up one's own brave deeds as enhancing *his* glory: this is the henchman's one great oath of fe-alty.[5] The chiefs fight for victory, the henchmen for their chief. If the state in which they are born should be growing sluggish through ease and a long peace, most of the noble young men seek of their own accord those nations which are then wag-ing war, both because a quiet life is hateful to this people, and because they can more easily distinguish themselves in perilous times, nor can they keep together a great train of henchmen, except by war and the strong hand.

For it is from the generosity of their chief that each henchman expects that mighty war-horse which he would bestride, that gory and victorious spear, which he would brandish. Banquets, too, and all the rough but plentiful appliances of the feast are

---

3. I think upon the whole "henchmen" is the best translation of this difficult word "*comites*." "Companions" is too indefinite; "comrades" implies too much equality with the chief.

4. *Comitatus*.

5. *Præcipuum sacramentum*.

47

taken as part of the henchman's pay; and the means of supplying all this prodigality must be sought by war and rapine. You would not so easily persuade them to plough the fields and wait in patience for a year's harvest, as to challenge an enemy and earn honourable wounds; since to them it seems always a slow and lazy process to accumulate by the sweat of your brow what you might win at once by the shedding of blood.

These words of Tacitus, written in the year 98 after Christ, describe with wonderful exactness the state of Ostrogothic society in the year 472. We are not expressly told of Theodoric's assumption of the shield and spear in the great council of the nation, but probably this ceremony immediately followed his return from Constantinople. Then we see the gathering together of the band of henchmen, the sudden march away from the peaceful land, growing torpid through two or three years of warlessness, the surprise of the Sclavonic king, the copious effusion of blood which was the preferred alternative to the sweat of the land-tiller, the return to the young chief's own land with spoils sufficient to support perhaps for many months the "generosity" expected by the henchmen.

There is one point, however, in which the description of the Germans given by Tacitus is probably not altogether applicable to the Goths of the fifth century: and that is, their invincible preference for the life of the warrior over that of the agriculturist. There are some indications that the Germans, when Tacitus wrote, had not long exchanged the nomadic life of a nation of shepherds and herdsmen (such as was led by the earlier generations of the Israelitish people) for the settled life which alone is consistent with the pursuits of the tiller of the soil. Hence the roving instinct was still strong within them, and this roving instinct easily allied itself with the thirst for battle and the love of the easy gains of the freebooter.

Four centuries, however, of agriculture and of neighbourhood to the great civilised stable Empire of Rome had apparently wrought some change in the Goths and in many of the other Teutonic nations. The work of agriculture was now not altogether odious in their eyes; they knew something of the joys of the husbandman as well as of the joys of the warrior; they began to feel something of that "land-hunger" which is the passion of a young, growing, industrious people. Still, however, the songs of the minstrels, the sagas of the bards, the fiery impulses of the young *princeps* surrounded by his *comitatus* pointed to war as the only occupation worthy of freemen. Hence we can perceive a double current in the ambitions of these nations which often perplexes the historian now, as it evidently then perplexed their mighty neighbour, the Roman Augustus, and the generals and lawyers who counselled him in his consistory. Sometimes the Teutonic king is roused by some real or imagined insult; the minstrels sing their battle-songs; the fiery henchmen gather round their chief; the barbarian tide rolls over the frontier of the Empire: it seems as if it must be a duel to the death between civilisation and its implacable foes. Then suddenly

> *he sinks*
> *To ashes who was very fire before.*

Food, not glory, seems to be the supreme object of the Teuton's ambition. He begs for land, for seed to sow in it, for a legal settle-ment within the limits of the Empire. If only these necessary things are granted to him, he promises, and not without intending to keep his promise, to be a peaceable subject, yes and a staunch defender, of the Roman Augustus. Had the Imperial statesmen truly understood this strange duality of purpose in the minds of their barbarian visitors, and had they set themselves loyally and patiently to foster the peaceful agricultural instincts of the Teuton, haply the Roman Empire might still be standing. As it was, the statesmen of the day, men of temporary shifts and expedients, living only as we say "from hand to mouth," saw, in the changing moods of the Germans, only the faithlessness of barbarism, which they met with the faithlessness of civilisation, and between the two the Empire—which no one really wished to destroy—was destroyed.

Even such a change it was which now came over the minds of the Ostrogothic people. There was dearth in Pannonia, partly, perhaps, the consequence of the frequent wars with the surrounding nations which had occurred during the twenty years of the Ostrogothic set-tlement. But even the cessation of those wars brought with it a loss of income to the warrior class. As the Gothic historian expresses it:

> From the diminution of the spoils of the neighbouring nations the Goths began to lack food and clothing, and to those men to whom war had long furnished all their sustenance peace began to be odious, and all the Goths with loud shouts approached their king Theudemir praying him to lead his army whither he would, but to lead it forth to war.

Here again it can hardly be doubted that Jordanes, writing about the fifth century, describes for us the same state of things as Tacitus writing about the first, and that this loudly shouted demand of the people for war was expressed in one of those national assemblies—the "Folc-motes" or "Folc-things" of Anglo-Saxon and German history—which formed such a real limitation to the power of the early Teutonic kings.

> Concerning smaller matters, (says Tacitus),[6] the chiefs deliberate; concerning greater matters, the whole nation; but in such wise that even those things which are in the power of the commonalty are discussed in detail by the chiefs. They come together, unless any sudden and accidental emergency have arisen, on fixed days determined by the new or full moon; for these times they deem the most fortunate for the transaction of business.
>
> An ill consequence flowing from their freedom is their want of punctuality in assembling; often two or three days are spent in waiting for the loiterers. When the crowd chooses, they sit down, arrayed in their armour (and commence business). Silence is called for by the priests, who have then the power even of keeping order by force. Then the king or one of the chiefs begins to speak, and is listened to in right either of his age, or his noble birth, or his glory in the wars, or his eloquence. In any case, he rather persuades than commands; not power, but weight of character procures the assent of his hearers.
>
> If they mislike his sentiments they express their contempt for them by groans, if they approve, they clash their spears together. Applause thus expressed by arms is the greatest tribute that can be paid to a speaker.

Before such an assembly of the nation in arms, the question, not of peace or war? but of war with whom? was debated. It was decided that the Empire should be the victim, and that East and West alike should feel the heavy hand of the Ostrogoths. The lot was cast (so said the national legend),[7] and it assigned to Theudemir the harder but, as it seemed, more profitable task of warring against Constantinople, while his younger brother Widemir was to attack Rome.

Of Widemir's movements there is little to tell. He died in Italy,

---

6. *Germania*, xi.

7. Köpke *Anfänge des Königthums*, (p. 146) throws doubt on this story of the decision by lot, and there seems something to be said on his side.

not having apparently achieved any brilliant exploits, and his son and namesake was easily persuaded to turn aside into Gaul, where he joined his forces to those of the kindred *Visigoths*, and became absorbed in their flourishing kingdom. This branch of Amal royalty henceforward bears no fruit in history.

More important, at any rate in its ultimate consequences, was the march of Theudemir and his people into the dominions of the Eastern Cæsar. They crossed the Save, and by their warlike array terrified into acquiescence the Sclavonic tribes which were settled in the neighbourhood of Belgrade.

Having pushed up the valley of the Morava, they captured the important city of Naissus (now Nisch), "the first city of Illyricum." Here Theudemir tarried for a space, sending on his son with a large and eager *comitatus* farther up the valley of the Morava. They reached the head of that valley, they crossed the watershed and the plain of Kossova, and descended the valley of the Vardar. Monastir in Macedonia, Larissa in Thessaly were taken and sacked; and a way having thus been made by these bold invaders into the heart of the Empire, a message was sent to Theudemir, inviting him to undertake the siege of Thessalonica. Leaving a few guards in Naissus, the old king moved southward with the bulk of his army, and was soon standing with his men before the walls of the Macedonian capital.

The Patrician Hilarianus held that city with a strong force, but when he saw it regularly invested by the Goths and an earthen rampart drawn all round it, he lost heart, and, despairing of a successful resistance, opened negotiations with the besiegers. The result of these negotiations (accompanied by handsome presents to the king) was that Theudemir abandoned the siege, resumed the often adopted, perhaps never wholly abandoned, position of a *fœderatus* or sworn auxiliary of the Empire, and received for himself and his people the unquestioned possession of six towns[8] and the surrounding country by the northeast corner of the Ægean, where the Vardar discharges itself into the Thermaic Gulf.

Thus ingloriously, thus unprofitably ended the expedition into Romania, which had been proposed amid such enthusiastic applause at the great council of the nation, and pressed with such loud acclamations and such brandishing of defiant spears upon the perhaps reluctant Theudemir. The Ostrogoths in 472 were an independent people, practically supreme in Pannonia. Those broad lands on the south and

---

8. The best known of these towns are Pella, Pydna, and Bercea.

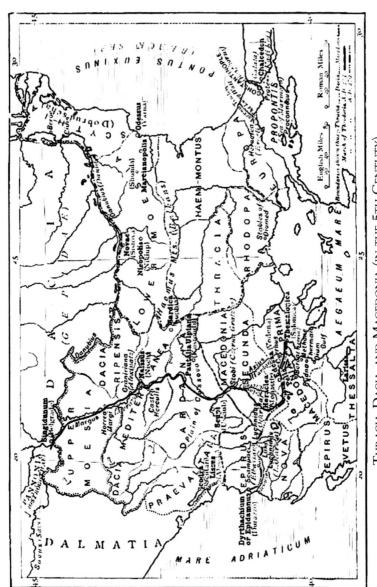

THRACIA, DACIA, AND MACEDONIA (IN THE 5TH CENTURY)

west of the Danube, rich in corn and wine, the very kernel of the Austrian monarchy of today, were theirs in absolute possession. Any tie of nominal dependence which attached Pannonia to the Empire was so merely theoretical, now that the Hun had ruled and ravaged it for a good part of a century, that it was not worth taking into consideration; it was in fact rather an excuse for claiming *stipendia* from the emperor than a bond of real vassalage. But now in 474 this great and proud nation, crowded into a few cities of Macedonia, with obedient subjects of the Empire all round them, had practically no choice between the life of peaceful provincials on the one hand and that of freebooters on the other. If they accepted the first, they would lose year by year something of their old national character.

The Teutonic speech, the Teutonic customs would gradually disappear, and in one or two generations they would be scarcely distinguishable from any of the other oppressed, patient, tax-exhausted populations of the great and weary Empire. On the other hand, if they accepted (which in fact they seem to have done) the other alternative, and became a mere horde of plunderers wandering up and down through the Empire, seeking what they might destroy, they abandoned the hope of forming a settled and stable monarchy, and, doing injustice to the high qualities and capacities for civilisation which were in them, they would sink lower into the depths of barbarism, and becoming like the Hun, like the Hun they would one day perish. Certainly, so far, the tumultuous decision of the Parliament on the shores of Lake Pelso was a false step in the nation's history.

CHAPTER 5

Storm and Stress

The imagination of a boy is healthy, and the mature imagination of a man is healthy, but there is a space of life between, in which the soul is in a ferment, the character undecided, the way of life uncertain, the ambition thick-sighted.
—Keats, Preface to *Endymion*.

The sentence thus written by the sensitive young poet, a child of London of the nineteenth century, was eminently exemplified in the history of the martial chief of the Ostrogoths. The next fourteen years in the life of Theodoric, which will be described in this chapter, were years of much useless endeavour, of marches and countermarches, of alliances formed and broken, of vain animosities and vainer reconciliations, years in which Theodoric himself seems never to understand his own purpose, whether it shall be under the shadow of the Empire or upon the ruins of the Empire, that he will build up his throne. Take the map of what is now often called "the Balkan peninsula," the region in which these fourteen years were passed; look at the apparently purpose, less way in which the mountain ranges of Hæmus, Rhodope, and Scardus cross, intersect, run parallel, approach, avoid one another; look at the strange entanglement of passes and watersheds and table-lands which their systems display to us. Even such as the ranges among which he was manœuvring—perplexed, purposeless, and sterile—was the early manhood of Theodoric.

About 474, soon after the great southward migration, Theudemir died at Cyrrhus in Macedonia, one of the new settlements of the Ostrogoths. When he was attacked by his fatal sickness he called his people together and pointed to Theodoric as the heir of his royal dignity. Kingship at this time among the Germanic nations was not purely hereditary, the consent of the people being required even in the most ordinary and natural cases of succession, such as that of a first-born son, full grown and a tried soldier succeeding to an aged father. In such cases, however, that consent was almost invariably given. Theodoric, at any rate, succeeded without disputes to the doubtful and precarious position of king of the Ostrogoths.

Almost at the same time a change was being made by death in the wearer of the Imperial diadem. In order to illustrate the widely different character of the Roman and the Gothic monarchies it will be well to cease for a little time to follow the fortunes of Theodoric and to sketch the history of Leo, the dying emperor, and of Zeno, who succeeded him.

Leo I., who reigned at Constantinople from 457 to 474, and who was therefore emperor during the whole time that Theodoric dwelt there as hostage, was not, as far as we can ascertain, a man of any great abilities in peace or war, or originally of very exalted station. But he was "curator" or steward in the household of Aspar, the successful barbarian adventurer who has been already alluded to.[1] As an Arian by religion, and a barbarian, or the son of a barbarian, by birth, Aspar could not himself assume the diadem, but he could give it to whom he would, and Leo the steward was the second of his dependants whom he had thus honoured.

Once placed upon the throne, however, Leo showed himself less obsequious to his old master than was expected. The post of *prefect* of the city became vacant; Aspar suggested for the office a man who, like himself, was tainted with the heresy of Arius. At the moment Leo promised acquiescence, but immediately repented, and in the dead of night privately conferred the important office on a senator who professed the orthodox faith.

Aspar in a rage laid a rough hand on the Imperial purple, saying to Leo: "Emperor! it is not fitting that one who wears this robe should tell lies." Leo answered with some spirit: "Neither is it fitting that an emperor should be bound to do the bidding of any of his subjects, and so injure the state."

After this encounter there were thirteen years of feud between king-maker and king, between Aspar and Leo. At length in 471 Aspar and his three valiant sons fell by the swords of the eunuchs of the palace. The foul and cowardly deed was perhaps marked by some circumstances of especial cruelty, which earned for Leo the title by which he

---

1. See Chapter 3.

was long after remembered in Constantinople, "The Butcher."[2]

In order to strengthen himself against the adherents of Aspar, Leo cultivated the friendship of a set of wild, uncouth mountaineers, who at this time played the same part in Constantinople which the Swiss of the Middle Ages played in Italy. These were the Isaurians, men from the rugged highlands of Pisidia, whose lives had hitherto been chiefly spent either in robbing or in defending themselves from robbery. At their head was a man named Tarasicodissa,—probably well born, if a chieftain from the Isaurian highlands could be deemed to be well born by the contemptuous citizens of Constantinople, no soldier, for we are told that even the picture of a battle frightened him, but a man whom the other Isaurians seem to have followed with clannish loyalty, like that which the Scottish Camerons showed even to the wily and unwarlike Master of Lovat.

With Tarasicodissa therefore the Emperor Leo entered into a compact of mutual defence. The Isaurian dropped his uncouth name and assumed the classical and philosophical-sounding name of Zeno; he received the hand of Ariadne, daughter of the emperor, in marriage, and as Leo had no male offspring, the little Leo, offspring of this marriage and therefore grandson of the aged emperor, was, in this monarchy which from elective was ever becoming more strictly hereditary, generally accepted as his probable successor.

As it had been planned so it came to pass. Leo the Butcher died (3rd Feb. 474); the younger Leo, a child of seven years old, was hailed by senate and people as his successor: Zeno came at the head of a brilliant train of senators, soldiers, and magistrates, to "adore" the new emperor, and the child, carefully instructed by his mother in the part which he had to play, placed on the bowed head of his father the Imperial diadem. This act of "association" as it was called, generally practised upon a son or nephew by a veteran emperor anxious to be relieved from some of the cares of reigning, required to be ratified by the acclamations of the soldiery; but no doubt these acclamations, which could generally be purchased by a sufficiently liberal *donative*, were not wanting on this occasion.

Zeno, otherwise called Tarasicodissa the Isaurian, was now emperor, and nine months after, when his child-partner died, he became sole ruler of the Roman world, except in so far as his dignity might be considered to be shared by the phantom emperors of the West, who at this time were dethroning and being dethroned with fatal rapidity at

---

2. Leo Macellus.

Rome and Ravenna.

Thus mean and devious were the paths by which an adventurer could climb in the fifth century to that which was still looked upon as the pinnacle of earthly greatness. For however unworthy a man might feel himself to be, and however unworthy all his subjects might know him to be of the highest place in the Empire, when once he had obtained it his power was absolute and the honours rendered to him were little less than divine.

All laws were passed by his "sacred providence"; all officers, military and civil, received their authority from him. In the edicts which he put forth to the world he spoke of himself as "My Eternity," "My Mildness," "My Magnificence," and of course these expressions, or, if it were possible, expressions more adulatory than these, were used by his subjects when they laid their petitions at the footstool of "the sacred throne."

He lived, withdrawn from vulgar eyes, in the innermost recesses of the palace, a sort of Holy of Holies behind the first and the second veil. A band of pages, in splendid dress, waited upon his bidding; thirty stately *silentiarii*, with helmets and brightly burnished cuirasses, marched backwards and forwards before the second veil, to see that no importunate petitioner disturbed the silence of "the sacred cubicle." On the comparatively rare occasions when he showed himself to his subjects, he wore upon his head the diadem, a band of white linen, in which blazed the most precious jewels of the Empire. Hung round his shoulders and reaching down to his feet was that precious purple robe, for the sake of which so many crimes were committed, and which often proved itself a very "garment of Nessus" to him who dared to assume it without force sufficient to render his usurpation legitimate.

On the feet of the emperor were buskins which, like the diadem, were studded with precious stones, and like the robe were dyed with the Imperial purple. Thus gorgeously arrayed he took his place in the *podium*, the royal box in the amphitheatre, and from thence, while gazed upon by his subjects, gazed himself upon the savage beast-fight, or in the hippodrome, with difficulty restraining his eagerness for the success of the Blue or the Green faction, gave the sign for the chariot races to begin.

Or he sat surrounded by his court in the purple presence-chamber to consult upon public affairs with his *consistory*, a sort of Privy Council, composed of the great ministers of state. Conspicuous among these were the fifteen officers of highest rank, generals, judges, grand chamberlains, finance ministers, who had each the right to be addressed as "Illustrious."

When any subject of the emperor, were it one of these Illustrious ones himself, were it the son or brother of his predecessor, were it even a former patron, like Aspar, by whose favour he had been selected to wear the purple, was admitted to an audience of "Augustus" (that great name went as of right with the diadem), the etiquette of the court required that he should not merely bow nor kneel, but absolutely prostrate himself before the Sacred Majesty of the emperor, who, if in a gracious mood, then with outstretched hand raised him from the earth and permitted him to kiss his knee or the fringe of his Imperial mantle.

To this dizzy height of greatness—for such, however small Marcian or Leo or Zeno may now seem to us by the lapse of centuries, it was felt to be by the contemporary generations—it was possible under the singular combination of election and inheritance which regulated the succession to the throne, for almost any citizen of the Empire, if not of barbarian blood or heretical creed, to aspire. Diocletian, the second founder of the Empire, was the son of a slave; Justinian—an even greater name—was the nephew of a Macedonian peasant, who with a sheepskin bag containing a week's store of biscuit, his only property, tramped down from his native highlands to seek his fortune in the capital Zeno, as we have seen, though perhaps better born than either Diocletian or Justinian, was only a little Isaurian chieftain.

Thus the possibilities open to aspiring ambition were great in the Empire of the Cæsars. As any male citizen of the United States, born between the St. Lawrence and the Rio Grande, may one day be installed in the White House as President, so any "Roman" and orthodox inhabitant of the Empire, whether noble, citizen, or peasant, might flatter himself with the hope that he too should one day wear the purple of Diocletian, be saluted as Augustus, and see *Prefects* and Masters of the Soldiery prostrating themselves before "His Eternity." This was, in a sense, the better, the democratic side of the Roman monarchy. Power which was supposed to be conveyed by the will of the people (as expressed by the acclamations of the army) might be wielded by the arm of any member of that people.

On the other hand there was an evil in the habit thus engendered in men's minds, of humbling themselves before mere power without regard to the manner of its acquirement. When we compare the polity of Rome or Constantinople, where a century was a long time for the duration of a dynasty, with the far simpler polities of the Teutonic tribes which invaded the Empire, almost all of whom had their royal houses, reaching back into and even beyond the dawn of national history, supposed to be sprung from the loins of the gods, and rendered illustrious by countless deeds of valour recorded in song or saga, we see at once that in these ruder states we are in presence of a principle which the Empire knew not, but which mediæval Europe knew and glorified, the principle of *Loyalty*.

This principle, the same that bound Bayard to the Valois, and Montrose to the Stuart, has been, with all the follies and even crimes which it may have caused, an element of strength and cohesion in the states which have arisen on the ruins of the Roman Empire. The self-respecting but loving loyalty, with which the Englishman of today, (as at time of first publication), cherishes the name of the descendant of Cerdic, of Alfred, and of Edward Plantagenet, who wields the sceptre of his country, is utterly unlike the slavish homage offered by the adoring courtiers of Byzantium to the pinchbeck divinity of Zeno Tarasicodissa.

Raised as Zeno had been to the throne by a mere palace intrigue, and destitute as he was of any of the qualities of a great statesman or general, it is no wonder that his reign, which lasted for seventeen years, was continually disturbed by conspiracies and rebellions. In most of these rebellions his mother-in-law, Verina, widow of Leo, an ambitious and turbulent woman, played an important part.

It was only a year after Zeno's accession to sole power by the death of his son (Nov., 475) when he was surprised by the outbreak of a conspiracy, hatched by his mother-in-law, the object of which was to place her brother Basiliscus on the throne. Zeno fled by night, still wearing the Imperial robes which he had worn, sitting in the hippodrome, when the tidings reached him, and crossing the Bosphorus was soon in the heart of Asia Minor, safe sheltered in his native Isauria.

From thence, (July, 477) after nearly two years of exile, he was by a strange turn of the wheel of Fortune restored to his throne. Religious bigotry (for Basiliscus did not belong to the party of strict orthodoxy) and domestic jealousies and perfidies all contributed to this result. Zeno, who had fled twenty months before from the hippodrome, returned to the amphitheatre, and there, having commanded that the linen curtain should be drawn over the circus to exclude the too piercing rays of the July sun, gave the signal for the games to begin, while the populace shouted in Latin the regular official congratulations on his elevation and prayers for his continued triumph.[3]

Meanwhile his fallen rival, less fortunate than Zeno himself in planning an escape, was crouching in the baptistery of the great Church of Saint Sophia, whither with his wife and children he had fled for refuge. After all the emblems of Imperial dignity had been rudely stripped from them, Basiliscus was induced, by a promise from Zeno, "that their heads should be safe," to come forth with his family from the sacred asylum. The emperor "kept the word of promise to the ear," since no executioner with drawn sword entered the chamber of his rival. Basiliscus and they that were with him were sent away to a remote fortress in Cappadocia. The gate of the fortress was built up, a band of wild Isaurians guarded the enclosure, suffering no man to enter or to leave it, and in that bleak stronghold before long the fallen emperor and empress with their children perished miserably of cold and hunger.

Theodoric, who was at this time settled with his people, not on the shores of the Ægean, but in the region which we now call the Dobrudscha, between the mouths of the Danube and the Black Sea, had zealously espoused the cause of the banished Zeno, and lent an effectual hand in the counter-revolution which restored him to the throne (478). For his services in this crisis he was rewarded with the dignities of Patrician and Master of the Soldiery, high honours for a barbarian of twenty-four; and probably about this time he was also adopted as "*filius in arma*" by the emperor.

What the precise nature of this adopted "sonship-in-arms" may have been we are not able to say. It reminds us of the barbarian customs which in the course of centuries ripened into the mediæval ceremony of knighthood, and the whole transaction certainly sounds more Ostrogothic than Imperial. Zeno's own son and namesake (the offspring of a first marriage before his union with Ariadne) was apparently dead before this time; and possibly therefore the title of son thus conferred upon Theodoric may have raised in his heart wild hopes that he too might one day be saluted as Roman Emperor. Any such hopes were probably doomed to inevitable disappointment. Any other dignity in the state, the "Roman Republic," as it still called itself, was practically within reach of a powerful barbarian, but the diadem, as has

---

3. "*Zeno Imperator Tu Vincas*," would be, as we know from other similar instances, the most frequently uttered acclamation. It is a curious instance of "survival" that this was always shouted in Latin, though Greek was the vernacular tongue of the vast majority of the inhabitants of Constantinople.

been already said, could in this age of the world, only be worn by one of pure Roman, that is, non-barbarian, blood.

At this time, and for the next three years, the position of our Theodoric, both towards the emperor and towards his own people, was sorely embarrassed by the position and the claims of the other, the squinting Theodoric (son of Triarius), whom we met with seventeen years ago, and whose receipt of *stipendia* from the court of Constantinople, at the very time when their own were withheld, raised the wrath of Walamir and Theudemir. This Theodoric, it will be remembered, was of unkingly, perhaps of quite ignoble, birth, had risen to greatness by clinging to the skirts of Aspar, and had, so far as the emperor's favour was concerned, fallen with his fall.

Shortly before the death of Leo he had appeared in arms against the Empire, taking one city and besieging another, and had forced the emperor to concede to him high rank in the army (that of General of the Household Troops,[4] a subsidy of; £80,000 a year for himself and his people, and lastly a remarkable stipulation, "that he should be absolute ruler[5] of the Goths, and that the emperor should not receive any of them who were minded to revolt from him." This strange article of the treaty shows us, on the one hand, how thoroughly fictitious and illegitimate was *this* Theodoric's claim to kinship; since assuredly neither Alaric, nor Ataulfus, nor Theudemir, nor any of the genuine kings of the Goths, ever needed to bolster up their authority over their subjects by any such figment of an Imperial concession; and on the other hand, as it coincides in date with the time of Theudemir's and *his* Theodoric's entrance into the Empire, it shows us the distracting influences to which the large number of Gothic settlers south of the Danube, settled there before Theudemir's migration, were exposed by that event.

There can be little doubt that the Goths who were minded to revolt from the son of Triarius and who were not to be received into favour by the emperor, were Ostrogoths, still dimly conscious of the old tie which bound them to the glorious house of Amala, and more than half disposed to forsake the service of their squinting upstart chief in order to follow the banners of the young hero, son of Theudemir.

Then came the death of Leo (478), Zeno's accession and the insurrection of Basiliscus, in which the son of Triarius took part against the Isaurian Emperor. Soon after this insurrection was ended and Zeno

4. *Magister Equitum et Peditum Præsentalis.*

5. αὐτοκράτωρ.

was restored to his precarious throne, there came an embassy from the *fœderati* (as they called themselves) that is, from the unattached Goths who followed the Triarian standard, begging Zeno to be reconciled to their lord, and hinting that he was a truer friend to the Empire than the petted and pampered son of Theudemir.

After a consultation with "the Senate and People of Rome," in other words, with the nobles of Constantinople and the troops of the household, Zeno decided that to take *both* the Theodorics into his pay would be too heavy a charge on the treasury; that there was no reason for breaking with the young Amal, his ally, and therefore that the request of his rival must be refused. Open war followed, consisting chiefly of devastating raids by the son of Triarius into the valleys of Mœsia and Thrace. A message was sent to Theodoric the Amal, who was dwelling quietly with his people by the Danube. "Why are you lingering in your home? Come forth and do great deeds worthy of a Master of Roman Soldiery."

"But if I take the field against the son of Triarius," was the answer, "I fear that you will make peace with him behind my back." The emperor and Senate bound themselves by solemn oaths that he should never be received back into favour, and an elaborate plan of campaign was arranged, according to which the Amal marching with his host from Marcianople, (*Shumla*) was to be met by one general with twelve thousand troops, on the southern side of the Balkans, and by another with thirty thousand in the valley of the Hebrus (*Maritza*).

But the Roman Empire, in its feeble and flaccid old age, seemed to have lost all capacity for making war. Theodoric the Amal performed his share of the compact; but when with his weary army, encumbered with many women and children, he emerged from the passes of the Balkans he found no Imperial generals there to meet him, but, instead, Theodoric the Squinter with a large army of Goths encamped on an inaccessible hill. Neither chief gave the signal for combat; perhaps both were restrained by a reluctance to urge the fratricidal strife; but there were daily skirmishes between the light-armed horsemen at the foraging grounds and places for watering.

Every day, too, the son of Triarius rode round the hostile camp, shouting forth reproaches against his rival, calling him "a perjured boy, a madman, a traitor to his race, a fool who could not see whither the Imperial plans were tending. The Romans would stand by and look quietly on while Goth wore out Goth in deadly strife." Murmurs from the Amal's troops showed that these words struck home. Next day the son of Triarius climbed a hill overlooking the camp, and again raised his voice in bitter defiance. "Scoundrel! why are you leading so many of my kinsmen to destruction? why have you made so many Gothic wives widows? What has become of that wealth and plenty which they had when they first took service with you? Then they had two or three horses apiece; now without horses and in the guise of slaves, they are wandering on foot through Thrace. But they are free-born men surely, aye, as free-born as you are, and they once measured out the gold coins of Byzantium with a bushel."

When the host heard these words, all, both men and women, went to their leader Theodoric the Amal, and claimed from him with tumultuous cries that he should come to an accommodation with the son of Tnarius. The proposal must have been hateful to the Amal. To throw away the laboriously earned favour of the emperor, to denude himself of the splendid dignity of Master of the Soldiery, to leave the comfortable home-like fabric of Imperial civilisation and go out again into the barbarian wilderness with this insolent namesake who had just been denouncing him as a perjured boy: all this was gall and worm-wood to the spirit of Theodoric. But he knew the conditions under which he held his sovereignty—"king," as a recent French monarch expressed it, "by the grace of God and the will of the people," and he did not attempt to strive against the decision of his tumultuary parliament. He met his elderly competitor, each standing on the opposite bank of a disparting stream, and after speech had, they agreed that they would wage no more war on one another but would make common cause against Byzantium.

The now confederated Theodorics sent an embassy to Zeno, bearing their common demands for territory, *stipendia* and rations for their followers, and, in the case of Theodoric the Amal, charged with bitter complaints of the desertion which had exposed him to such dangers. The emperor replied with an accusation (which appears to have been wholly unfounded) that Theodoric himself had meditated treachery, and that this was the reason why the Roman generals had feared to join their forces to his. Still the emperor was willing to receive him again into favour if he would relinquish his alliance with the son of Triarius, and in order to lure him back the ambassadors were to offer him 1,000 pounds' weight of gold (£40,000), 10,000 of silver (£35,000), a yearly revenue of 10,000 *aurei* (£6,000), and the daughter of Olybrius, one of the noblest-born damsels of Byzantium, for his wife.

But the Amal king, having stooped so low as to make an alliance with the son of Triarius, was not going to stoop lower by breaking it. The ambassadors returned to Constantinople with their purpose unaccomplished, and Zeno began seriously to prepare for the apparently inevitable war with all the Gothic *fœderati* in his land, commanded by both the Theodorics. He summoned to the capital all the troops whom he could muster, and delivered to them a spirited oration, in which he exhorted them to be of good courage, declaring that he himself would go forth with them to war, and would share all their hardships and dangers. For nearly a hundred years, ever since the time of the great Theodosius, no Eastern emperor apparently had conducted a campaign in person; and the announcement that this inactivity was to be ended and that a Roman *Imperator* was again, like the *imperators* of old time, to march with the legions and to withstand the shock of battle, roused the soldiers to extraordinary enthusiasm.

The very men who, a little while before, had been bribing the officers to procure exemption from service, now offered larger sums of money in order to obtain an opportunity of distinguishing themselves under the eyes of the emperor. They pressed forward past the long wall which at about sixty miles from Constantinople crossed the narrow peninsula and defended the capital of the Empire; they caught some of the forerunners of the Gothic host, the Uhlans, if we may call them so, of Theodoric: everything foreboded an encounter, more serious and perhaps more triumphant than any that had been seen since the days of Theodosius. Then, as in a moment, all was changed. Zeno's old spirit of sloth and cowardice returned. He would not undergo the fatigue of the long marches through Thrace, he would not look upon the battlefield, the very pictures of which he found so terrible; it was publicly announced that the emperor would not go forth to war. The soldiers, enraged, began to gather in angry groups, rebuking one another for their over-patience in submitting to be ruled by such a coward. "How? Are we men, and have we swords in our hands, and shall we any longer bear with such disgraceful effeminacy, by which the might of this great Empire is sapped, so that every barbarian who chooses may carve out a slice from it?"

These clamours were rapidly growing seditious, and in a few days an anti-emperor would probably have been proclaimed; but Zeno, more afraid of his soldiers than even of the Goths, adroitly moved them into their widely-scattered winter-quarters, leaving the invaded provinces to take care of themselves for a little time, while he tried by his own natural weapons of bribery and intrigue to detach the *other* and older Theodoric from the new confederacy.

On this path he met with unmerited success. The son of Triarius, who had lately been uttering such noble sentiments about Gothic kinship, and the folly of Gothic warriors playing into the hands of their hereditary enemies, the crafty courtiers of Constantinople, soon came to terms with the emperor, and on receiving the command of two brigades of household troops,[6] his restoration to all the dignities which he had held under Basiliscus, the military office which his rival had forfeited, and rations and allowances for 13,000 of his followers, broke his alliance with Theodoric the Amal, and entered the service of the Emperor of New Rome.

Theodoric the Amal, who was now in his own despite (479) an outlaw from the Roman state, burst in fierce wrath into Macedonia, into the region where he and his people had been first quartered five years before. Again he marched down the valley of the Vardar, he took Stobi, putting its garrison to the sword, and threatened the great city of Thessalonica. The citizens, fearing that Zeno would abandon them to the barbarians, broke out into open sedition, threw down the statues of the emperor, took the keys of the city from the *prefect* and entrusted them to the safer keeping of their Bishop. Zeno sent ambassadors reproaching the Amal for his ungrateful requital of the unexampled favours and dignities which had been conferred upon him, and inviting him to return to his old fidelity.

Theodoric showed himself not unwilling to treat, sent ambassadors to Constantinople, and ordered his troops to refrain from murder and conflagration, and to take only the absolute necessaries of life from the provincials. He then quitted the precincts of Thessalonica and moved westwards to the city of Heraclea (*Monastir*), which lies at the foot of the great mountain range that separates Macedonia from Epirus. While talking of peace he was already meditating a new and brilliant stroke of strategy, but he was for some time hindered from accomplishing it by the illness of his sister, who, perhaps fatigued by the hardships of the march, had fallen sick in the camp before Heraclea. This time of enforced delay was occupied by negotiations with the emperor. But the emperor had really nothing to offer worth the Ostrogoth's acceptance.

A settlement on the Pantalian plain, a bleak upland among the Balkans, about forty miles south of Sardica (*Sofia*), and a payment of two

---

6. Scholæ.

65

hundred pounds' weight of gold (£8,000) as subsistence-money for the people till they should have had time to till the land and reap their first harvest, this was all that Zeno offered to the chief, who already in imagination saw the rich cities of the Adriatic lying defenceless at his feet. For during this time of inaction the Amal had opened communications with a Gothic landowner, named Sigismund, who dwelt near Dyrrhachium (*Durazzo*), and was a man of influence in the province of Epirus; and Sigismund, though nominally a loyal subject of the emperor, was doing his best to sow fear and discouragement in the hearts of the citizens of Dyrrhachium and to prepare the way for the advent of his countrymen.

At length the Gothic princess died, and her brother, the Amal, having vainly sought to put Heraclea to ransom (the citizens had retired to a strong fortress which commanded it), burned the deserted city, a deed more worthy of a barbarian than of one bred up in the Roman Commonwealth. Then with all his nation-army he started off upon the great Egnatian Way, which, threading the rough passes of Mount Scardus, leads from Macedonia to Epirus, from the shores of the Ægean to the shores of the Adriatic. His light horsemen went first to reconnoitre the path; then followed Theodoric himself with the first division of his army. Soas, his second in command, ordered the movements of the middle host; last of all came the rear-guard, commanded by Theodoric's brother, Theudimund, and protecting the march of the women, the cattle, and the waggons. It was a striking proof both of their leader's audacity and of his knowledge of the decay of martial spirit among the various garrisons that lined the Egnatian Way, that he should have ventured with such a train into such a perilous country, where at every turn were narrow defiles which a few brave men might have held against an army.

The Amal and his host passed safely through the defiles of Scardus and reached the fortress of Lychnidus overlooking a lake now known as Lake Ochrida. Here Theodoric met with his first repulse. The fortress was immensely strong by nature, was well stored with corn, and had springing fountains of its own, and the garrison were therefore not to be frightened into surrender. Accordingly, leaving the fortress untaken, Theodoric with his two first divisions pushed rapidly across the second and lower range, the Candavian Mountains, leaving Theudimund with the waggons and the women to follow more slowly. In this arrangement there was probably an error of judgement which Theodoric had occasion bitterly to regret.

For the moment, however, he was completely successful. Descending into the plain he took the towns of Scampæ (*Elbassan*) and Dyrrhachium (Durazzo), both of which, probably owing to the discouraging counsels of Sigismund, seem to have been abandoned by their inhabitants.

Great was the consternation at Edessa (a town about thirty miles west of Thessalonica and the headquarters of the Imperial troops) when the news of this unexpected march of Theodoric across the mountains was brought into the camp. Not only the general-in-chief, Sabinianus, was quartered there, but also a certain Adamantius, an official of the highest rank, who had been charged by Zeno with the conduct of the negotiations with Theodoric, and whose whole soul seems to have been set on the success of his mission. He contrived to communicate with Theodoric, and advanced with Sabinianus through the mountains as far as Lychnidus in order to conduct the discussion at closer quarters. Propositions passed backwards and forwards as to the terms upon which a meeting could be arranged.

Theodoric sent a Gothic priest; Adamantius in reply offered to come in person to Dyrrhachium if Soas and another Gothic noble were sent as hostages for his safe return. Theodoric was willing to send the hostages if Sabinianus would swear that they should return in safety. This, however, for some reason or other, the general surlily and stubbornly refused to do, and Adamantius saw the earnestly desired interview fading away into impossibility. At length, with courageous self-devotion, he succeeded in finding a by-path across the mountains, which brought him to a fort, situated on a hill and strengthened by a deep ditch, in sight of Dyrrhachium. From thence he sent messengers to Theodoric earnestly soliciting a conference; and the Amal, leaving his army in the plain, rode with a few horsemen to the banks of the stream which separated him from Adamantius' stronghold.

Adamantius, too, to guard against a surprise, placed his little band of soldiers in a circle round the hill, and then descended to the stream, and with none to listen to their speech, commenced the long-desired colloquy. How Adamantius may have opened his case we are not informed, but the Ostrogoth's reply is worth quoting word for word:

> It was my choice to live altogether out of Thrace, far away towards Scythia, where I should disturb no one by my presence, and yet should be ready to go forth thence to do the emperor's bidding. But you having called me forth, as if for war against

the son of Tnarius, first of all promised that the General of Thrace should immediately join me with his forces (he never appeared); and then that Claudius, the Steward of the Goth-money,[7] should meet me with the pay of the mercenaries (him I never saw); and thirdly, you gave me guides for my journey, but what sort of guides? Men who, leaving untrodden all the easier roads into the enemy's country, led me by a steep path and along the sharp edges of cliffs, where, had the enemy attacked us, travelling as we were bound to do with horsemen and wag-gons and all the lumber of our camp, it had been a marvel if I and all my folk had not been utterly destroyed. Hence I was forced to make such terms as I could with the foes, and in fact I owe them many thanks that, when you had betrayed and they might have consumed me, they nevertheless spared my life.

Adamantius went over the old story about the great benefits which the emperor had bestowed on Theodoric, the Patriciate, the Master-ship, the rich presents, and all the other evidences of his fatherly regard. He attempted to answer the charges brought by Theodoric, but in this even the Greek historian[8] who records the dialogue thinks that he failed. With more show of reason he complained of the march across the mountains and the dash into Epirus, while negotiations were pro-ceeding with Constantinople. He recommended him to make peace with the Empire while it was in his power, and assuring him that he would never be allowed to lord it over the great cities of Epirus nor to banish their citizens from thence to make room for his people, again pressed him to accept the emperor's offer of "Dardania" (the Pantal-ian plain), "where there was abundance of land, beside that which was already inhabited, a fair and fertile territory lacking cultivators, which his people could till, so providing themselves in abundance with all the necessaries of life."

Theodoric refused with an oath to take his toil-worn people who had served him so faithfully, at that time of year (it was now perhaps autumn) into Dardania. No! they must all remain in Epirus for the winter; then if they could agree upon the rest of the terms he might be willing in spring to follow a guide sent by the emperor to lead them to their new abode. But more than this, he was ready to deposit

7. **Τὸν τοῦ Γοτθικοῦ ταμίαν**. Probably the *Gothicum* was a fund set apart for subsidising the Goths.
8. Malchus of Philadelphia.

his baggage and all his unwarlike folk in any city which the emperor might appoint, to give his mother and his sister as hostages for his entire fidelity, and then to advance at once with ten thousand of his bravest warriors into Thrace, as the emperor's ally. With these men and the Imperial armies now stationed in the Illyrian provinces, he would undertake to sweep Thrace clear of all the Goths who followed the son of Triarius. Only he stipulated that in that case he should be clothed with his old dignity of Master of the Soldiery, which had been taken from him and bestowed on his rival, and that he should be received into the Commonwealth and allowed to live—as he evidently yearned to live—as a Roman citizen.

Adamantius replied that he was not empowered to treat on such terms while Theodoric remained in Epirus, but he would refer his proposal to the emperor, and with this understanding they parted one from the other.

Meanwhile, important, and for the Goths disastrous, events had been taking place in the Candavian mountains. Over these the rearguard of Theodoric's army, with the waggons and the baggage, had been slowly making its way, in a security which was no doubt chiefly caused by the facility of the previous marches, but to which the knowledge of the negotiations going forward between king and emperor may partly have contributed. In any case, security was certainly insecure with such a fort as Lychnidus untaken in their rear. The garrison of that fort had been reinforced by many cohorts of the regular army who had flocked thither at the general's signal, and with these Sabinianus prepared a formidable ambuscade. He sent a considerable number of infantry round by unfrequented paths over the mountains, and ordered them to take up a commanding but concealed position, and to rush forth from thence at a given signal.

He himself started with his cavalry from Lychnidus at nightfall, and rode rapidly along the Egnatian Way. At dawn the pursuing horsemen attacked the Goths, who were just descending the last mountain slopes into the plain. Theudimund, with his mother, was riding near the head of the long line of march. Too anxious perhaps for her safety, and fearing to meet the reproachful looks of Theodoric if aught of harm happened to her, he hurried her across the last bridge, spanning a deep defile, which intervened between the mountains and the plain, and then broke down the bridge behind him to prevent pursuit. Pursuit was indeed rendered impossible, and the mother of Theodoric was saved, but at what a cost! The Goths turned back to fight, with the courage of despair, the pursuing cavalry.

At that moment the infantry in ambush, having received the signal, began to attack them from the rocks above. The position was a terrible one, and many brave men fell in the hopeless battle. Quarter, however, was given by the Imperial soldiers, for we are told that more than five thousand of the Goths were taken prisoners. The booty was large; and all the waggons of the barbarians, two thousand in number, were of course captured, but the soldiers, misliking the toil of dragging them back over all those jagged passes to Lychnidus, burned them there as they stood upon the Candavian mountains.

I have copied with some minuteness the account given us by the Greek historian of this mountain march of Theodoric, because it brings before us with more than usual vividness the conditions under which the campaigns of the barbarians were conducted. It will have been noticed that the Gothic army is not only an army but a nation, and that the campaign is also a migration. The mother and the sister of Theodoric are accompanying him. There is evidently a long train of non-combatants, old men, women, and children, following the army in those two thousand Gothic waggons. The character attributed by Horace to the

> *Campestres Scythæ,*
> *Quorum plaustra vagas rite trahunt domos*

still survives. Still

> *The waggon holds the Scythian's wandering home.*

The Goth, a terrible enemy to those outside the pale of his kinship, is a home-lover at heart, and even in war will not separate himself from his wife and children. This makes his impact slow, his campaigns unscientific. It prepares for him frequent defeats, such as that of the Candavian Mountains, which a celibate army would have avoided. But it makes his conquests, when he does conquer, more enduring, while it explains those perpetual demands for land, for a settlement within the Empire, almost on any terms, with which, as was before shown, the barbarian inroads so often close. We need not follow the tedious story of the negotiations with Adamantius, which were interrupted by this sudden success of the Imperial arms.

In fact at this point our best authority,[9] who has been unusually

---

9. Malchus of Philadelphia, from whose history certain *Extracts concerning Embassies* were made by order of the Emperor Constantine Porphyrogemtus.

full and graphic for the events of 478 and 479, suddenly fails us, and we have scarcely anything but dry and scanty annalistic notices for the next nine years of the life of Theodoric. He seems not to have maintained his footing in Epirus, but to have returned to the neighbourhood of the Danube, where he fought and conquered the king of the Bulgarians, a fresh horde of barbarians who at this time made their first appearance in "the Balkan peninsula" Whether the much desired reconciliation with the Empire took place we know not. It seems probable that this may have been the case, as in the year 481 we find his rival, the other Theodoric, in opposition, and planning an invasion of Greece.

But the career of the son of Triarius was about to come to an untimely close. Marching westwards, he had reached a station on the Egnatian Way, near the frontiers of Thrace and Macedonia, called "The Stables of Diomed," and there pitched his camp. One morning he would fain mount his horse for a gallop across the plain, but before he was securely seated in the saddle the horse reared. The rider, afraid to grasp the bridle firmly lest he should pull the creature over upon him, clung tightly to his seat, but could not guide the horse, which, in its dancing and prancing, came sidling past the door of the tent. There was hanging, in barbarian fashion, a spear fastened by a thong. The horse shied up against the spear, whose point gored his master's side. He was not killed on the spot, but died soon after of the wound. After some domestic dissensions and bloodshed, the leadership of his band passed to his son Recitach, apparently a hot-tempered and tyrannical youth.

Three years after his father's death (484), Recitach, now an enemy of the Empire, was put to death by Theodoric the Amal, acting under the orders of Zeno. The band of Triarian Goths, thirty thousand fighting men in number, was joined to the army of Theodoric, an important addition to his power, but also to his cares, to the ever-present difficulty of finding food for his followers.

(481-487) Backwards and forwards between peace and war with the Empire, Theodoric wavered during the six years which followed his rival's death. The settlement of his people at this time seems to have been on the southern shore of the Danube, in part of the countries now known as Servia and Wallachia, with Novæ (*Sistova*) for his headquarters. One year (482) he is making a raid into Macedonia and Thessaly and plundering Larissa. The next (483) he is again clothed with his old dignity of Master of the Soldiery and keeps his Goths

71

rigidly within their allotted limits. The next (484) he is actually raised to the Consulate, an office which, though devoid of power, is still so radiant with the glory of the illustrious men who have held it for near a thousand years, from the days of Brutus and Collatinus, that emperors covet the possession of it and the mightiest barbarian chiefs in their service long for no higher reward.

Two years after this (486) he is again in rebellion, ravaging Thrace; the next year (487) he has broken through the Long Walls and penetrates within fourteen miles of Constantinople. In all this wearisome period of Theodoric's life his action seems to be merely destructive; there is nothing constructive, no fruitful or fertilising thought to be found in it. Had this been a fair sample of his life, there could be no reason why he should not sink into the oblivion which covers so many forgotten freebooters. But in 488 a change came over the spirit of his dream. A plan was agreed upon between him and the emperor (by which of them it was first suggested we cannot now say) for the employment of all this wasted and destructive force in another field, where its energies might accomplish some result beneficent and enduring.

That new field was Italy, and in order to understand the conditions of the problem which there awaited Theodoric, we must briefly recount the chief events which had happened in that peninsula since Attila departed from untaken Rome in compliance with the petition of Pope Leo.

GOLDEN *SOLIDUS*. (LEO II ZENO)

CHAPTER 6

Italy Under Odovacar

In former chapters I have very briefly sketched the fortunes of the Italian peninsula during two great barbarian invasions—that of Alaric (407-410) and that of Attila (452). The monarch who ruled the Western Empire at the date of the last invasion was Valentinian III., grandson of the great Theodosius. He dwelt sometimes at Rome, sometimes at Ravenna, which latter city, protected by the waves of the Adriatic and by the innumerable canals and pools through which the waters of two rivers [1] flowed lazily to the sea, was all but impregnable by the barbarians. A selfish and indolent voluptuary, Valentinian III. made no valuable contribution to the defence of the menaced Empire, some stones of which were being shaken down every year by the tremendous blows of the Teutonic invaders.

Any wisdom that might be shown in the councils of the state was due to his mother, Galla Placidia, who, till her death in 451, was the real ruler of the Empire. Any strength and valour that was displayed in its defence was due to the great minister and general, Aëtius, a man who had himself, probably, many drops of barbarian blood in his veins, though he has been not unfitly styled "the last of the Romans." It was Aëtius who, as we have seen, in concert with the Visigothic king, fought the fight of civilisation against Hunnish barbarism on the Catalaunian battle-plain. It was to "Aëtius, thrice Consul," that "the groans of the Britons" were addressed when "the Barbarians drove them to the sea, and the sea drove them back on the Barbarians."

When Attila was dead, the weak and worthless emperor seems to have thought that he might safely dispense with the services of this too powerful subject. Inviting Aëtius to his palace, he debated with him a scheme for the marriage of their children (the son of the gen-

---

1. The Ronco and the Montone.

eral was to wed the daughter of the emperor), and when the debate grew warm, with calculated passion he snatched a sword from one of his guardsmen, and with it pierced the body of Aëtius. The bloody work was finished by the courtiers standing by, and the most eminent of the friends and counsellors of the deceased statesman were murdered at the same time.

The foul assassination of this great defender of the Roman State was requited next year by two barbarians of his train, men who no doubt cherished for Aëtius the same feelings of personal loyalty which bound the members of a Teutonic "*Comitatus*" to their chief, and who deemed life a dishonour while their leader's blood remained unavenged. On a day in March, while Valentinian was watching intently the games in the Campus Martius of Rome, these two barbarians rushed upon him and stabbed him, slaying at the same time the eunuch, who had been his chief confederate in the murder of Aëtius.

With Valentinian III. the line of Theodosius, which had swayed the Roman sceptre for eighty-six years, came to an end. None of the men who after him bore the great title of Augustus in Rome (I am speaking, of course, of the fifth century only) succeeded in founding a dynasty. Not only was no one of them followed by a son: scarcely one of them was suffered to end his own reign in peace. Of the nine emperors who wore the purple in Italy after the death of Valentinian, only two ended their reigns in the course of nature, four were deposed, and three met their death by violence.

Only one reigned for more than five years; several could only measure the duration of their royalty by months. Even the short period (455-476) which these nine reigns occupy is not entirely filled by them, for there were frequent *interregna*, one lasting for a year and eight months. And the men were as feeble as their kingly life was short and precarious. With the single exception of Majorian, (457-461), a brave and strong man, and one who, if fair play had been given him, would have assuredly done something to stay the ruin of the Empire, all of these nine men (with whose names there is no need to burden the reader's memory) are fitly named by a German historian "the Shadow Emperors."

During sixteen years of this time (456-472), supreme power in the Empire was virtually wielded by a nobleman of barbarian origin, but naturalised in the Roman State, the proud and stern "Patrician" Ricimer. This man, descended from the chiefs of the Suevi[2] grandson

2. A widely spread German nation, the largest fragment of which was at this time settled in the west of Spain and in Portugal.

of a Visigothic king, and brother-in-law of a king of the Burgundians, was doubtless able to bring much barbaric influence to support the cause which, from whatever motives, he had espoused,—the cause of the defence of that which was left to Rome of her Empire in the west of Europe.

Many Teutonic tribes had by this time settled themselves in the Imperial lands. Spain was quite lost to the Empire: some fragments of Gaul were still bound to it by a most precarious tie; but the loss which threatened the life of the state most nearly was the loss of Africa. For this province, the capital of which was the restored and Romanised city of Carthage, had been for generations the chief exporter of corn to feed the pauperised population of Rome, and here now dwelt and ruled, and from hence (428-432) sallied forth to his piratical raids against Italy, the deadliest enemy of the Roman name, the king of the Vandals, Gaiseric.[3] The Vandal conquest of Africa was, at the time which we have now reached, a somewhat old story, nearly a generation having elapsed since it occurred,[4] but the Vandal sack of Rome, which came to pass immediately after the death of Valentinian III., and which marked the beginning of the period of the "Shadow Emperors" was still near and terrible to the memories of men.

No Roman but remembered in bitterness of soul how in June, 455, the long ships of the Vandals appeared at the mouth of the Tiber, how Gaiseric and his men landed, marched to the Eternal City, and entered it unopposed, how they remained there for a fortnight, not perhaps slaying or ravishing, but with calm insolence plundering the city of all that they cared to carry away, stripping off what they supposed to be the golden roof of the Capitol, removing the statues from their pedestals, transporting everything that seemed beautiful or costly, and stowing away all their spoils in the holds of those insatiable vessels of theirs which lay at anchor at Ostia.

The remembrance of this humiliating capture and the fear that it might at any moment be repeated, probably with circumstances of greater atrocity, were the dominant emotions in the hearts of the Roman Senate and people during the twenty-one years which we are now rapidly surveying. It was doubtless these feelings which induced

---

3. Commonly but incorrectly called Genseric. The form used above, which is that found in nearly all contemporary historians, is now almost universally employed by German scholars.
4. The capture of Carthage, which completed the conquest, did not take place till 439.

them to submit more patiently than they would otherwise have done to the scarcely veiled autocracy of an imperfectly Romanised Teuton such as Ricimer. He was a barbarian, it was true; probably he could not even speak Latin grammatically; but he was mighty with the barbarian kings, mighty with the *fœderati* the rough soldiers gathered from every German tribe on the other side of the Alps, who now formed the bulk of the Imperial army; let him be as arrogant as he would to the Senate, let him set up and pull down one "Shadow Emperor" after another, if only he would keep the streets of Rome from being again profaned by the tread of the terrible Vandal.

(456-468) To a certain extent the confidence reposed in Ricimer was not misplaced. He inflicted a severe defeat on the Vandals in a naval engagement near the island of Corsica; he raised to the throne the young and valiant Majorian, who repelled a Vandal invasion of Campania; he planned, in conjunction with the Eastern emperor, a great expedition against Carthage, which failed through no fault of his, but by the bad generalship of Basiliscus, whose brother-in-law, Leo, had appointed him to the command. But the rule of a barbarian like Ricimer exercised on the sacred soil of Italy, and the brutal arrogance with which he dashed down one of his puppet-emperors after another when they had served his purpose, must have done much to break the spirit of the Roman nobles and the Roman commonalty, and to prepare the way for the Teutonic revolution which occurred soon after his death. Above all, we have reason to think that, during the whole time of Ricimer's ascendancy, the barbarian *fœderati* were becoming more absolutely dominant in the Roman army, and with waxing numbers were growing more insolent in their demeanour, and more intolerable In their demands.

The ranks of the *fœderati* were at this time recruited, not from one of the great historic nationalities—Visigoth, Ostrogoth, Frank, or Burgundian,—but chiefly from a number of petty tribes, known as the Rugii, Scyri, Heruli, and Turcilingi, who have failed to make any enduring mark in history. These tribes, which upon the break-up of Attila's Empire had established themselves on the shore of the Middle Danube, north and west of the lands occupied by the Ostrogoths, were continually sending their young warriors over the passes of Noricum (*Salzburg, Styria,* and *Carinthia*) to seek their fortune in Italy. One of these recruits, on his southward journey, stepped into the cave of a holy hermit named Severinus, and stooping his lofty stature in the lowly cell, asked the saint's blessing. When the blessing was given, the youth said: "Farewell." "Not farewell, but fare forward",[5] answered Severinus. "Onward into Italy: skin-clothed now, but destined before long to enrich many men with costly gifts." The name of this young recruit was Odovacar.[6]

Odovacar probably entered Italy about 465. He attached himself to the party of Ricimer, and before long became a conspicuous captain of *fœderati* After the death of Ricimer (18th August, 472), there was a series of rapid revolutions in the Roman State. Olybrius, the then reigning nonentity, died in October of the same year.

(June, 474) After five months' *interregnum*, a yet more shadowy shadow, Glycerius, succeeded him, and after fifteen months of rule was thrust from the throne by Julius Nepos, who had married the niece of Verina, the mischief-making Augusta of the East, and who was, therefore, supported by all the moral influence of Constantinople.

Nepos, after fourteen months of Empire, in which he distinguished himself only by the loss of some (Oct., 475) Gaulish provinces to the Visigoths, was in his turn dethroned by the Master of the Soldiery, Orestes, who had once held a subordinate situation in the court of Attila. Nepos fled to Dalmatia, which was probably his native land, and lived there for four years after his dethronement, still keeping up some at least of the state which belonged to a Roman emperor.

We know very little of the pretexts for these rapid revolutions, or the circumstances attending them, but there cannot be much doubt that the army was the chief agent in what, to borrow a phrase from modern Spanish politics, were a series of *pronunciamentos*. For some reason which is dim to us, Orestes, though a full-blooded Roman citizen, did not set the diadem on his own head, but placed it on that of his son, a handsome boy of some fourteen or fifteen years, named Romulus, and nicknamed "the little Augustus." For himself, he took the dignity of "Patrician," which had been so long worn by Ricimer, and was associated in men's minds with the practical mastery of the Empire. But a ruler who has been raised to the throne by military sedition soon finds that the authors of his elevation are the most exacting of masters.

The *fœderati*, who knew themselves now absolute arbiters of the destiny of the Empire, and who had the same craving for a settlement within its borders which we have met with more than once among

---

5. "*Vale.*" "*Vade.*"
6. This is the form of the name used by contemporary historians; Odoacer is a later and less authentic form.

the followers of Theodoric, presented themselves before the Patrician Orestes, and demanded that one-third of the lands of Italy should be assigned to them as a perpetual inheritance. This was more than Orestes dared to grant, and, on his refusal, Odovacar said to the mercenaries: "Make me king and I will obtain for you your desire."

(23rd Aug., 476) The offer was accepted; Odovacar was lifted high on a shield by the arms of stalwart barbarians, and saluted as king by their unanimous acclamations.

When the *fœderati* were gathered out of the "Roman" army, there seems to have been nothing left that was capable of making any real defence of the Empire. The campaign, if such it may be called, between Odovacar and Orestes was of the shortest and most perfunctory kind. Ticinum (*Pavia*), in which Orestes had taken refuge, was taken, sacked, and partly burnt by the barbarians. The Master of the Soldiery himself fled to Placentia, but was there taken prisoner and beheaded, only five days after the elevation of Odovacar. A week later his brother Paulus, who had not men enough to hold even the strong city of Ravenna, was taken prisoner, and slain in the great pine-forest outside that city. At Ravenna the young puppet-emperor, Romulus, was also taken prisoner. The barbarian showed himself more merciful, perhaps also more contemptuous, towards his boy-rival than was the custom of the Emperors of Rome and Constantinople towards the sons of their competitors.

Odovacar, who pitied the tender years of Augustulus, and looked with admiration on his beautiful countenance, spared his life and assigned to him for a residence the palace and gardens of Lucullus, the conqueror of Mithridates, who five and a half centuries before had prepared for himself this beautiful home (the Lucullanum) in the very heart of the lovely Bay of Naples. The building and the fortifying of a great commercial city have utterly altered the whole aspect of the bay, but in the long egg-shaped peninsula, on which stands today the Castel dell' Ovo, we can still see the outlines of the famous Lucullanum, in which the last Roman Emperor of Rome ended his inglorious days. His conqueror generously allowed him a pension of £3,600 *per annum*, but for how long this pension continued to be a charge on the revenues of the new kingdom we are unable to say. There is one doubtful indication of his having survived his abdication by about thirty years,[7] but clear historical notices of his subsequent life and of

---

7 I allude here to a letter in the Vanarum of Cassiodorus (iii., 35), written between 504 and 525, and addressed to Romulus and his mother. But we can by no means prove that this is Romulus Augustulus.

the date of his death are denied us; a striking proof of the absolute nullity of his character.

This then was the event which stands out in the history of Europe as the "Fall of the Western Empire" The reader will perceive that it was no great and terrible invasion of a conquering host like the Fall of the Eastern Empire in 1453; no sudden overthrow of a national polity like the Norman Conquest of 1066; not even a bloody overturning of the existing order by demagogic force like the French Revolution of 1792. It was but the continuance of a process which had been going forward more or less manifestly for nearly a century,—the recognition of the fact that the *fœderati*, the so-called barbarian mercenaries of Rome, were really her masters. If we had to seek a parallel for the event of 476, we should find it rather in the deposition of the last Mogul emperor at Delhi, and the public assumption by the British Queen of the "*Raj*" over the greater part of India, than in any of the other events to which we have alluded.

Reflecting on this fact, and seeing that the Roman Empire still lived on in the East for nearly a thousand years, that the Eastern Cæsar never for many generations relinquished his claim to be considered the legitimate ruler of the Old Rome, as well as of the New, and sometimes asserted that claim in a very real and effective manner, and considering too that Charles the Great, when he (in modern phrase) "restored the Western Empire" in 800, never professed to be the successor of Romulus Augustulus, but of Constantine VI., the then recently deposed emperor of the East; the latest school of historical investigators, with scarcely an exception, minimise the importance of the event of 476, and some even object to the expression "Fall of the Western Empire" as fitly describing it. The protest is a sound one and was greatly needed. Perhaps now the danger is in the other direction, and there is a risk of our making too little of an event in which after all the sceptre did manifestly depart from Rome.

During the whole interval between Odovacar's accession and Belisarius' occupation of Rome (476-536), no Roman, however proud or patriotic, could blind himself to the fact that a man of barbarian blood was the real, and in a certain sense the supreme, ruler of his country. Ricimer might be looked upon as an eminent servant of the Emperor who had the misfortune to be of barbarian birth. Odovacar and Theodoric were, without all contradiction, kings; if not "kings of Italy," at any rate "kings in Italy," sometimes actually making war on the Cæsar of Byzantium, and not caring, when they did so, to set up the phantom of a rival emperor in order to legitimise their opposition. But in a matter so greatly debated as this it will be safer not to use our own or any modern words.

This is how Count Marcellinus, an official of the Eastern Empire, writing his annals about fifty-eight years after the deposition of Romulus, describes the event:

> Odovacar killed Orestes and condemned his son Augustulus to the punishment of exile in the Lucullanum, a castle of Campania. The Hesperian (Western) Empire of the Roman people, which Octavianus Augustus first of the Augusti began to hold in the 709th year of the building of the city (B.C. 44), perished with this Augustulus in the 522nd year of his predecessors (A.D. 476), the kings of the Goths thenceforward holding both Rome and Italy.[8]

Of the details of Odovacar's rule in Italy we know very little. Of course the *fœderati* had their will, at any rate in some measure, with reference to the assignment of land in Italy, but no historian has told us anything as to the social disorganisation which such a redistribution of property must have produced. There are some indications that it was not thoroughly carried into effect, at any rate in the South of Italy, and that the settlements of the *fœderati* were chiefly in the valley of the Po, and in the districts since known as the Romagna.

The old Imperial machinery of government was taken over by the new ruler, and in all outward appearance things probably went on under King Odovacar much as they had done under Count Ricimer. No great act of cruelty or oppression stains the memory of Odovacar. He lost Provence to the Visigoths, but, on the other hand, he by judicious diplomacy recovered Sicily from the Vandals. Altogether it is probable that Italy was, at any rate, not more miserable under the sway of this barbarian king than she had been at any time since Alaric's invasion, in 408, proclaimed her helplessness to the world.

One piece of solemn comedy is worth relating, namely, the embassies despatched to Constantinople by the rival claimants to the dominion of Italy. It was probably towards the end of 477, or early in

8. "*Orestem Odoacer llico trucidavit, Augustulum filium Orestis Odoacer in Lucullano Campania castello exilii poena damnavit. Hesperium Romana gentis imperium, quod septingentesimo nono urbis condita anno primus Augustorum Octavianus Augustus tenere cœpit, cum hoc Augustulo periit, anno decessorum regni Imperatorum DXXII. Gothorum dehinc regibus Romam tenentibus.*" It will be seen that there is an error of two years in the calculation.

478, that Zeno, then recently returned from exile after the usurpation of Basiliscus, received two embassies from two deposed emperors of the West. First of all came the ambassadors of Augustulus, or rather of the Roman Senate, sent nominally by the orders of Augustulus, really by those of Odovacar.

These men, great Roman nobles, represented "that they did not need an emperor of their own. One absolute ruler was sufficient to guard both East and West; but they had, moreover, chosen Odovacar, who was well able to protect their interests, being a man wise in counsel and brave in war. They therefore prayed the emperor to bestow on him the dignity of *patrician*, and to entrust to him the administration of the affairs of Italy."

At the same time (apparently) they brought the ornaments of the Imperial dignity, the diadem, the purple robe, the jewelled buskins, which had been worn by all the "Shadow Emperors" who flitted across the stage, and requested that they might be laid up in the Imperial palace at Constantinople.

Simultaneously there came ambassadors from Nepos, the Imperial refugee, the nephew by marriage of Verina. From his Dalmatian exile he congratulated his kinsman Zeno on his recent restoration to the throne, and begged him to lend men and money to bring about the like happy result for him by replacing him on the Western throne.

To these embassies Zeno returned ambiguous answers, which seemed to leave the question as to the legitimacy of Odovacar's rule an open one. The Senate were sharply rebuked for having acquiesced in the dethronement of Nepos, and a previous emperor who had been sent to them from the East.[9] Odovacar was recommended to seek the coveted dignity from Nepos, and to co-operate for his return. At the same time, the moderation of Odovacar's rule, and his desire to conform himself to the maxims of Roman civilisation, received the Emperor's praise.

The nature of the reply to Nepos is not recorded, but it was no doubt made plain to him that sympathy and good wishes were all that he would receive from his Eastern colleague. The letters addressed to Odovacar bore the superscription "To the Patrician Odovacar," and that was all that the barbarian really cared for. With such a title as this, every act, even the most high-handed, on the part of the barbarian king was rendered legitimate.

Nepos and Augustulus were equally excluded as useless encum-

---

9. Anthemius.

brances to the state, and the kings *de jure* and *de facto* became practically one man, and that man Odovacar.

HALF-*SILIQUA* OF SILVER. (*ODOVACAR*.)

CHAPTER 7

The Conquest of Italy

The friendly relations between Odovacar and the Eastern emperor which had been established by the embassy last described were gradually altered into estrangement. In the year 480, Nepos, the dethroned Emperor of Rome, was stabbed by two treacherous courtiers in his palace near Salona. Odovacar led an army into Dalmatia, and avenged the murder, but also apparently annexed the province of Dalmatia to his dominion, thus coming into nearer neighbourhood with Constantinople (487-488) This may have been one cause of alienation, but a more powerful one was the negotiation which was commenced in the year 484 between Odovacar and Illus, the last of the many insurgent generals who disturbed the reign of Zeno. At first Odovacar held himself aloof from the proposed confederacy, but afterwards (486) he was disposed, or Zeno believed that he was disposed, to accept the alliance of the insurgent general.

In order to find him sufficient occupation nearer home, the Emperor fanned into a flame the smouldering embers of discord between Odovacar and Feletheus, king of the Rugians, the most powerful ruler of those Danubian lands from which the Italian king himself had migrated into Italy. The Rugian war was short, and Odovacar's success was decisive. In 487 he vanquished the Rugian army and carried Feletheus and his wife prisoners to Ravenna. In 488 an attempt to raise again the standard of the Rugian monarchy, which was made by Frederic, the son of Feletheus, was crushed, and Frederic, an exile and a fugitive, betook himself to the camp of Theodoric, who was then dwelling at Novæ(*Sistova?*), on the Danube.

When the attempt to weaken Odovacar by means of his fellow-barbarians in "Rugiland" failed, Zeno feigned outward acquiescence, offering congratulations on the victory and receiving presents out of the Rugian spoils, but in his heart he felt that there must now be war to the death between him and this too powerful ruler of Italy. The news came to him at a time when Theodoric was in one of his most turbulent and destructive moods, when he had penetrated within fourteen miles of Constantinople and had fired the towns and villages of Thrace, perhaps even within sight of the capital. It was a natural thought and not altogether an unstatesmanlike expedient to play off one disturber of his peace against the other, to commission Theodoric to dethrone the "tyrant" Odovacar, and thus at least earn repose for the provincials of Thrace, perhaps secure an ally at Ravenna. Theodoric, we may be sure, with those instincts of civilisation and love for the Empire which had been in his heart from boyhood, though often repressed and disobeyed, needed little exhortation to an enterprise which he may himself have suggested to the emperor.

Thus then it came to pass that a formal interview was arranged between emperor and king (perhaps at Constantinople, though it seems doubtful whether Theodoric could have safely trusted himself within its walls), and at this interview the terms of the joint enterprise were arranged, an enterprise to which Theodoric was to contribute all the effective strength and Zeno the glamour of Imperial legitimacy.

When the high contracting parties met, Theodoric lamented the hapless condition of Italy and Rome: Italy once subject to the predecessors of Zeno; Rome, once the mistress of the world, now harassed and distressed by the usurped authority of a king of Rugians and Turcilingians. If the emperor would send Theodoric thither with his people, he would be at once relieved from the heavy charges of their *stipendia* which he was now bound to furnish, while Theodoric would hold the land as of the free gift of the emperor, and would reign there as king, only till Zeno himself should arrive to claim the supremacy.[1]

In the autumn of the year 488, Theodoric with all his host set forth from Sistova on the Danube on his march to Italy. His road was the same taken by Alaric and by most of the barbarian invaders; along the Danube as far as Belgrade, then between the rivers Drave and Save or along the banks of one of them till he reached the Julian Alps (not

1. The account of this important interview is combined from two sources: Jordanes, the Gothic historian, who naturally magnifies Theodoric's share in the inception of the enterprise; and a chronicler known as "*Anonymus Valesii*," who evidently writes in the interest of Zeno. It is from the latter only that we have any hint of an intended visit of Zeno to Italy, a visit which certainly never took place. Procopius, who also writes from the Byzantine point of view, attributes the conception of the design to Zeno.

far from the modern city of Laibach), then down upon Aquileia and the Venetian plain. As in the Macedonian campaign, so now, he was accompanied by all the members of his nation, old men and children, mothers and maidens, and doubtless by a long train of waggons.

We have no accurate information whatever as to the number of his army, but various indications, both in earlier and later history, seem to justify us in assuming that the soldiers must have numbered fully 40,000; and if this was the case, the whole nation cannot have been less than 200,000. The difficulty of finding food for so great a multitude in the often desolated plains of Pannonia and Noricum must have been enormous, and was no doubt the reason of the slowness of Theodoric's progress. Very probably he divided his army into several portions, moving on parallel lines; foragers would scour the country far and wide, stores of provisions would be accumulated in the great Gothic waggons, which would be laboriously driven over the rough mountain passes.

Then all the divisions of the army which had scattered in search of food would have to concentrate again when they came into the neighbourhood of an enemy, whether Odovacar or one of the barbarian kings who sought to bar their progress. All these operations consumed much time, and hence it was that though the Goths started on their pilgrimage in 488 (probably in the autumn of that year) they did not descend into the plains of Italy even at its extreme north-eastern corner, till July, 489.

There was one fact which probably facilitated the progress of Theodoric, and prevented his expedition with such a multitude from being condemned as absolute foolhardiness. His road lay, for the most part, through regions with which he was already well acquainted, through a land which might almost be called his native land, and both the resources and the difficulties of which were well known to him. The first considerable city that he came to, Singidunum (the modern Belgrade), was the scene of his own first boyish battle. The Gepidæ, who were his chief antagonists on the road, had swarmed over into that very province of Pannonia where his father's palace once stood; and though they showed themselves bitter foes, they were doubtless surrounded by foes of their own who would be friends to the Ostrogoths.

Probably, too, Frederic, the Rugian refugee, brought with him many followers who knew the road and could count on the assistance of some barbarian allies, eager to overturn the throne of Odovacar.

Thus it will be seen that though the perils of the Ostrogothic march were tremendous, the danger which in those mapless days was so often fatal to an invading army—ignorance of the country—was not among them.

We are vaguely told of countless battles fought by the Ostrogoths with Sclavonic and other tribes that lay across their line of march, but the only battle of which we have any details (and those only such as we can extract from the cloudy rhetoric of a popular preacher[2] is one which was fought with the Gepidse, soon after the Goths had emerged from the territory of the friendly Empire, near the great mere or river which went by the name of Hiulca Palus, in what is now the crown-land of Sclavonia. When the great and over-wearied multitude approached the outskirts of the Gepid territory, their leader sent an embassy to Traustila, king of the Gepidæ, entreating that his host might have an unmolested passage, and offering to pay for the provisions which they would require.

To this embassy Traustila returned a harsh and insulting answer:

He would yield no passage through his dominions to the Ostrogoths; if they would go by that road they must first fight with the unconquered Gepidæ

Traustila then took up a strong position near the Hiulca Palus, whose broad waters, girdled by fen and treacherous morass, made the onward march of the invaders a task of almost desperate danger. But the Ostrogoths could not now retreat; famine and pestilence lay behind them on their road; they must go forward, and with a reluctant heart Theodoric gave the signal for the battle.

It seemed at first as if that battle would be lost, and as if the name and fame of the Ostrogothic people would be swallowed up in the morasses of the reedy Hiulca. Already the van of the army, floundering in the soft mud, and with only their wicker shields to oppose to the deadly shower of the Gepid arrows, were like to fall back in confusion. Then Theodoric, having called for a cup of wine, and drunk to the fortunes of his people, in a few spirited words called to his soldiers to follow his standard—the standard of a king who would carve out the way to victory. Perchance he may have discerned some part of the plain where the road went over solid ground, and if that were beset by foes, at any rate the Gepid was less terrible than the morass.

---

2. Ennodius, Bishop of Pavia, whose Panegyric on Theodoric, spoken about 506, is our chief authority for this part of the history.

So it was that he charged triumphantly through the hostile ranks, and, being followed by his eager warriors, achieved a signal victory. The Gepidæ were soon wandering over the plain, a broken and dispirited force. Multitudes of them were slain before the descent of night saved the remaining fugitives, and so large a number of the Gepid store-waggons fell into the hands of the Ostrogoths that throughout the host one voice of rejoicing arose that Traustila had been willing to fight. So had a little Gothic blood bought food more than they could ever have afforded money to purchase.

Thus, through foes and famine, hardships of the winter and hardships of the summer, the nation-army held on its way, and at length (as has been already said) in the month of August (489) the last of the waggons descended from the highlands, which are an outpost of the Julian Alps, and the Ostrogoths were encamped on the plains of Italy. Odovacar, who apparently had allowed them to accomplish the passage of the Alps unmolested, stood ready to meet them on the banks of the Isonzo, the river which flows near the ruins of the great city of Aquileia.

He had a large army, the kernel of which would doubtless be those mercenaries who had raised him on the shield thirteen years before, and among whom he had divided one-third part of the soil of Italy. But many other barbarians had flocked to his standard, so that he had, as it were, a little court of kings, chieftains serving under him as supreme leader. He himself, however, was now in the fifty-sixth year of his age, and his genius for war, if he ever had any, seems to have failed him.

He fought (as far as we can discern his conduct from the fragmentary notices of the analysts and panegyrists) with a sort of sullen savageness, like a wild beast at bay, but without skill either of strategy or tactics. The invaders, encumbered with the waggons and the non-combatants, had greatly the disadvantage of position. Odovacar's camp had been long prepared, was carefully fortified, and protected by the deep and rapid Isonzo.

But Theodoric's soldiers succeeded in crossing the river, stormed the camp, defended as it was by a strong earthen rampart, and sent its defenders flying in wild rout over the plains of Venetia. Odovacar fell back on the line of the Adige, and the beautiful north-eastern corner of Italy, the region which includes among its cities Udine, Venice, Vicenza, Padua, now accepted without dispute the rule of Theodoric, and perhaps welcomed him as a deliverer from the stern sway of Odovacar.[3] From this time forward it is allowable to conjecture that the most pressing of Theodoric's anxieties, that which arose from the difficulty of feeding and housing the women and children of his people, if not wholly removed was greatly lightened. Odovacar took up a strong position near Verona, separated from that city by the River Adige.

Theodoric, though not well provided with warlike appliances,[4] rightly judged that it was of supreme importance to his cause to follow up with rapidity the blow struck on the banks of the Isonzo, and accordingly, towards the end of September, he, with his army, stood before the *fossatum* or entrenched camp at Verona. In order to force his soldiers to fight bravely, Odovacar had, in defiance of the ordinary rules of war, placed his camp where retreat was almost hopelessly barred by the swift stream of the Adige, and he addressed his army with stout words full of simulated confidence in victory.

On the morning of the 30th of September, when the two armies were about to join in what must evidently be a most bloody encounter, the mother and sister of Theodoric, Erelieva and Amalfrida, sought his presence and asked him with some anxiety what were the chances of the battle. With words, reminding us of the Homeric saying that "the best omen is to fight bravely for one's country," Theodoric reassured their doubting hearts. On that day, he told his mother, it was for him to show that she had given birth to a hero on the day when the Ostrogoths did battle with the Huns. Dressed in his most splendid robes, those robes which their hands had adorned with bright embroidery, he would be conspicuous both to friend and foe, and would give a noble spoil to his conqueror if any man could succeed in slaying him. With these words he leapt on his horse, rushed to the van, cheered on his wavering troops, and began a series of charges, which at length, but not till thousands of his own men as well as of the enemy were slain, carried the *fossatum* of Odovacar.

The battle once gained, of course the dispositions which Odovacar had made to ensure the resistance of his soldiers, necessitated their ruin, and the swirling waters of the Adige probably destroyed as many as the Ostrogothic sword. Odovacar himself, again a fugitive, sped across the plain south-eastward to Ravenna, compelled like so many Roman emperors before him to shelter himself from the invad-

---

3. I cannot put this as more than a conjecture. We have singularly little information, even from *the panegyrical Ennodius*, as to the feelings of the Italian provincials during this crisis of their fate.

4. *Expers bellicis rebus (Continuatio Prosperi: Codex Havniensis)*

er behind its untraversable network of rivers and canals. It would seem from the scanty notices which remain to us that in this Battle of Verona, the bloodiest and most hardly fought of all the battles of the war, the original army of *fœderati*, the men who had crowned Odovacar king, and divided the third part of Italy between them, was, if not annihilated, utterly broken and dispirited, and Theodoric, who now marched westward with his people, and was welcomed with blessing and acclamations by the bishop and citizens of Milan, received also the transferred allegiance of the larger part of the army of his rival.

It seemed as if a campaign of a few weeks had secured the conquest of Italy, but the war was in fact prolonged for three years and a half from this time by domestic treachery, foreign invasion, and the almost absolute impregnability of Ravenna.

1. At the head of the soldiers of Odovacar who had apparently with enthusiasm accepted the leadership of his younger and more brilliant rival, was a certain Tufa, Master of the Soldiery among the *fœderati* Either he had extraordinary powers of deception, or Theodoric, short of generals, accepted his professions of loyalty with most unwise facility; for so it was that the Ostrogothic king entrusted to Tufa's generalship the army which assuredly he ought to have led himself to the siege of Ravenna. When Tufa arrived at Faventia, about eighteen miles from Ravenna, his old master came forth to meet him; the instinct of loyalty to Odovacar revived (if indeed he had not all along been playing a part in his alleged desertion), and Tufa carried over, apparently, the larger part of the army under his command to the service of Theodoric's rival.

Worst of all, he surrendered to his late master the chief members of his staff the so-called *comites* (henchmen) of Theodoric some of whom had probably helped him in his early adventure against Singidunum, and had shared his hardships in many a weary march through Thrace and Macedonia. These men were all basely murdered by Odovacar, a deed which Theodoric inwardly determined should never be forgiven (492).

Such an event as the defection of Tufa, carrying with him a considerable portion of his troops, was a great blow to the Ostrogothic cause. Sometime later another and similar event took place. Frederic the Rugian, whose father had been dethroned, and who had been himself driven into exile by the armies of Odovacar, for some unexplained and most mysterious reason, quitted the service of Theodoric and entered that of his own deadliest enemy. The sympathy of scoundrels seems to have drawn him into a special intimacy with Tufa, with whom he probably wandered up and down through Lombardy (as we now call it) and Venetia, robbing and slaying in the name of Odovacar, but not caring to share his hardships in blockaded and famine-stricken Ravenna. Fortunately, the Nemesis which so often waits on the friendship of bad men was not wanting in this case.

The two traitors quarrelled about the division of the spoil and a battle took place between them, in the valley of the Adige above Verona, in which Tufa was slain. Frederic, with his Rugian countrymen, occupied the strong city of Ticinum (*Pavia*), where they spent two dreadful years, "Their minds," says an eye-witness,[5] in after-time the Bishop of that city, "were full of cruel energy which prompted them to daily crimes. In truth, they thought that each day was wasted which they had not made memorable by some sort of outrage." In 494, with the general pacification of Italy, they disappear from view: and we may conjecture, though we are not told, that Pavia was taken, and that Frederic received his deserts at the hands of Theodoric.

2. In the year 490 Gundobad, king of the Burgundians, crossed the Alps and descended into Italy to mingle in the fray as an antagonist of Theodoric. In the same year, probably at the same time, Alaric II., king of the Visigoths, entered Italy as his ally. A great battle was fought on the river Adda, ten miles east of Milan, in which Odovacar, who had emerged from the shelter of Ravenna, was again completely defeated. He fled once more to Ravenna, which he never again quitted.

While these operations were proceeding, Theodoric's own family and the non-combatants of the Ostrogothic nation were in safe shelter, though in somewhat narrow quarters, in the strong city of Pavia, whose bishop, Epiphanius, was the greatest saint of his age, and one for whom Theodoric felt an especial veneration. No doubt they must have left that city before the evil-minded Rugians entered it (492), but we hear nothing of the circumstances of their flight or removal.

As for the Burgundian king, he does not seem to have been guided by any high considerations of policy in his invasion of Italy, and having been induced to conclude a treaty with Theodoric, he returned to his own royal city of Lyons with goodly spoil and a long train of hapless captives torn from the fields of Liguria.

3. These disturbing elements being cleared away, we may now turn

---

5. Ennodius (writing the life of Bishop Epiphanius).

our attention to the true key of the position and the central event of the war, the siege of Odovacar in Ravenna. After Tufa's second change of sides, and during the Burgundian invasion of Italy, there was no possibility of keeping up an Ostrogothic blockade of the city of the marshes. Odovacar emerged thence, won back the lower valley of the Po, and marching on Milan, inflicted heavy punishment on the city, for the welcome given to Theodoric.

In the Battle of the Adda, 11 August, 490, however, as has been already mentioned, he sustained a severe defeat, in which he lost one of his most faithful friends and ablest counsellors, a Roman noble named Pierius. After his flight to Ravenna, which immediately followed the battle of the Adda, there seems to have been a general movement throughout Italy, headed by the Catholic clergy, for the purpose of throwing off his yoke, and if we do not misread the obscure language of the Panegyrist, this movement was accompanied by a wide-spread popular conspiracy, somewhat like the Sicilian Vespers of a later day, to which the *fœderati*, the still surviving adherents of Odovacar, scattered over their various domains in Italy, appear to have fallen victims.

Only two cities, Cæsena and Rimini, beside Ravenna, now remained to Odovacar, and for the next two years and a half (from the autumn of 490 to the spring of 493) Ravenna was straitly besieged. Corn rose to a terrible famine price (seventy-two shillings a peck), and before the end of the siege the inhabitants had to feed on the hides of animals, and all sorts of foul and fearful aliments, and many of them perished of hunger. A sortie made in 491 by a number of barbarian recruits whom Odovacar had by some means attracted to his standard, was repelled after a desperate encounter. During all this time Theodoric, from his entrenched camp in the great pine-wood of Ravenna, was watching jealously to see that no provisions entered the city by land, and in 492, after taking Rimini, he brought a fleet of swift vessels thence to a harbour about six miles from Ravenna, and thus completed its investment by sea.

In the beginning of 493 the misery of the besieged city became unendurable, and Odovacar, with infinite reluctance, began to negotiate for its surrender. His son Thelane was handed over as a hostage for his fidelity, and the parleying between the two rival chiefs began on the 25th of February. On the following day Theodoric and his Ostrogoths entered Classis, the great naval emporium, about three miles from the city; and on the 27th, by the mediation of the bishop, peace was formally concluded between the warring kings.

The peace, the surrender of the city, the acceptance of the rule of "the new King from the East," were apparently placed under the especial guardianship of the church. "The most blessed man, the Archbishop John," says a later ecclesiastical historian,[6] "opened the gates of the city, 5 March, 493, which Odovacar had closed, and went forth with crosses and thuribles and the Holy Gospels, seeking peace. While the priests and the rest of the clergy round him intoned the psalms, he, falling prostrate on the ground, obtained that which he desired. He welcomed the new king coming from the East, and peace was granted unto him, including not only the citizens of Ravenna, but all the other Romans[7], for whom the blessed John made entreaty."

The chief clause of the treaty was that which assured Odovacar not only life but absolute equality of power with his conqueror. The fact that Theodoric should have, even in appearance, consented to an arrangement so precarious and unstable, is the strongest testimony to the impregnability of Ravenna, which after three years' strict blockade, could still be won only by so mighty a concession. But of course there was not, there could not be, any real peace on such terms between the two queen-bees in that swarming hive of barbarians. Theodoric received information—so we are told—that his rival was laying snares for his life, and being determined to anticipate the blow, invited Odovacar to a banquet at "the Palace of the Laurel-grove," on the southeast of the city (15th March, 493).

When Odovacar arrived, two suppliants knelt before him and clasped his hands while offering a feigned petition. Some soldiers who had been stationed in two side alcoves stepped forth from the ambush to slay him, but at the last moment their hearts failed them, and they could not strike. If the deed was to be done, Theodoric must himself be the executioner or the assassin. He raised his sword to strike. "Where is God?" cried the defenceless but unterrified victim. "Thus didst thou to my friends," answered Theodoric, reminding him of the treacherous murder of the "henchmen." Then with a tremendous stroke of his broadsword he clove his rival from the shoulder to the loin. The barbarian frenzy, which the Scandinavian minstrels call the "fury of the Berserk," was in his heart, and with a savage laugh at his own too impetuous blow, he shouted as the corpse fell to the ground: "I think the weakling had never a bone in his body."

---

6. Agnellus (writing in the ninth century). His use of the term Archbishop is itself a sign of a later age.
7. The non-barbarian population of Italy.

The body of Odovacar was laid in a stone coffin, and buried near the synagogue of the Jews. His brother was mortally wounded while attempting to escape through the palace-garden. His wife died of hunger in her prison. His son, sent for safe-keeping to the king of the Visigoths in Gaul, afterwards escaped to Italy and was put to death by the orders of Theodoric. Thus perished the whole short-lived dynasty of the captain of the *fœderati*.

In his long struggle for the possession of Italy, Theodoric had shown himself patient in adversity, moderate in prosperity, brave, resourceful, and enduring. But the memory of all these noble deeds is dimmed by the crime which ended the tragedy, a crime by the commission of which Theodoric sank below the level of the ordinary morality of the barbarian, breaking his plighted word, and sinning against the faith of hospitality.

CHAPTER 8

Civilitas

Thus far we have followed the fortunes of a Teutonic warrior of the fifth century of our era, marking his strange vacillations between friendship and enmity to the great civilised Empire under the shattered fabric whereof he and his people were dwelling, and neither concealing nor extenuating any of his lawless deeds, least of all that deed of treachery and violence by which he finally climbed to the pinnacle of supreme power in Italy. Now, for the next thirty years, we shall have to watch the career of this same man, ruling Italy with unquestioned justice and wise forethought, making the welfare of every class of his subjects the end of all his endeavours, and cherishing civilisation (or, as it was called in the language of his chosen counsellors, *civilitas* with a love and devotion almost equal to that which religious zeal kindles in the hearts of its surrendered votaries.

The transformation is a marvellous one. Success and unquestioned dominion far more often deprave and distort than ennoble and purify the moral nature of man. But something like this transformation was seen when Octavian, the crafty and selfish intriguer, ripened into the wise and statesmanlike Augustus. Nor have our own days been quite ignorant of a similar phenomenon, when the stern soldier-politician of Germany, the man who once seemed to delight in war and whose favourite motto had till then been "*blood and iron*" having secured for his master the hegemony of Europe, strove (or seems to have striven), during twenty difficult years, to maintain peace among European nations, like one convinced in his heart that War is the supreme calamity for mankind.

It is a threadbare saying, "*Happy is the nation that has no annals*," and the miserable historians of the time tell us far too little about the thirty years of peace which Italy enjoyed under the wise rule of Theodoric;

still we are told enough to enable us in some degree to understand both what he accomplished and how he accomplished it. And one thing which makes us accept the statements of these historians with unquestioning belief is that they have no motive for the praises which they so freely bestow on the great Ostrogoth. They are not his countrymen, nor his fellow-religionists.

Our chief authorities are Roman and Orthodox, and bitterly condemn Theodoric for the persecution of the Catholics, into which, as we shall see, he was provoked in the last two years of his reign. Still, over the grave of this dead barbarian and heretic, when they have nothing to gain by speaking well of him, they cannot forbear to praise the noble impartiality and anxious care for the welfare of his people, which, for the space of one whole generation, gave happiness to Italy. It will be well to quote here one or two of these testimonies, borne by impartial witnesses.

Our chief authority,[1] who is believed to have been a Catholic bishop of Ravenna, says:

He was an illustrious man, and full of good-will towards all. He reigned thirty-three (really thirty-two) years, and during thirty of these years so great was the happiness of Italy that even the wayfarers were at peace. For he did nothing wrong. So did he govern the two nations, the Goths and Romans, as if they were one people, belonging himself to the Arian sect, yet he ordained that the civil administration should remain for the Romans as it had been under their emperors. He gave presents and rations to the people, yet, though he found the Treasury ruined, he brought it round, by his own hard work, into a flourishing state. He attempted nothing (during these first thirty years) against the Catholic faith.

Exhibiting games in the circus and amphitheatre, he received from the Romans the names of Trajan and Valentinian (the happy days of which most prosperous emperors he did in truth seek to restore), and, at the same time, the Goths rendered true obedience to their valiant king, according to the edict which he had promulgated for them."

He gave one of his daughters in marriage to the king of the Visigoths in Gaul, another to the son of the Burgundian king; his sister to the king of the Vandals, and his niece to the king

---

1. "*Anonymus Valesii*" (probably Bishop Maximian).

ITALY
Under the Ostrogoths.

English Miles
0   25   50   100

Roman Miles
0   25   50   100

RAETIA
ALAMANNI

NORICUM

SAVIA

DALMATIA

Addadfl.

Comun
(Como)
Mediolanum
(Milan)
G.U.R.
Ticinum (Pavia)
Dertona (Tortona)
ALPES
COTTIAE
(Genua)
(Genoa)
Via Aurelia

VENETIA ET HISTRIA
Aquileia
Verona
Rivus Altus
(Venice)
Pola
Padus fl.
Ravenna
Ariminum (Rimini)

Scardonia
Sebenico
Salona

Sinus
Ligusticus

Faesula
(Fiesole)
Florentia

TUSCIA
Clusium
(Chiusi)
UMBRIA
Perusia
(Perugia)
Spoletum
Narni
VALERIA
Tibor

FLAMINIA
AEMILIA
PICENUM
ANNONARIA
Ancona
Auximum
(Osimo)
Firmum (Fermo)
Asculum (Ascoli)

MARE ADRIATICUM

CORSICA

Centumcellae
(Civita Vecchia)
Ostia
Antium
Tarracina

ROME
Albanum

SAMNIUM
CAMPANIA

Cannae
Beneventum
Canusium
(Canosa)
Acheronta
LUCANIA

Brundusium
(Brindisi)
Tarentum
Hydruntum
(Otranto)

SARDINIA

MARE
TYRRHENUM

Neapolis
(Naples)
Pompeii

Nucetia

Lipari Is.

Panormus
(Palermo)
Lilybaeum
(Marsala)

Messana

SICILIA

Sybaris
Roscianum
(Rossano)
Crotona
BRUTTII
Scyllacium
(Squillace)
Rhegium

Carthage

AFRICA

Syracuse

Thurii

of the Thuringians. Thus he pleased all the nations round him, for he was a lover of manufactures and a great restorer of cities. He restored the aqueduct of Ravenna, which Trajan had built; and again, after a long interval, brought water into the city. He completed, but did not dedicate, the palace, and finished the porticoes round it. At Verona he erected baths and a palace, and constructed a *portico* from the gate to the palace. The aqueduct, which had been long destroyed, he renewed, and brought in water through it. He also surrounded the city with new walls. At Ticinum (*Pavia*) too he built a palace, baths, and an amphitheatre, and erected walls round the city. On many other cities also he bestowed similar benefits.

Thus he so charmed the nations near him that they entered into a league with him, hoping that he would be their king. The merchants, too, from divers provinces, flocked to his dominions, for so great was the order which he maintained, that if any one wished to leave gold or silver on his land (in his country house) it was as safe as in a walled city.

A proof of this was the fact that he never made gates for any city of Italy, and the gates already existing were not closed. Anyone who had business to transact could do it as safely by night as by day.

In his time men bought wheat at 60 pecks for a *solidus* (12 shillings a quarter), and 30 *amphoræ* of wine for the same price (*2s. 4d.* a gallon).

So far the supposed bishop of Ravenna. Now let us hear Procopius, an official in the Imperial army which brought the Ostrogothic kingdom to ruin:

Theodoric was an extraordinary lover of justice, and adhered rigorously to the laws. He guarded the country from barbarian invasions, and displayed the greatest intelligence and prudence. There was in his government scarcely a trace of injustice towards his subjects, nor would he permit any of those under him to attempt anything of the kind, except that the Goths divided among themselves the same proportion of the land of Italy which Odovacar had allotted to his partisans. Thus then Theodoric was in name a tyrant (that is, an irregular, because barbarian, ruler), but indeed a true king (or emperor), not inferior to the best of his predecessors, and his popularity grew greatly, both among Goths and Italians, and this fact (that he was popular with both nations) was contrary to the ordinary fashion of human affairs. For generally, as different classes in the State want different things, the government which pleases one party has to incur the odium of those who do not belong to it.

After a reign of thirty-seven years[2] he died, having been a terror to all his enemies, but leaving a deep regret for his loss in the hearts of his subjects.

So much for the general aspect of Theodoric's rule in Italy. Now let us consider rather more in detail what was his precise position in that country. And first as to the title by which he was known. It is singularly difficult to say what this title was. It is quite clear that Theodoric never claimed to be emperor of the West, the successor of Honorius and Augustulus. But there are grave reasons for doubting whether he called himself, as has been often stated, "King of Italy." In the fifth century territorial titles of this kind were, if not absolutely unknown, at least very uncommon. The various Teutonic rulers generally took their titles from the nations whom they led to battle, Gaiseric being "King of the Vandals and Alans," Gundobad, "King of the Burgundians," Clovis, "King of the Franks," and so forth. Upon the whole, it seems most probable that Theodoric's full title was *King of the Goths and Romans in Italy*[3] and that the allusion to *Romans* in his title explains some of the conflict of testimony as to the source from whence he derived his title of king.

It is quite true that a Teutonic sovereign like Theodoric, sprung from a long line of royal ancestors, and chosen by the voice of his people to succeed their king, his father, would not need, and except under circumstances of great national humiliation would not accept, any grant of the kingly title, as ruler over his own nation, from the Augustus at New Rome.

But when it came to claiming by the same title the obedience of Romans as well as Goths, especially in that country which had once been the heart of the Empire,—Theodoric, king of the Goths, might well be anxious to strain all the resources of diplomacy in order to obtain from the legitimate head of the Roman world the confirmation of those important words "and Romans," which appeared in his

---

2. Really thirty-two years and a half from the death of Odovacar, thirty-seven from the descent into Italy, thirty-eight from Theodoric's departure from Novæ.
3. *Per Italiam.*

regal title.[4]

In the year 490, probably soon after the battle of the Adda, Theodoric sent Faustus, an eminent Roman noble and "Chief of the Senate," on an embassy to Zeno, "hoping that he might receive from that emperor permission to clothe himself with the royal mantle." It will be remembered that in the compact between Roman and Teuton, which preceded Theodoric's invasion of Italy, words had been used which implied that he was only to rule as "*locum tenens*" of the emperor till he himself should arrive to claim the supremacy. Now, with that conquest apparently almost completed, and with his rival fast sealed up in Ravenna, Theodoric sends a report of his success of the enterprise undertaken "on joint account," and desires to legalise his position by a formal grant of the mantle of royalty from the Autocrat of the World.

The time of the arrival of Theodoric's embassy at Constantinople was unpropitious, as the Emperor Zeno was already stricken by mortal illness. On the 9th of April, 491, he died, and was succeeded by the handsome but elderly life-guardsman, Anastasius, to whom Ariadne, widow of Zeno, gave her hand in marriage. The rights and duties which pertained to the compact between Theodoric and Zeno were perhaps considered as of only personal obligation. It might plausibly be contended by the emperor's successor that he was not bound to recognise the new royalty of his predecessor's, "*filius in arma*," and by Theodoric that the conditional estate in Italy granted to him to hold "till Zeno should himself arrive" became absolute, now that by the death of Zeno that event was rendered impossible.

However this may be, we hear no more of negotiations between the Gothic camp and the court of Constantinople till the death of Odovacar(493). Then the Goths, apparently in some great assembly of the nation, "confirmed Theodoric to themselves as king," without waiting for the orders of the new emperor.[5] Whatever this ceremony may have imported, it must have in some way conferred on Theodoric a fuller kingship, perhaps more of a territorial and less of a tribal sovereignty than he had possessed when he was wandering with his followers over the passes of the Balkans.

---

4. The chief advocates of the two opposite views here indicated are Prof. Dahn (in his *Könige der Germanen; Abtheilung iv.*) and Prof. Gaudenzi (*Sui rapporti tra e l'Italia l'Impero d'Oriente*). I believe that the view which is suggested above is the true reconciliation of both theories.

5. *Gothi sibi confirmaverunt regem Theodericum, non expectatâ jussione novi principis* (*Anastasii*).—Anon.Vales., 57.

Though Theodoric had not consulted the emperor before taking this step, he sent an ambassador, again Faustus, who now held the important post of "Master of the Offices",[6] to Constantinople, probably in order to give a formal notification of his self-assumed accession of dignity.[7]

No messages or embassies, however, could yet soothe the wounded pride of Anastasius. There was deep resentment at the Eastern Court, and for three or four years there seems to have been a rupture of diplomatic relations between Constantinople and Ravenna. At length, in the year 497, Theodoric sent another ambassador, Festus, (also an eminent Roman noble and Chief of the Senate,) to Anastasius. This messenger, more successful than his predecessor, "made peace with Anastasius concerning Theodoric's premature assumption of royalty, and brought back all the ornaments of the palace which Odovacar had transmitted to Constantinople."[8]

(497) This final ratification of the Ostrogoth's sovereignty in Italy is so vaguely described to us that it is difficult to see how much it may have implied. Probably it was to a certain extent convenient to both parties that it should be left vague. The emperor would not abandon any hope, however shadowy, of one day winning back full possession of "the Hesperian kingdom." The king might hope that, in the course of years or generations, he himself, or his descendants, might sever the last link of dependence on Constantinople, perhaps might one day establish themselves as full-blown emperors of Rome. The claims thus left in vagueness were the seeds of future difficulties, and bore fruit forty years later in a bloody and desolating war, but meanwhile the position, as far as we can ascertain it, seems to have been something like this.

Theodoric, "King of the Goths and Romans in Italy," was absolute ruler of the country de facto, except in so far as the Gothic nation, assembled under arms at its periodical parades, may have exercised some check on his full autocracy. He made peace and war, he nominated the high officers of state, even one of the two consuls, who still kept alive the fiction of the Roman Republic; he probably regulated the

---

6. The *Magister Officiorum*, who was at the head of the civil service of the Empire (or Kingdom), combined some of the duties of our Home Secretary with some of those of the Secretary for Foreign Affairs.

7. Faustus was accompanied by another nobleman—Irenæus. We are not definitely informed of the object of their mission, but may fairly infer it from the date of their departure.

8. *Anon. Valesii.*

admissions to the Senate; he was even in the last resort arbiter of the fortunes of the Roman Church.

On the other hand, he did not himself coin gold or silver money with his effigy; but in this he was not singular, for it was not till a generation or two had elapsed that any of the new barbarian royalties thought it worthwhile to claim this attribute of sovereignty. Though dressed in the purple of royalty, by assuming the title of king only, he accepted a position somewhat lower than that of the emperor of the New Rome. He sent the names of the consuls whom he had appointed to Constantinople, an act which might be represented as a mere piece of formal courtesy, or as a request for their ratification, according to the point of view of the narrator. With a similar show of courtesy, or submission, the accession of Theodoric's descendants to the throne was, when the occasion arose, notified to the then reigning emperor.

And there were many limitations which the good sense and statesmanlike feeling of the Ostrogothic king imposed on his exercise of the royal power, but which might be, perhaps were, represented as part of the fundamental compact between him and the emperor of Rome. Such were the employment of men of Roman birth by preference, in all the great offices of the state; absolute impartiality between the rival creeds, Catholic and Arian (to the latter of which Theodoric himself was an adherent); and a determination to abstain as much as possible from all fresh legislation which might modify the rights and duties of the Roman inhabitants of Italy, the legislative power being chiefly exercised in order to provide for those new cases which arose out of the settlement of so large a number of newcomers of alien blood within the borders of the land.

After all the attempts which have been made to explain and to systematise the relation between the new barbarian royalties and the old and tottering Empire, much remains which is absolutely incapable of definition, but perhaps an historical parallel, though not strictly accurate, may somewhat aid our comprehension of the subject. It is well-known how for the first hundred years of the English *Raj* in India the power which actually resided in an association of traders, the old East India Company, and which was wielded under their orders by a Clive, a Hastings, or a Wellesley, was theoretically vested in an emperor, the descendant of "the Great Mogul," who lived in seclusion in his palace at Delhi, and who, though nominally all-powerful, had really, as Macaulay has said, "less power to help or to hurt than the youngest civil servant of the Company." Now assuredly Anastasius and Justin,

101

the Imperial contemporaries of Theodoric, were no mere phantoms of royalty, like the last Mogul Emperors of Delhi, but as far as actual efficacious share in the government of Italy went, the parallel holds good. Such deference as was paid to their name and authority was a mere courteous form; the whole power of the state—subject, as has been said, to the limitations still imposed by the popular institutions of the Goths—was gathered up in the hands of Theodoric.

What then, it may be said, was gained by keeping up the fiction that Italy still formed part of the Roman Empire, and that Theodoric ruled in any sense as the delegate of the emperor? For the present, much (though at the cost of future entanglements and complications), since it facilitated that union of "Romania" and "Barbaricum," which was the next piece of work obviously necessary for Europe. If the reader will recur to that noble sentence of Ataulfus, which was quoted in the introduction to this book,[9] he will see that the reasoning of that great chieftain took this shape:

A Commonwealth must have laws. The Goths, accustomed for generations to their tameless freedom, have not acquired the habit of obedience to the laws. Till they acquire that habit, the administration of the State must be left in Roman hands, and all the authority of the King must be used in defence of Roman organisation.

These principles, though he may never have read the passage of Orosius which expounded them, were essentially the principles of Theodoric. So long as he remained in antagonism to the Empire, he could not reckon on the hearty co-operation of Roman officials in the task of government. The brave, through patriotism, and the cowardly, through fear of coming retribution, would decline to be known as his adherents, and would stand aloof from his work of re-organization. But when it was known that even the great Augustus at Constantinople, "Our Lord Anastasius, Father of his Country" (as the coins styled him), recognised the royalty of Theodoric, and had in some sort confided to him the government of Italy, all the great army of civil servants, who performed the functions of that highly specialised organism, the Roman State, could, without fear and without reproach, accept office under the newcomer, and could look forward again, as they had done before, to a fortunate official career, to the honours and emoluments which were the recognised reward of the successful civil

9. See chapter 1.

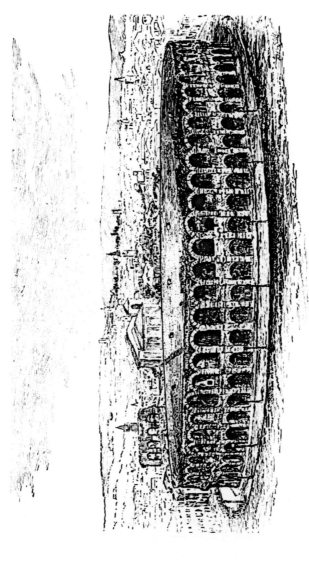

The Arena of Verona (condition at time of first publication)

servant.

In the next chapter, I shall describe with a little more detail the character and the duties of some of these Roman officials. For the present we will rather consider the nature of the work which Theodoric accomplished through their instrumentality. We have already heard from a nearly contemporary chronicler, the story of some of the great civilising works which he wrought in the wasted land, the aqueducts of Ravenna and Verona, the walls of Verona and Pavia, the baths, the palace, and the amphitheatre. More important for the great mass of his subjects was the perfect security which he gave to the merchant for his commerce, to the husbandman for the fruit of his toil. Corn, as we have seen, sank to the extraordinarily low price of twelve shillings a quarter. But this low price did not mean, as it might in our country, the depression of the agricultural interest, through the rivalry of the foreign producer.

On the contrary, the great economic symptom of Theodoric's reign—and under the circumstances a most healthy symptom—was that Italy, from a corn-importing became a corn-exporting country. Under the old emperors, whose rule was a most singular blending of autocracy and demagogy, in fact a kind of crowned socialism, every nerve had been strained to bring from Alexandria and Carthage the corn which was distributed gratuitously to the idle population of Rome. Under such hopeless competition as this, together with the demoralising influence of slave labour, large tracts of Italy had actually gone out of cultivation. Now, by political changes, the merit of which must not be claimed for the Ostrogothic government, both Egypt and Africa had become unavailable for the supply of the necessities of Rome. Theodoric and his ministers may however be praised for that prevalence of order and good government, which enabled the long prostrate agriculture of Italy to spring up like grass after a summer shower.

The conditions of prosperity were there, and only needed the removal of adverse influences and mistaken benevolence to bring forth their natural fruit. The grain-*largesses* to the people of Rome were indeed still continued in a modified form, but the stores thus dispensed seemed to have been brought almost entirely from Italy.[10] When Gaul was visited with famine, the ship-masters along the whole western

---

10. Once they are mentioned as coming from Spain (Cassiodorus, Var., v., 35), but this seems to be an exception. 11. Cass. Var., x., 27. This is some years after the death of Theodoric.

coast of Italy were permitted and encouraged to take the surplus of the Italian crops to the suffering province. Even in a time of dearth and after war had begun, corn was sold by the state to the impoverished inhabitants of Liguria at sixteen shillings a quarter.[11] Altogether we seem justified in asserting that the economic condition of Italy, both as to the producers and the consumers of its food-supplies, was more prosperous under Theodoric than it had been for centuries before, or than it was to be for centuries afterwards.

I have already made some reference to aqueducts, which were among the noblest and most beneficial works that any ruler of Italy could accomplish. Ravenna, situated in an unhealthy swamp where water fit for drinking was proverbially dearer than wine[12] was preeminently dependent on such supplies of the precious fluid as could be brought fresh and sparkling from the distant Apennines. Theodoric issued an order to all the farmers dwelling along the course of the aqueduct to eradicate the shrubs growing by its side, which would otherwise fix their roots in the bed of the stream, loosen the masonry, and cause many a dangerous leak. "This being done," said the Secretary of State, "we shall again have baths that we may look upon with pleasure, water which will cleanse, not stain, water after using which we shall not require again to wash ourselves: drinking-water, the mere sight of which will not take away our appetite."[12]

Similar care was needed to preserve the great Aqueducts which were the glory of Imperial Rome, as even now their giant arches, striding for miles over the desolate Campagna, are her most impressive monument. At Rome also the officer who was specially charged with the maintenance of these noble works, the "Count of the Aqueducts," was exhorted to show his zeal by rooting up hurtful trees, and by at once repairing any part of the masonry that seemed to be falling into decay through age. He was warned against peculation and against connivance at the frauds which often marked the distribution of the water supply, and he was assured that the strengthening of the aqueducts would constitute his best claim on the favour of his sovereign.[13]

But while in most parts of Italy water is a boon eagerly craved for, in some places it is a superabundance and a curse. At Terracina on the

---

11. There is a well known epigram of Martial, in which he complains of an innkeeper of Ravenna for diluting his water with wine, when the poet had paid for pure water.

12. Cass. Var., v., 38.

13. *Ibid.*, vii., 6.

Latian coast there still stands in the *piazza* a slab of marble with a long inscription, setting forth that "The most illustrious lord and renowed king, Theodoric, triumphant conqueror, ever Augustus, born for the good of the Commonwealth, guardian of liberty and propagator of the Roman name, subduer of the nations," ordered that nineteen miles of the Appian Way, being the portion extending from Three-bridges (*Tripontium*) to Terracina should be cleared of the waters which had flowed together upon it from the marshes on either side. A nobleman of the very highest rank, Consul, Patrician, and *Prefect* of the City, Cæcina Maurus Basilius Decius, successfully accomplished this work under the orders of his sovereign, and for the safety thus afforded to travellers, was rewarded by a large grant of the newly-drained lands.[14]

We have seen that Theodoric's anonymous panegyrist calls him "a lover of manufactures and a great restorer of cities." Of the manufactures encouraged by the Ostrogothic king, we should have been glad to receive a fuller account. All that I have been able to discover in the published state-papers of himself and his successors at all bearing on this subject is some instructions with reference to the opening of gold mines in Bruttii (the modern Calabria), and iron mines in Dalmatia, a concession of potteries to three senators, who are promised the royal protection if they will prosecute the work diligently, and permission to another nobleman to erect a row of workshops or manufactories overlooking the Roman Forum.[15] The whole tenour of these state papers, however, shows that public works were being diligently pushed on in every quarter of Italy, and is entirely consistent with the praise awarded to Theodoric "as a lover of manufactures."

His zeal for the restoration of cities is by the same documents abundantly manifested. At one time we find him giving orders for the transport of marble slabs and columns to Ravenna, at another, directing the repair of the walls of Catana, now rebuilding the walls and towers of Arles, and now relieving the distress of Naples and Nola, which have been half ruined by an eruption of Vesuvius.[16] His care for the adornment of the cities of Italy with works of art is manifest, as well as his zeal for their material enrichment. He hears with great disgust that a brazen statue has been stolen from the city of Como.

"It is vexatious" says his secretary, "that while we are labouring to increase the ornaments of our cities, those which antiquity has be-

---

14. Cass.,Var., ii., 32, 33.
15. Cass.,Var., ix., 3; iv., 30; iii., 25; ii., 23.
16. *Ibid.*, iii., 9, 10, 49, 44; iv., 50.

queathed to us should be diminished by such deeds as this." A reward of 100 *aurei* (£60), and a free pardon is offered to any accomplice who will assist in the discovery of the chief offender.[17]

But it is above all for Rome, for the glory and magnificence of Rome, that this Ostrogothic king, in a certain sense the kinsman and successor of her first ravager, Alaric, shows a tender solicitude. Her Aqueducts, as we have seen, are to be repaired, her Cloacæ, those still existing memorials of the civilisation of the earliest, the regal, Rome, are to be carefully upheld; the thefts of brass and lead from the public buildings, which have become frequent during the disorders of the past century, are to be sternly repressed[18]; a spirited patrician[19] who has restored the mighty theatre of Pompeius is encouraged and rewarded, the *Prefect* of the City is stimulated to greater activity in the repair of all the ruined buildings therein. "In Rome, praised beyond all other cities by the world's mouth, it is not right that anything should be found either sordid or mediocre."

In all these counsels for the material well-being of Italy, and for the repair of the ravages of anarchy and war, Theodoric was undoubtedly much assisted by his ministers of Roman extraction, some of whom I shall endeavour to portray in a later chapter. Still, though the details of the work may have been theirs, it cannot be denied that the initiative was his. A barbarian, thinking only barbarous thoughts, looking upon war and the chase as the only employments worthy of a free man, would not have chosen such counsellors, and, if he had found them in his service, would not have kept them.

Therefore, remembering those years of boyhood, which he passed at Constantinople, at a time when the character is most susceptible of strong and lasting impressions, I cannot doubt that notwithstanding the frequent relapses into barbarism which marked his early manhood, he was at heart a convert to civilisation, that his desire was to obtain for "the Hesperian land" all that he had seen best and greatest in the social condition of the city by the Bosphorus, and that his secretary truly expressed his deepest and inmost thoughts when he made him speak of himself as one "whose whole care was to change everything for the better."[20]

I shall close this chapter with a few anecdotes—far too few have

---

17. *Ibid.*, ii., 35.
18. Cass.,Var., iii., 30, 31.
19 Symmachus.
20. *Nos quibus cordi est in melius cuncta mutare.*—Cass.,Var., ii., 21.

been preserved to us—which serve to show what manner of man he appeared to his contemporaries. Again I borrow from the anonymous author, the supposed bishop of Ravenna.

He was, we are told, unlettered,[21] though fond of the converse of learned men, and so clumsy with his pen that after ten years of reigning he was still unable to form without assistance the four letters (THEO) which were affixed as his sign-manual to documents issued in his name. In order to overcome this difficulty he had a golden plate prepared with the necessary letters perforated in it, and drew his pen through the holes.[22] But, though he was unlettered, his shrewdness and mother-wit caused both his sayings and doings to be much noted and remembered by his subjects.

In one difficult case which came before him, he discovered the truth by a sudden device which probably reminded the bystanders of the judgement of Solomon. A young man who as a child had been brought up by a friend of his deceased father, returned to his home and claimed a share of his inheritance from his mother. She, however, was on the point of marriage with a second husband, and under her suitor's influence she disowned the son whom she had at first welcomed with joy and had entertained for a month in her house. As the suitor persisted in his demand that the son should be turned out of doors, and the son refused to leave his paternal abode, the case came before the King's Court,[23] where the widow still persisted in her assertion that the young man was not her son, but a stranger whom she had entertained merely out of motives of hospitality. Suddenly the king turned round upon her and said: "This young man is to be thy husband, I command thee to marry him." The horror-stricken mother then confessed that he was indeed her son.

Some of Theodoric's sayings passed into proverbs among the common people. One was: "*He who has gold and he who has a devil can neither of them hide what he has got*" Another: "*The Roman when in misery imitates the Goth and the Goth in comfort imitates the Roman.*"

We have unfortunately no description of the great Ostrogoth's outward appearance, though the indications in his history would lead

---

21. Agrammatus.

22. I have a slight distrust of this story, because it is told in almost the same words of the contemporary Justin I., Emperor of the East.

23. I conjecture that the mother and son in this case were Goths, possibly the suitor a Roman, and that this may have been the reason why the case came to the King's Court instead of going before the *Prætorian Prefect*.

us to suppose that he was a man of stalwart form and soldierly bearing. Nor is this deficiency adequately made up to us by his coins, since, as has been already said, the gold and silver pieces which were circulated in his reign bore the impress of the Eastern emperor, and the miserable little copper coins which bear his effigy do not pretend to portraiture.

HALF-*SILIQUA* OF THEODORIC (SILVER)
BEARING THE HEAD OF ANASTASIUS.

Roman Officials—Cassiodorus

I have said that one of the most important characteristics of Theodoric's government of Italy was that it was conducted in accordance with the traditions of the Empire and administered mainly by officials trained in the Imperial school. To a certain extent the same thing is true of all the Teutonic monarchies which arose in the fifth century on the ruins of the Empire. In dealing with the needs and settling the disputes of the large, highly-organised communities, into whose midst they had poured themselves, it was not possible, if it had been desirable, for the rulers to remain satisfied with the simple, sometimes barbarous, principles of law and administration which had sufficed for the rude farmer-folk who dwelt in isolated villages beyond the Rhine and the Danube.

Nor was this necessity disliked by the rulers themselves. They soon perceived that the Roman law, with its tendency to derive all power from the Imperial head of the state, and the Roman official staff, an elaborate and well-organised hierarchy, every member of which received orders from one above him and transmitted orders to those below, were far more favourable to their own prerogative and gave them a far higher position over against their followers and comrades in war, than the institutions which had prevailed in the forests of Germany. Hence, as I have said, all the new barbarian royalties, even that of the Vandals in Africa (in some respects more anti-Roman than any other), preserved much of the laws and machinery of the Roman Empire; but Theodoric's Italian kingdom preserved the most of all.

It might in fact almost be looked upon as a mere continuation of the old Imperial system, only with a strong, laborious, martial Goth at the head of affairs, able and willing to keep all the members of the official hierarchy sternly to their work, instead of the ruler whom the last three generations had been accustomed to behold, a man decked with the purple and diadem, but too weak, too indolent, too nervously afraid of irritating some powerful captain of *fœderati*, or some wealthy Roman noble, to be able to do justice to all classes of his subjects.

The composition of the official hierarchy of the Empire is, from various sources,[1] almost as fully known to us as that of any state of modern Europe.

Pre-eminent in dignity over all the rest rose the "Illustrious" *Prætorian Prefect*, the vicegerent of the sovereign, a man who held towards emperor or king nearly the same position which a Grand *Vizier* holds towards a Turkish *Sultan*. Like his sovereign he wore a purple robe (which reached however only to his knees, not to his feet), and he drove through the streets in a lofty official chariot. It was for him to promulgate the Imperial laws, sometimes to put forth edicts of his own. He proclaimed what taxes were to be imposed each year, and their produce came into his "*Prætorian* chest." He suggested to his sovereign the names of the governors of the provinces, paid them their salaries, and exercised a general superintendence over them, having even power to depose them from their offices. And lastly, he was the highest Judge of Appeal in the land, even the emperor himself having generally no power to reverse his sentences.

There was another "Illustrious" minister, who, during this century both in the Eastern and Western Empire, was always treading on the heels of the *Prætorian Prefect*, and trying to rob him of some portion of his power. This was the *Master of the Offices* the intermediary between the sovereign and the great mass of the civil servants, to whom the execution of his orders was entrusted. *A swarm of Agentes in Rebus* (king's messengers, bailiffs, sheriff's officers; we may call them by all these designations) roved through the provinces, carrying into effect the orders of the sovereign, always magnifying their "master's" dignity, (whence they derived their epithet of "*Magistriani*",) and seeking to depress the *Prætorian cohorts*, who discharged somewhat similar duties under the *Prætorian prefect*. The Master of the Offices, besides sharing the counsels of his sovereign in relation to foreign states, had also the arsenals under his charge, and there was transferred to him from his rival, the *prefect*, the superintendence of the *cursus publicus*, the great postal service of the Empire.

Again, somewhat overlapping, as it seems to us, the functions of

---

1. Chiefly the *Notitia Utriusque Imperii* (a sort of official Red-book of the time of Honorius,) but also the *Various Letters* of Cassiodorus, to be described below.

the Master of the Offices, came the "Illustrious" *quæstor*, the head-rhetorician of the state, the official whose business it was to put the thoughts of the sovereign into fitting and eloquent words, either when he was replying to the ambassadors of foreign powers, or when he was issuing laws and proclamations to his own subjects. As his duties and qualifications were of a more personal kind than those of his two brother-ministers already described, he had not like them a large official staff waiting upon his orders.

There were two great financial ministers, *the Count of Sacred Largesses* ("sacred," of course, is equivalent to "Imperial"), and the *Count of Private Domains*, whose duties practically related in the former case to the personal, in the latter to the real, estate of the sovereign. Or perhaps, for it is difficult exactly to define the nature of their various duties, it would be better to think of the Count of Sacred Largesses as the Imperial Chancellor of the Exchequer, and the Count of Private Domains as the Chief Commissioner of Woods and Forests.

The *Superintendent of the Sacred Dormitory* was the Grand Chamberlain of the Empire, and commanding, as he did, the army of pages, grooms of the bed-chamber, vestiaries, and life-guardsmen, who ministered to the myriad wants of an Arcadius or a Honorius, he was not the least important among the chief officers of the state.

These great civil ministers, eight in number under the Western Emperors (for there were three *Prætorian prefects*, one for the Gauls, one for Italy, and one for the city of Rome), formed, with the military officers of highest rank (generally five in number), the innermost circle of "*Illustres*," who may be likened to the Cabinet of the emperor. At this time the Cabinet of *Illustres* may have been smaller by one or two members, on account of the separation of the Gaulish provinces from Rome, but we are not able to speak positively on this point.

Nearly every one of these great ministers of state had under him a large, ambitious, and often highly-paid staff of subordinates, who were called his *Officium*. The civil service was at least as regular and highly specialised a profession under the emperors and under Theodoric as it is in any modern state. It is possible that we should have to go to the Celestial Empire of China to find its fitting representative. A large number of *singularii, rationalii, clavicularii,* and the like (whom we should call policemen, subordinate clerks, and gaolers) formed the "Unlettered Staff" (*Militia Illiterata*), who stood on the lowest stage of the bureaucratic pyramid. Above these was the lettered staff, beginning with the humble chancellor (*cancellarius*), who sat by the *cancelli* (latticework), at the bottom of the court (to prevent importunate suitors from venturing too far), and rising to the dignified *princeps* or *cornicularius*, who was looked upon as equal in rank to a count, and who expected to make an income of not less than £600 a year, equivalent to two or three times that amount in our day.

All this great hierarchy of officials wielded powers derived, mediately or immediately, from the emperor (or in the Ostrogothic monarchy from the king), and great as was their brilliancy in the eyes of the dazzled multitudes who crouched before them, it was all reflected from him, who was the central sun of their universe. But there were still two institutions which were in theory independent of emperor or king, which were yet held venerable by men, and which had come down from the days of the great world-conquering republic, or the yet earlier days of Romulus and Numa. These two institutions were the Consulship and the Senate.

The consuls, as was said in an earlier chapter, still appeared to preside over the Roman Republic, as they had in truth presided, wielding between them the full power of a king, when Brutus and Collatinus, a thousand years before Theodoric's commencement of the siege of Ravenna, took their seat upon the *curule* chairs, and donned the *trabea* of the consul. Still, though utterly shorn of its power, the glamour of the venerable office remained. The emperor himself seemed to add to his dignity when he allowed himself to be nominated as consul, and in nothing was the cupidity of the tyrant emperors and the moderation of the patriot emperors better displayed than in the number of consulships which they claimed or forbore from claiming. Ever since the virtual division of the Empire into an Eastern and Western portion, it had been usual, though not absolutely obligatory, for one consul to be chosen out of each half of the *Orbis Romanus*, and in reading the contemporary chronicles we can almost invariably tell to which portion the author belongs by observing to which consul's name he gives the priority.

As has been already stated, after the resumption of friendly relations between Ravenna and Constantinople, Theodoric, while naming the Western Consul, sent a courteous notification of the fact to the emperor, by whom his nomination seems to have been always accepted without question. The great Ostrogoth, having once worn the consular robes and distributed largess to "the Roman people" in the streets of Constantinople, does not seem to have cared a second time to assume that ancient dignity, but in the year 519, towards the end of his reign, he named his son-in-law, Eutharic, consul, and the splendour of Eutharic's year of office was enhanced by the fact that he had the then reigning emperor, Justin, for his colleague. As for the *Senate*, it too was still in appearance what it had ever been,—the highest council in the state, the assembly of kings which overawed the ambassador of Pyrrhus, the main-spring, or, if not the main-spring, at any rate the balance-wheel, of the administrative machine. This it was in theory, for there had never been any formal abolition of its existence or abrogation of its powers.

In practice it was just what the sovereign, whether called emperor or king, allowed it to be. A self-willed and arbitrary monarch, like Caligula or Domitian, would reduce its functions to a nullity. A wise and moderate emperor, like Trajan or Marcus Aurelius, would consult it on all important state-affairs, and, while reserving to himself both the power of initiation and that of final control, would make of it a real Council of State, a valuable member of the governing body of the Empire. The latter seems to have been the policy of Theodoric. Probably the very fact of his holding a somewhat doubtful position towards the emperor at Constantinople made him more willing to accept all the moral support that could be given him by the body which was in a certain sense older and more august than any emperor, the venerable Senate of Rome.

At any rate, the letters in which he announces to the Senate the various acts, especially the nomination of the great officials of his kingdom, in which he desires their concurrence, are couched in such extremely courteous terms, that sometimes civility almost borders on servility. Notwithstanding this, however, it is quite plain that it was always thoroughly understood who was master in Italy, and that any attempt on the part of the Senate to wrest any portion of real power from Theodoric would have been instantly and summarily suppressed.

I have said that it was only by the aid of officials, trained in the service of the Empire that Theodoric, or indeed any of the new barbarian sovereigns, could hope to keep the machine of civil government in working order. We have, fortunately, a little information as to some of these officials, and an elaborate self-drawn picture of one of them.

Liberius had been a faithful servant of Odovacar; and had to the last remained by the sinking vessel of his fortunes. This fidelity did not injure him in the estimation of the conqueror. When all was over, he came, with no eagerness, and with unconcealed sorrow for the death of his former master, to offer his services to Theodoric, who gladly accepted them, and gave him at once the pre-eminent dignity of *Prætorian prefect*. His wise and economical management of the finances filled the royal exchequer without increasing the burdens of the tax-payer, and it is probable that the early return of prosperity to Italy, which was described in the last chapter, was, in great measure, due to the just and statesmanlike administration of Liberius.

In the delicate business of allotting to the Gothic warriors the third part of the soil of Italy, which seems to have been their recognised dividend on Theodoric's Italian speculation, he so acquitted himself as to win the approbation of all. It is difficult for us to understand how such a change of ownership can have brought with it anything but heart-burning and resentment. But (*1*) there are not wanting indications that, owing to evil influences both economic and political, there was actually a large quantity of good land lying unoccupied in Italy in the fifth century; and (*2*) there had already been one expropriation of the same kind for the benefit of the soldiers of Odovacar. In so far as this allotment of Thirds[2] merely followed the lines of that earlier redistribution, but little of a grievance was caused to the Italian owner. An Ostrogoth, the follower of Theodoric, stepped into the position of a slain Scyrian or Turcilingian, the follower of Odovacar, and the Italian owner suffered no further detriment.

Still there must have been some loss to the provincials and some cases of hardship which would be long and bitterly remembered, before every family which crossed the Alps in the Gothic waggons was safely settled in its Italian home. It is therefore not without some qualification that we can accept the statement of the official panegyrist[3] of the Gothic *régime*, who declares that in this business of the allotment of the Thirds "Liberius joined both the hearts and the properties of the two nations, Gothic and Roman. For whereas neighbourhood often proves a cause of enmity, with these men communion of farms proved a cause of concord.[4] Thus the division of the soil promoted the concord of the owners; friendship grew out of the loss of the provincials, and the land gained a defender, whose possession of part

---

2. *Deputatio Tertiarum.*
3. Cassiodorus, *Var.*, ii., 16.
4. *Nam cum se homines soleant de vicinitate collidere, istis prædiorum communio causam noscitur præstitisse concordiæ. Sic enim contigit ut utraque natio, dum commumater vivit ad unum velle convenerit.*

guaranteed the quiet enjoyment of the remainder."

It is possible that there was some foundation of truth for the last statement. After the fearful convulsions through which the whole Western Empire had passed, and with the strange paralysis of the power of self-defence which had overtaken the once brave and hardy population of Italy, it is possible that the presence, near to each considerable Italian landowner, of a Goth whose duty to his king obliged him to defend the land from foreign invasion, and to suppress with a strong hand all robbery and brigandage, may have been felt in some cases as a compensation even for whatever share of the soil of Italy was transferred to Goth from Roman by the chief commissioner, Liberius.

Two eminent Romans, whom in the early years of his reign Theodoric placed in high offices of state, were the two successive ambassadors to Constantinople, *Faustus* and *Festus*. Both seem to have held the high dignity of *Prætorian prefect*. We do not, however, hear much as to the career of Festus, and what we hear of Faustus is not altogether to his credit. He had been for several years practically the prime minister of Theodoric, when in an evil hour for his reputation he coveted the estate of a certain Castorius, whose land adjoined his own. Deprived of his patrimony, Castorius appealed, not in vain, to the justice of Theodoric, whose ears were not closed, as an emperor's would probably have been, to the cry of a private citizen against a powerful official.

We are determined, (says Theodoric, in his reply to the petition of Castorius), to assist the humble and to repress the violence of the proud. If the petition of Castorius prove to be well-founded, let the spoiler restore to Castorius his property and hand over besides another estate of equal value. If the Magnificent Faustus have employed any subordinate in this act of injustice, bring him to us bound with chains that he may pay for the outrage in person, if he cannot do so in purse. If on any future occasion that now known craftsman of evil (Faustus) shall attempt to injure the aforesaid Castorius, let him be at once fined fifty pounds of gold (£2,000). Greatest of all punishments will be the necessity of beholding the untroubled estate of the man whom he sought to ruin.

Behold herein a deed which may well chasten and subdue the hearts of all our great dignitaries when they see that not even a *Prætorian prefect* is permitted to trample on the lowly, and that when we put forth our arm to help, such an one's power of injuring the wretched fails him. From this may all men learn how great is our love of justice, since we are willing to diminish even the power of our judges, that we may increase the contentment of our own conscience.

This edict was followed by a letter to the Illustrious Faustus himself, in which that grasping governor was reminded that human nature frequently requires a change, and permission was graciously given him to withdraw for four months into the country. At the end of that time he was without fail to return to the capital, since no Roman Senator ought to be happy if permanently settled anywhere but at Rome. It is tolerably plain that the four months' *villeggiatura* was really a sentence of temporary banishment, and we may probably conclude that the Magnificent Faustus never afterwards held any high position under Theodoric.

The letters announcing the king's judgement in this matter, like all the other extant state-papers of Theodoric, were written by a man who was probably by the fall of Faustus raised a step in the official hierarchy, and who was certainly for the last twenty years of the reign of Theodoric one of the most conspicuous of his Roman officials. This was Cassiodorus, or, to give him his full name, *Magnus Aurelius Cassiodorus Senator*, a man, whose life and character require to be described in some detail.

Cassiodorus was sprung from a noble Roman family, which had already given three of its members in lineal succession (all bearing the name Cassiodorus) to the service of the state. His great-grandfather, of "Illustrious" rank, defended Sicily and Calabria from the incursions of the Vandals. His grandsire, a Tribune in the army, was sent by the Emperor Valentinian III. on an important embassy to Attila. His father filled first one and then the other of the two highest financial offices in the state under Odovacar. On the overthrow of that chieftain, he, like Liberius, transferred his services to Theodoric, who employed him as governor first of Sicily, then of Calabria, and finally, about the year 500, conferred upon him the highest dignity of all, that of *Prætorian prefect*.

The ancestral possessions of the Cassiodori were situated in that southernmost province, sometimes likened to the toe of Italy, which was then called Bruttii, and is now called Calabria. It was a land rich in cattle, renowned for its cheese and for its aromatic, white Palmatian wine; and veins of gold were said to be in its mountains. Here, in the old Greek city of Scyllacium (*Sguillace*), "a city perched upon a high hill overlooking the sea, sunny yet fanned by cool Mediterranean breezes, and looking peacefully on the cornfields, the vineyards, and the olive-groves around her",[5] Cassiodorus was born, about the year 480. He was therefore probably some twelve or thirteen years of age when the long strife between Odovacar and Theodoric was ended by the murder scene in the palace at Ravenna.

Like all the young Roman nobles who aspired to the honours and emoluments of public life, Cassiodorus studied philosophy and rhetoric, and, according to the standard of the age, a degraded standard, he acquired great proficiency in both lines of study. When his father was made *Prætorian prefect* (about the year 500), the young rhetorician received an appointment as *Consiliarius*, or Assessor in the *prefect's* court, at a salary which probably did not exceed forty or fifty pounds. While he was holding this position, it fell to his lot to pronounce a laudatory oration on Theodoric (perhaps on the occasion of one of his visits to Rome), and the eloquence of the young *Consiliarius* so delighted the king, that he was at once made an "Illustrious" *quæstor*, thus receiving what we should call cabinet-rank while he was still considerably under thirty years of age.

The *quæstor*, as has been said, was the public orator of the state. It devolved upon him to reply to the formal harangues in which the ambassadors of foreign nations greeted his master, to answer the petitions of his subjects, and to see that the edicts of the sovereign were expressed in proper terms. The post exactly fitted the intellectual tendencies of Cassiodorus, who was never so happy as when he was wrapping up some commonplace thought in a garment of sonorous but turgid rhetoric; and the simple honesty of his moral nature, simple in its very vanity and honest in its childlike egotism, coupled as it was with real love for his country and loyal zeal for her welfare, endeared him in his turn to Theodoric, with whom he had many "*gloriosa colloquia*" (as he calls them), conversations in which the young, learned, and eloquent Roman poured forth for his master the stored up wine of generations of philosophers and poets, while the kingly barbarian doubtless unfolded some of the propositions of that more difficult science, the knowledge of men, which he had acquired by long and arduous years of study in the council-chamber, on the mountain-march, and on the battlefield.

We can go at once to the fountain-head for information as to the character of Cassiodorus. When he was promoted, soon after the

---

5. The description is taken from Cassiodorus, *Var.*, xii., 15.

death of Theodoric, to the rank of *Prætorian prefect*, it became his duty, as *quæstor* to the young King Athalaric (Theodoric's successor), to inform himself by an official letter of the honour conferred upon him. In writing this letter, he does not deviate from the usual custom of describing the virtues and accomplishments which justify the new minister's promotion. Why indeed should he keep silence on such an occasion? No one could know the good qualities of Cassiodorus so well or so intimately as Cassiodorus himself, and accordingly the *quæstor* sets forth, with all the rhetoric of which he had such an endless supply, the virtues and the accomplishments which his observant eye has discovered in himself, the new *Prætorian prefect*.

Such a course would certainly not be often pursued by a modern statesman, but there is a pleasing ingenuousness about it which to some minds will be more attractive than our present methods, the "inspired" article in a hired newspaper, or the feigned reluctance to receive a testimonial which, till the receiver suggested it, no one had dreamed of offering.

This then is how Cassiodorus, in 533, describes his past career[6]:

> You came (his young sovereign, Athalaric, is supposed to be addressing him) in very early years to the dignity of *quæstor*, and my grandfather's (Theodoric's) wonderful insight into character was never more abundantly proved than in your case, for he found you to be endued with rare conscientiousness, and already ripe in your knowledge of the laws. You were in truth the chief glory of your times, and you won his favour by arts which none could blame, for his mind, by nature anxious in all things, was able to lay aside its cares while you supported the weight of the royal counsels with the strength of your eloquence.
>
> In you he had a charming secretary, a rigidly upright judge, a minister to whom avarice was unknown. You never fixed a scandalous tariff for the sale of his benefits; you chose to take your reward in public esteem, not in riches. Therefore it was that this most righteous ruler chose you to be honoured by his glorious friendship, because he saw you to be free from all taint of corrupt vices. How often did he fix your place among his white-haired counsellors; inasmuch as they, by the experience of years, had not come up to the point from which you had started! He found that he could safely praise your excellent

---

6. *Variæ*, ix., 24.

disposition, open-handed in bestowing benefits, tightly closed against the vices of avarice.

Thus you passed on to the dignity of Master of the Offices,[7] which you obtained, not by a pecuniary payment, but as a testimony to your character. In that office you were ever ready to help the *quæstors*, for when pure eloquence was needed men always resorted to you; and, in fact, when you were at hand and ready to help, there was no accurate division of labour among the various offices of the state.[8] No one could find an occasion to murmur aught against you, although you bore all the unpopularity which accompanies the favour of a prince."

Your detractors were conquered by the integrity of your life; your adversaries, bowing to public opinion, were obliged to praise even while they hated you.

To the lord of the land you showed yourself a friendly judge and an intimate minister. When public affairs no longer claimed him, he would ask you to tell him the stories in which wise men of old have clothed their maxims, that by his own deeds he might equal the ancient heroes. The courses of the stars, the ebb and flow of the sea, the marvels of springing fountains,—into all these subjects would that most acute questioner inquire, so that by his diligent investigations into the nature of things, he seemed to be a philosopher in the purple.

This sketch of the character of the minister throws light incidentally on that of the monarch who employed him. Of course, as a general rule, history cannot allow the personages with whom she deals to write their own testimonials, but in this case there is reason to think that the self-portraiture of Cassiodorus is accurate in its main outlines, though our modern taste would have suggested the employment of somewhat less florid colouring.

One literary service which Cassiodorus rendered to the Ostrogothic monarchy is thus described by himself, still speaking in his young king's name and addressing the Roman Senate.[9]

He was not satisfied with extolling surviving kings, from whom

---

7. The date of Cassiodorus' first promotion to this dignity is uncertain, but it was probably about 518.

8. *Non enim proprios fines sub te ulla dignitas custodivit.* (Of course there is a certain anachronism in representing a statesman of the sixth century as using the phrase "division of labour.")

9. *Variæ* ix., 25.

their panegyrist might hope for a reward. He extended his labours to our remote ancestry, learning from books that which the hoary memories of our old men scarcely retained. He drew forth from their hiding-place the kings of the Goths, hidden by long forgetfulness. He restored the Amals in all the lustre of their lineage, evidently proving that we have kings for our ancestors up to the seventeenth generation. He made the origin of the Goths part of Roman history, collecting into one wreath the flowers which had previously been scattered over the wide plains of literature. Consider, therefore, what love he showed to you (the Senate) in uttering our praises, while teaching that the nation of your sovereign has been from ancient time a marvellous people: so that you who from the days of your ancestors have been truly deemed noble are also now ruled over by the long-descended progeny of kings.

These sentences relate to the *Gothic History* of Cassiodorus, which once existed in twelve books, but is now unfortunately lost. A hasty abridgment of it, made by an ignorant monk named Jordanes, is all that now remains. Even this, with its many faults, is a most precious monument of the early history of the Teutonic invaders of the Empire, and it is from its pages that much of the information contained in the previous chapters is drawn. The object of the original statesman-author in composing his *Gothic History* is plainly stated in the above sentences. He wishes to heal the wound given to Roman pride by the fact of the supremacy in Italy of a Gothic lord; and in order to effect this object he strings together all that he can collect of the *Sagas* of the Gothic people, showing the great deeds of the Amal progenitors of Theodoric, whose lineage he traces back into distant centuries. "It is true" he seems to say to the Senators of Rome, "that you, who once ruled the world, are now ruled by an alien; but at least that alien is no newcomer into greatness.

He and his progenitors have been crowned kings for centuries. His people, who are quartered among you and claim one-third of the soil of Italy, are an old, historic people. Their ancestors fought under the walls of Troy; they defeated Cyrus, king of Persia; they warred not ingloriously with Perdiccas of Macedonia."

These classical elements of the Gothic history of Cassiodorus (which rest chiefly on a misunderstanding of the vague and unscientific term "Scythians") are valueless for the purposes of history; but

121

the old Gothic Sagas, of which he has evidently also preserved some fragments, are both interesting and valuable. When a nation has played so important a part on the theatre of the world as that assigned to the Goths, even their legendary stories of the past are precious. Whether these early Amal kings fought and ruled and migrated as the *Sagas* represent them to have done, or not, in any case the belief that these were their achievements was a part of the intellectual heritage of the Gothic peoples. The songs to whose lullaby the cradle of a great nation is rocked are a precious possession to the historian.

The other most important work of Cassiodorus is the collection of letters called the *Variæ*, in twelve books. This collection contains all the chief state-papers composed by him during the period (somewhat more than thirty years) which was covered by his official life. Five books are devoted to the letters written at the dictation of Theodoric; two to the *Formulæ* or model-letters addressed to the various dignitaries of the State on their accession to office; three to the letters written in the name of Theodoric's immediate successors (his grandson, daughter, and nephew); and two to those written by Cassiodorus himself in his own name when he had attained the crowning dignity of *Prætorian prefect*.

I have already made some extracts from this collection of *Various Epistles* and the reader, from the specimens thus submitted to him, will have formed some conception of the character of the author's style. That style is diffuse and turgid, marked in an eminent degree with the prevailing faults of the sixth century, an age of literary decay, when the language of Cicero and Virgil was falling into its dotage. There is much ill-timed display of irrelevant learning, and a grievous absence of simplicity and directness, in the *Various Epistles*. It must be regarded as a misfortune for Theodoric that his maxims of statesmanship, which were assuredly full of manly sense and vigour, should have reached us only in such a shape, diluted with the platitudes and false rhetoric of a scholar of the decadence.

Still, even through all these disguises, it is easy to discern the genuine patriotism both of the great king and of his minister, their earnest desire that right, not might, should determine every case that came before them, their true insight into the vices and the virtues of each of the two different nations which now shared Italy between them, their persevering endeavour to keep *civilitas* intact, their determination to oppose alike the turbulence of the Goth and the chicane of the scheming Roman.

As specimens of the rhetoric of Cassiodorus when he is trying his highest flights, the reader may care to peruse the two following letters. The first[10] was written to Faustus the *Prætorian prefect*, to complain of his delay in forwarding some cargoes of corn from Calabria to Rome:

What are you waiting for? (says Cassiodorus, writing in his master's name). Why are your ships not spreading their sails to the breeze? When the South-wind is blowing and your oarsmen are urging on your vessels, has the sucking-fish (Echeneis) fastened its bite upon them through the liquid waves? Or have the shell-fishes of the Indian Sea with similar power stayed your keels with their lips: those creatures whose quiet touch is said to hold back, more than the tumultuous elements can possibly urge forward? The idle bark stands still, though winged with swelling sails, and has no way on her though the breeze is propitious; she is fixed without anchors; she is moored without cables, and these tiny animals pull back, more than all such favouring powers can propel. Therefore when the subject wave would hasten the vessel's course, it appears that it stands fixed on the surface of the sea: and in marvellous style the floating ship is retained immovable, while the wave is hurried along by countless currents.

But let us describe the nature of another kind of fish. Perhaps the crews of the aforesaid ships have been benumbed into idleness by the touch of a torpedo, by which the right hand of him who attacks it is so deadened—even through the spear by which it is itself wounded—that while still part of a living body it hangs down benumbed without sense or motion. I think some such misfortunes must have happened to men who are unable to move themselves.

But no. The sucking-fish of these men is their hindering corruption. The shell-fishes that bite them are their avaricious hearts. The torpedo that benumbs them is lying guile. With perverted ingenuity they manufacture delays, that they may seem to have met with a run of ill-luck.

Let your greatness, whom it especially behoves to take thought for such matters, cause that this be put right by speediest rebuke: lest the famine, which will otherwise ensue, be deemed

---

10. *Var.*, i., 35.

to be the child of negligence rather than of the barrenness of the land.

The occasion of the second letter (*Var.*, x., 30.) was as follows. Some brazen images of elephants which adorned the Sacred Street of Rome were falling into ruin, Cassiodorus, writing in the name of one of Theodoric's successors, to the *prefect* of the city, orders that their gaping limbs should be strengthened by hooks, and their pendulous bellies should be supported by masonry. He then proceeds to give to the admiring *prefect* some wonderful information as to the natural history of the elephant. He regrets that the metal effigies should be so soon destroyed, when the animal which they represent is accustomed to live more than a thousand years.

The living elephant (he says), when it is once prostrate on the ground, cannot rise unaided, because it has no joints in its feet. Hence when they are helping men to fell timber, you see numbers of them lying on the earth till men come and help them to rise. Thus this creature, so formidable by its size, is really more helpless than the tiny ant. The elephant, wiser than all other creatures, renders religious adoration to the Ruler of all: also to good princes, but if a tyrant approach, it will not pay him the homage which is due only to the virtuous. It uses its *proboscis*, that nose-like hand which Nature has given it in compensation for its very short neck, for the benefit of its master, accepting the presents which will be profitable to him. It always walks cautiously, remembering that fatal fall into the hunter's pit which was the beginning of its captivity. When requested to do so, it exhales its breath, which is said to be a remedy for the headache.

When it comes to water, it sucks up a vast quantity in its trunk, and then at the word of command squirts it forth like a shower. If any one have treated its demands with contempt, it pours forth such a stream of dirty water over him that one would think that a river had entered his house. For this beast has a wonderfully long memory, both of injury and of kindness. Its eyes are small but move solemnly, so that there is a sort of royal majesty in its appearance: and it despises scurrile jests, while it always looks with pleasure on that which is honourable.

It must be admitted that if the official communications of modern statesmen thus anxiously combined amusement with instruction, the dull routine of "I have the honour to inform" and "I beg to remain your obedient humble servant," would acquire a charm of which it is now destitute.

I have translated two letters which show the ludicrous side of the literary character of Cassiodorus. In justice to this honest, if somewhat pedantic, servant of Theodoric, I will close this sketch of his character with a state-paper of a better type, and one which incidentally throws some light on the social condition of Italy under the Goths.

THEODORIC TO THE ILLUSTRIOUS NEUDES.[10]

We were moved to sympathy by the long petition of Ocer but yet more by beholding the old hero, bereft of the blessing of sight, inasmuch as the calamities which we witness make more impression upon us than those of which we only hear. He, poor man, living on in perpetual darkness, had to borrow the sight of another to hasten to our presence in order that he might feel the sweetness of our clemency, though he could not gaze upon our countenance.

He complains that Gudila and Oppas (probably two Gothic nobles or a Gothic chief and his wife) have reduced him to a state of slavery, a condition unknown to him or his fathers, since he once served in our army as a free man. We marvel that such a man should be dragged into bondage who (on account of his infirmity) ought to have been liberated by a lawful owner. It is a new kind of ostentation to claim the services of such an one, the sight of whom shocks you, and to call that man a slave, to whom you ought rather to minister with divine compassion.

He adds also that all claims of this nature have been already judged invalid after careful examination by Count Pythias, a man celebrated for the correctness of his judgements.

But now overwhelmed by the weight of his calamity, he cannot assert his freedom by his own right hand, which in the strong man is the most effectual advocate of his claims.

We, however, whose peculiar property it is to administer justice indifferently, whether between men of equal or unequal condition, do by this present mandate decree, that if, in the judgement of the aforesaid Pythias, Ocer have proved himself free-born, you shall at once remove those who are harassing him with their claims, nor shall they dare any longer to mock at the calamities of others: these people who once convicted ought to

125

have been covered with shame for their wicked designs

—*Var.*, v., 29.

THEODORIC'S KINDRED.

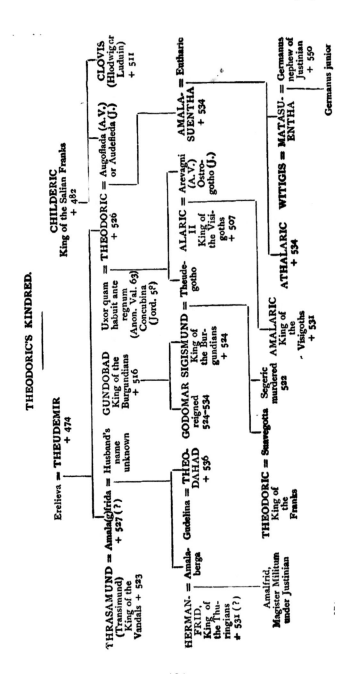

CHAPTER 10

The Arian League

The position of Theodoric in relation both to his own subjects and to the Empire was seriously modified by one fact to which hitherto I have only alluded casually, the fact that he, like the great majority of the Teutonic invaders of the Empire, was an adherent of the Arian form of Christianity. In order to estimate at its true value the bearing of religion, or at least of religious profession, on politics, at the time of the fall of the Roman State, we might well look at the condition of another dominion, founded under the combined influence of martial spirit and religious zeal, which is now going to pieces under our very eyes, I mean the Empire of the Ottomans.

In the lands which are still under the sway of the *Sultan*, religion may not be a great spiritual force, but it is at any rate a great political lever. When you have said that a man is a Moslem or a Druse, a member of the Orthodox or of the Catholic Church, an Armenian or a Protestant, you have almost always said enough to define his political position. Without the need of additional information you have already got the elements of his civic equation, and can say whether he is a loyal subject of the Porte, or whether he looks to Russia or Greece, to France, Austria, or England as the sovereign of his future choice. In fact, as has been often pointed out, in the East at this day "Religion is Nationality."

Very similar to this was the condition of the ancient world at the time when the general movement of the Northern nations began. The battle with heathenism was virtually over, Christianity being the unquestioned conqueror; but the question, which of the many modifications of Christianity devised by the subtle Hellenic and Oriental intellects should be the victor, was a question still unsettled, and debated with the keenest interest on all the shores of the Mediterranean.

So keen indeed was the interest that it sometimes seems almost to have blinded the disputants to the fact that the Roman Empire, the greatest political work that the world has ever seen, was falling in ruins around them. When we want information about the march of armies and the fall of states, the chroniclers to whom we turn for guidance, withholding that which we seek, deluge us with trivial talk about the squabbles of monks and bishops, about Timothy the Weasel and Peter the Fuller, and a host of other self-seeking ecclesiastics, to whose names, to whose characters, and to whose often violent deaths we are profoundly and absolutely indifferent.

But though a feeling of utter weariness comes over the mind of most readers, while watching the theological sword-play of the fourth and fifth centuries, the historical student cannot afford to shut his eyes altogether to the battle of the creeds, which produced results of such infinite importance to the crystallising process by which mediæval Europe was formed out of the Roman Empire.

As I have just said, Theodoric the Ostrogoth, like almost all the great Teutonic swarm-leaders, like Alaric the Visigoth, like Gaiseric the Vandal, like Gundobad the Burgundian, was an Arian. On the other hand, the emperors, Zeno, for instance, and Anastasius, and the great majority of the population of Italy and of the provinces of the Empire, were Catholic. What was the amount of theological divergence which was conveyed by these terms Arian and Catholic, or to speak more judicially (for the Arians averred that they were the true Catholics and that their opponents were heretics) Arian and Athanasian?

As this is not the place for a disquisition on disputed points of theology, it is sufficient to say that, while the Athanasian held for truth the whole of the Nicene Creed, the Arian—at least that type of Arian with whom we are here concerned—would, in that part which relates to the Son of God, leave out the words "being of one substance with the Father," and would substitute for them "being like unto the Father in such manner as the Scriptures declare." He would also have refused to repeat the words which assert the Godhead of the Holy Spirit. These were important differences, but it will be seen at once that they were not so broad as those which now generally separate "orthodox" from "heterodox" theologians.

The reasons which led the barbarian invaders of the Empire to accept the Arian form of Christianity are not yet fully disclosed to us. The cause could not be an uncultured people's preference for a simple faith, for the Arian champions were at least as subtle and technical in their theology as the Athanasian, and often surpassed them in these qualities. It is possible that some remembrances of the mythology handed down to them by their fathers made them willing to accept a subordinate Christ, a spiritualised "Balder the Beautiful," divine yet subject to death, standing as it were upon the steps of his father's throne, rather than the dogma, too highly spiritualised for their apprehension, of One God in Three Persons. But probably the chief cause of the Arianism of the German invaders was the fact that the Empire itself was to a great extent Arian when they were in friendly relations with it, and were accepting both religion and civilisation at its hands, in the middle years of the fourth century.

The most powerful factor in this change, the man who more than all others was responsible for the conversion of the Germanic races to Christianity, in its Arian form, was the Gothic Bishop, Ulfilas (311-381), whose construction of an Alphabet and translation of the Scriptures into the language of his fellow-countrymen have secured for him imperishable renown among all who are interested in the history of human speech. Ulfilas, who has been well termed "The Apostle of the Goths," seems to have embraced Christianity as a young man when he was dwelling in Constantinople as a hostage (thus in some measure anticipating the part which one hundred and thirty years later was to be played by Theodoric), and having been ordained first Lector (Reader) and afterwards (341) Bishop of Gothia, he spent the remaining forty years of his life in missionary journeys among his countrymen in Dacia, in collecting those of his converts who fled from the persecution of their still heathen rulers, and settling them as colonists in Mœsia, and, most important of all, in his great work of the translation of the Bible into Gothic.

Of this work, as is well known, some precious fragments still remain; most precious of all, the glorious Silver Manuscript of the Gospels (*Codex Argenteus*), which is supposed to have been written in the sixth century, and which, after many wanderings and an eventful history, rests now in a Scandinavian land, in the library of the university of Upsala, It is well worth while to make a pilgrimage to that friendly and hospitable Swedish city, if for no other purpose than to see the letters (traced in silver on parchment of rich purple dye) in which the skilful amanuensis laboriously transcribed the sayings of Christ rendered by Bishop Ulfilas into the language of Alaric. For that *Codex Argenteus* is oldest of all extant monuments of Teutonic speech, the first fruit of that mighty tree which now spreads its branches over half the civilised world.

With the theological bearings of the Arian controversy we have no present concern; but it is impossible not to notice the unfortunate political results of the difference of creed between the German invaders and the great majority of the inhabitants of the Empire. The cultivators of the soil and the dwellers in the cities had suffered much from the misgovernment of their rulers during the last two centuries of Imperial sway; they could, to some extent, appreciate the nobler moral qualities of the barbarian settlers—their manliness, their truthfulness, their higher standard of chastity; nor is it idle to suppose that if there had been perfect harmony of religious faith between the newcomers and the old inhabitants they might soon have settled down into vigorous and well-ordered communities, such as Theodoric and Cassiodorus longed to behold, combining the Teutonic strength with the Roman reverence for law.

Religious discord made it impossible to realise this ideal. The orthodox clergy loathed and dreaded the invaders "infected," as they said, "with the Arian pravity." The barbarian kings, unaccustomed to have their will opposed by men who never wielded a broadsword, were masterful and high-handed in their demand for absolute obedience, even when their commands related to the things of God rather than to the things of Cæsar; and the Arian bishops and priests who stood beside their thrones, and who had sometimes long arrears of vengeance for past insult or oppression to exact, often wrought up the monarch's mind to a perfect frenzy of fanatical rage, and goaded him to cruel deeds which made reconciliation between the warring creeds hopelessly impossible. In Africa, the Vandal kings set on foot a persecution of their Catholic subjects which rivalled, nay exceeded, the horrors of the persecution under Diocletian.

Churches were destroyed, bishops banished, and their flocks forbidden to elect their successors: nay, sometimes, in the fierce quest after hidden treasure, eminent ecclesiastics were stretched on the rack, their mouths were filled with noisome dirt, or cords were twisted round their foreheads or their shins. In Gaul, under the Visigothic King Euric, the persecution was less savage, but it was stubborn and severe. Here, too, the congregations were forbidden to elect successors to their exiled bishops; the paths to the churches were stopped up with thorns and briers; cattle grazed on the grass-grown altar steps, and the rain came through the shattered roofs into the dismantled *basilicas*.

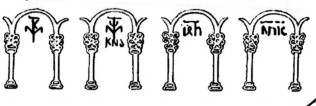

A PAGE OF THE GOTHIC GOSPELS
(CODEX ARGENTEUS)
MARK VII 3-7

Thus all round the shores of the Mediterranean there was strife and bitter heart-burning between the Roman provincial and his Teutonic "guest," not so much because one was or called himself a Roman, while the other called himself Goth, Burgundian, or Vandal, but because one was Athanasian and the other Arian. With this strife of creeds Theodoric, for the greater part of his reign, refused to concern himself. He remained an Arian, as his fathers had been before him, but he protected the Catholic Church in the privileges which she had acquired, and he refused to exert his royal authority to either threaten or allure men into adopting his creed. So evenly for many years did he hold the balance between the rival faiths, that it was reported of him that he put to death a Catholic priest who apostatised to Arianism in order to attain the royal favour; and though this story does not perhaps rest on sufficient authority, there can be no doubt that the general testimony of the marvelling Catholic subjects of Theodoric would have coincided with that already quoted (See chapter 8) from the bishop of Ravenna that "he attempted nothing against the Catholic faith."

Still, though determined not to govern in the interests of a sect, it was impossible that Theodoric's political relations should not be, to a certain extent, modified by his religious affinities. Let us glance at the position of the chief States with which a ruler of Italy at the close of the fifth century necessarily came in contact.

First of all we have *the Empire*, practically confined at this time to "the Balkan peninsula" south of the Danube, Asia Minor, Syria, and Egypt, and presided over by the elderly, politic, but unpopular Anastasius. This state is Catholic, though, as we shall hereafter see, not in hearty alliance with the Church of Rome.

Westward from the Empire, along the southern shore of the Mediterranean, stretches the great kingdom of the Vandals, with Carthage for its capital. They have a powerful navy, but their kings, Gunthamund (484-496) and Thrasamund (496-523), do not seem to be disposed to renew the buccaneering expeditions of their grandfather, the great Vandal Gaiseric. They are decided Arians, and keep up a stern, steady pressure on their Catholic subjects, who are spared, however, the ruthless brutalities practised upon them by the earlier Vandal kings. The relations of the Vandals with the Ostrogothic kingdom seem to have been of a friendly character during almost the whole reign of Theodoric. Thrasamund, the fourth king who reigned at Carthage, married Amalafrida, Theodoric's sister, who brought with her, as dowry, possession of the strong fortress of Lilybæum (*Marsala*), in the west of Sicily, and who was accompanied to her new home by a brilliant train of one thousand Gothic nobles with five thousand mounted retainers.

In the north and west of Spain dwell the nation of the *Suevi*, Teutonic and Arian, but practically out of the sphere of European politics, and who, half a century after the death of Theodoric, will be absorbed by their Visigothic neighbours.

This latter state, the kingdom of the *Visigoths*, is apparently, at the end of the fifth century, by far the most powerful of the new barbarian monarchies. All Spain, except its north-western corner, and something like half of Gaul—namely, that region which is contained between the Pyrenees and the Loire, owns the sway of the young king, whose capital city is Toulouse, and who, though a stranger in blood, bears the name of the great Visigoth who first battered a breach in the walls of Rome, the mighty Alaric. This Alaric II. (485-507), the son of Euric, who had been the most powerful sovereign of his dynasty, inherited neither his father's force of character (485-507) nor the bitterness of his Arianism. The persecution of the Catholics was suspended, or ceased altogether, and we may picture to ourselves the congregations again wending their way by unblockaded paths to the house of prayer, the churches once more roofed in and again made gorgeous by the stately ceremonial of the Catholic rite.

In other ways, too, Alaric showed himself anxious to conciliate the favour of his Roman subjects. He ordered an abstract of the Imperial Code to be prepared, and this abstract, under the name of the *Breviarium Alaricianum*[1] is to this day one of our most valuable sources of information as to Roman law. He is also said to have directed the construction of the canal, which still bears his name (*Canal d'Alaric*), and which, connecting the Adour with the Aisne, assists the irrigation of the meadows of Gascony. But all these attempts to close the feud between the king and his orthodox subjects were vain. When the day of trial came, it was seen, as it had long been suspected, that the sympathies and the powerful influence of the bishops and clergy were thrown entirely on the side of the Catholic invader.

Between the Visigothic and Ostrogothic courts there was firm friendship and alliance, the remembrance of their common origin and of many perils and hardships shared together on the shores of the Euxine and in the passes of the Balkans being fortified by the knowledge of the dangers to which their common profession of Ari-

---

1. Sometimes called the *Breviarium Aniani*, from the name of the registrar whose signature attested each copy of the *Breviarium*.

anism exposed them amidst the Catholic population of the Empire. The alliance, which had served Theodoric in good stead when the Visigoths helped him in his struggle with Odovacar, was yet further strengthened by kinship, the young king of Toulouse having received in marriage a princess from Ravenna, whose name is variously given as Arevagni or Ostrogotho.

A matrimonial alliance also connected Theodoric with the king of the *Burgundians*. These invaders, who were destined so strangely to disappear out of history themselves, while giving their name to such wide and rich regions of mediæval Europe, occupied at this time the valleys of the Saone and the Rhone, as well as the country which we now call Switzerland. Their king, Gundobad, a man somewhat older than Theodoric, had once interfered zealously in the politics of Italy, making and unmaking emperors and striking for Odovacar against his Ostrogothic rival. Now, however, his whole energies were directed to extending his dominions in Gaul, and to securing his somewhat precarious throne from the machinations of the Catholic bishops, his subjects. For he, too, was by profession an Arian, though of a tolerant type, and though he sometimes seemed on the point of crossing the abyss and declaring himself a convert to the Nicene faith. Theudegotho, sister of Arevagni, was given by her father, Theodoric in marriage to Sigismund, the son and heir of Gundobad.

The event which intensified the fears of all these Arian kings, and which left to each one little more than the hope that he might be the last to be devoured, was the conversion to Catholicism of Clovis,[2] the heathen king of the *Franks*, that fortunate barbarian who, by a well-timed baptism, won for his tribe of rude warriors the possession of the fairest land in Europe and the glory of giving birth to one of the foremost nations in the world.

As we are here come to one of the common-places of history, I need but very briefly remind the reader of the chief stages in the upward course of the young Frankish king. Born in 466, he succeeded

---

2. I call the Frankish king by the name by which he is best known in history, though no doubt the more correct form is either Hlodwig or Chlodovech. It is of course the same name with Ludovicus or Louis I do not know whether the barbarian sound of Hlodwig offended the delicate taste of Cassiodorus, but in the *Various Letters* he addresses the king of the Franks as Ludum. It seems probable that there was some harsh guttural before the L which Gregory of Tours endeavoured to represent by Ch (Chlodovech), while Cassiodorus, receiving the name from the Frankish barbarians, thought it safer to leave it unrepresented (Ludum). In any case his *n* must have been due to some defective understanding of the final sound.

his father, Childeric, as one of the kings of the Salian Franks in 481. The lands of the Salians occupied but the extreme northern corner of modern France, and a portion of Flanders, and even here Clovis was but one of many kinglets allied by blood but frequently engaged in petty and inglorious wars one with another.

For five years the young Salian chieftain lived in peace with his neighbours. In the twentieth year of his age (486) he sprang with one bound into fame and dominion by attacking and overcoming the Roman Syagrius, who with ill-defined prerogatives, and bearing the title not of emperor or of *prefect*, but of king, had succeeded amidst the wreck of the Western Empire in preserving some of the fairest districts of the north of Gaul from barbarian domination. With the help of some of his brother chiefs, Clovis overthrew this "King of Soissons." Syagrius took refuge at the court of Toulouse, and the Frankish king now felt himself strong enough to send to the young Alaric, who had ascended the throne only a year before, a peremptory message, insisting, under the penalty of a declaration of war, on the surrender of the Roman fugitive. The Visigoth was mean-spirited enough to purchase peace by delivering up his guest, bound in fetters, to the ambassadors of Clovis, who shortly after ordered him to be privily done to death. From that time, we may well believe, Clovis felt confident that he should one day vanquish Alaric.

About seven years after this event (493) came his memorable marriage with Clotilda,[3] a Burgundian princess, who, unlike her Arian uncle, Gundobad, was enthusiastically devoted to the Catholic faith, and who ceased not by private conversations and by inducing him to listen to the sermons of the eloquent Bishop Remigius, to endeavour to win her husband from the religion of his heathen forefathers to the creed of Rome and of the Empire. Clovis, however, for some years wavered. Sprung himself, according to the traditions of his people, from the sea-god Meroveus, he was not in haste to renounce this fabulous glory, nor to acknowledge as Lord, One who had been reared in a carpenter's shop at Nazareth. He allowed Clotilda to have her eldest son baptised, but when the child soon after died, he took that as a sign of the power and vengeance of the old gods. A second son was born, was baptised, fell sick. Had that child died, Clovis would probably have remained an obstinate heathen, but the little one recovered, given back, as was believed, to the earnest prayers of his mother.

It was perhaps during these years of indecision as to his future re-

3. More accurately Chrotchildis.

ligious profession, that Clovis consented to a matrimonial alliance between his house and that of the Arian Theodoric. The great Ostrogoth married, probably about the year 495, the sister of Clovis, Augofleda, who, as we may reasonably conjecture, renounced the worship of the gods of her people, and was baptised by an Arian bishop on becoming "Queen of the Goths and Romans." Unfortunately the meagre annals of the time give us no hint of the character or history of the princess who was thus transferred from the fens of Flanders to the marshes of Ravenna. Every indication shows that she came from a far lower level of civilisation than that which her husband's people occupied. Did she soon learn to conform herself to the stately ceremonial which Ravenna borrowed from Constantinople? Did she too speak of *civilitas* and the necessity of obeying the Roman laws, and did she share the "glorious colloquies" which her husband held with the exuberant Cassiodorus?

When war came between the Ostrogoth and the Frank, did she openly show her sympathy with her brother Clovis, or did she "forget her people and her father's house" and cleave with all her soul to the fortunes of Theodoric? As to all these interesting questions the *Various Letters*, with all their diffuseness, give us no more information than the most *jejune* of the analysts. The only fact upon which we might found a conjecture is the love of literature and of Roman civilisation displayed by her daughter, Amalasuentha, which inclines us to guess that the mother may have thrown off her Frankish wildness when she came into the softening atmosphere of Italy.

We return to the event so memorable in the history of the world, Clovis' conversion to Christianity. In the year 486 he went forth to fight his barbarian neighbours in the south-east, the Alamanni, The battle was a stubborn and a bloody one, as well it might be when two such thunder-clouds met, the savage Frank and the savage Alaman. Already the Frankish host seemed wavering, when Clovis, lifting his eyes to heaven and shedding tears in the agony of his soul, said:

> O Jesus Christ! whom Clotilda declares to be the son of the living God, who art said to give help to the weary, and victory to them that trust in thee, I humbly pray for thy glorious aid, and promise that if thou wilt indulge me with the victory over these enemies, I will believe in thee and be baptised in thy name. For I have called on my own gods and have found that they are of no power and do not help those who call upon

them.

Scarcely had he spoken the words when the tide of battle turned. The Franks recovered from their panic, the Alamanni turned to flight. Their king was slain, and his people submitted to Clovis, who, returning, told his queen how he had called upon her God in the day of battle and been delivered.

Then followed, after a short consultation with the leading men of his kingdom, which made the change of faith in some degree a national act, the celebrated scene in the cathedral of Rheims, where the king, having confessed his faith in the Holy Trinity, was baptised in the name of the Father and the Son and the Holy Ghost, the poetical bishop uttering the well-known words: "Bow down thy head in lowliness, O Sicambrian; adore what thou hast burned and burn what thou hast adored." The streets of the city were hung with bright banners, white curtains adorned the churches, and clouds of sweet incense filled all the great basilica in which "the new Constantine" stooped to the baptismal water. He entered the cathedral a mere "Sicambrian" chieftain, the descendant of the sea-god: he emerged from it amid the acclamations of the joyous provincials, "the eldest son of the Church."

The result of this ceremony was to change the political relations of every state in Gaul. Though the Franks were among the roughest and most uncivilised of the tribes that had poured westwards across the Rhine, as Catholics they were now sure of a welcome from the Catholic clergy of every city, and where the clergy led, the "Roman" provincials, or in other words the Latin-speaking laity, generally followed. Immediately after his baptism Clovis received a letter of enthusiastic welcome Into the true fold, written by Avitus, Bishop of Vienne, the most eminent ecclesiastic of the Burgundian kingdom.

I regret, (says Avitus), that I could not be present in the flesh at that most glorious solemnity. But as your most sublime Humility had sent me a messenger to inform me of your intention, when night fell I retired to rest already secure of your conversion. How often my friends and I went over the scene in our imaginations! We saw the band of holy prelates vying with one another in the ambition of lowly service, each one wishing to comfort the royal limbs with the water of life. We saw that head, so terrible to the nations, bowed low before the servants of God; the hair which had grown long under the helmet now

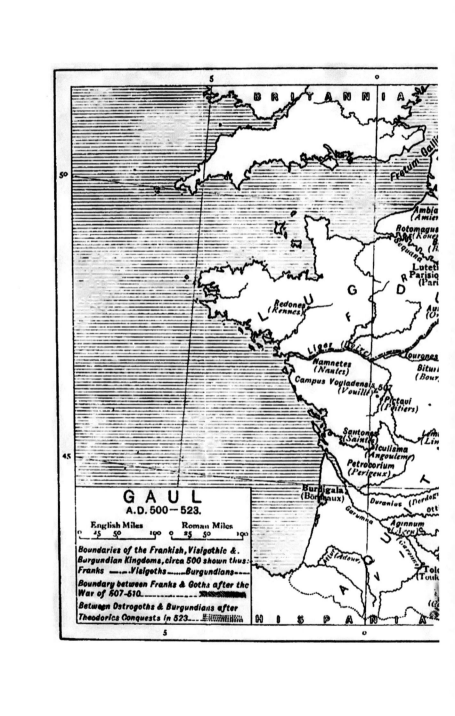

5   0

B R I T A N N I A

50

Freium Galli

Ambia
(Amiens)

Rotomagus
(Rouen)
Sequana

Lutetia
Parisio...
(Pari...

U   G   D

U

Redones
(Rennes)

L

Aur
(O...

Liger (Loire)

Namnetes
(Nantes)

Tourones

Bituri
(Bour...

Campus Vogladensis 507
(Vouillé)

Pictavi
(Poitiers)

Santones
(Saintes)

Lim
Lin

Iculisma
(Angoulem)

45

Petrocorium
(Perigeux)

Burdigala
(Bordeaux)

Duranius (Dordo...

ott...

G A U L
A.D. 500 — 523.

English Miles   Roman Miles
0   25   50   100   0   25   50   100

Aginnum

Garumna

Boundaries of the Frankish, Visigothic &.
Burgundian Kingdoms, circa 500 shown thus:
Franks —·—· Visigoths —— Burgundians - - - -
Boundary between Franks & Goths after the
War of 507-510. ············ 〰〰〰〰
Between Ostrogoths & Burgundians after
Theodorics Conquests in 523... 〰〰〰〰

Adour

U

V

Tol
Toul...

H   I   S   P   A   N   I   A

5   0

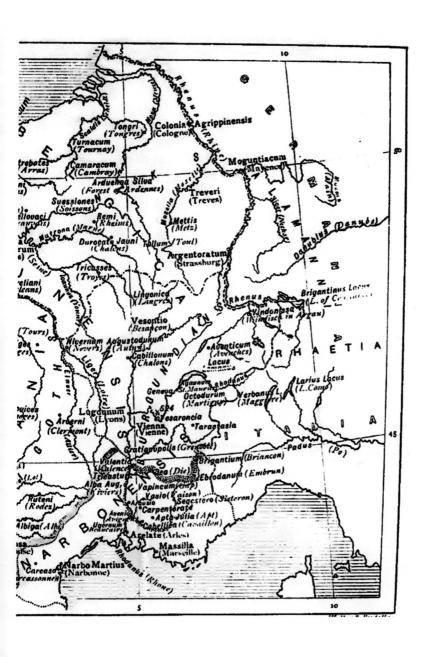

A map of Roman Gaul showing cities and geographic features with both Latin and modern names, including:

Rhenus Fluvius (Rhine)
Tongri (Tongres)
Colonia Agrippinensis (Cologne)
Scaldis fluvia
Turnacum (Tournay)
Camaracum (Cambray)
Atrebates (Arras)
Arduenna Silva (Forest of Ardennes)
Moguntiacum (Mayence)
Treveri (Treves)
Suessiones (Soissons)
Bellovaci
Remi (Rheims)
Mosella (Moselle)
Mettis (Metz)
Matrona (Marne)
Durocata Jauni (Chalons)
Tollum (Toul)
Argentoratum (Strasburg)
Tricasses (Troyes)
Aureliani (Orleans)
Sequana (Seine)
Lingonica (Langres)
Rhenus
Brigantinus Lacus (L. of Constance)
Vesontio (Besançon)
Vindonissa (Windisch in Aargau)
Nivernum (Nevers)
Augustodunum (Autun)
Avanticum (Avenches)
RHAETIA
Cabillonum (Chalons)
Liger (Loire)
Lacus
Larius Lacus (L. Como)
Geneva
Agaunum
St. Maurice
Rhodanus
Octodurum (Martigny)
Verbanus L. (Maggiore)
Lugdunum (Lyons)
Arverni (Clermont)
Caesaroncia
Vienna (Vienne)
Tarantasia
Padus (Po)
Gratianopolis (Grenoble)
Valentia (Valence)
Brigantium (Briancon)
Tricastini
Dea (Die)
Ebrodanum (Embrun)
Alba Aug. (Riviers)
Vapincum (Gap)
Ruteni (Rodez)
Vasio (Vaison)
Segestero (Sisteron)
Arausio (Orange)
Carpentorate
Apta Julia (Apt)
Avenio
Ugernum
Heauouire
Cabellio (Cavaillon)
Albiga (Albi)
Arelate (Arles)
Massilia (Marseille)
Narbo Martius (Narbonne)
Careaso (Carcassonne)
Rhodanus (Rhone)
NARBONENSIS
AQUITANIA
GOTHI
LUGDUNENSIS
Danubius (Danube)
Rhenus (Main)

crowned with the diadem of the holy anointing; the coat of mail laid aside and the white limbs wrapped in linen robes as white and spotless as themselves.

One thing only have I to ask of you, that you will spread the light which you have yourself received to the nations around you. Scatter the seeds of faith from out of the good treasure of your heart, and be not ashamed, by embassies directed to this very end, to strengthen in other states the cause of that God who has so greatly exalted your fortunes. Shine on, forever, upon those who are present, by lustre of your diadem, upon those who are absent, by the glory of your name. We are touched by your happiness; as often as you fight in those (heretical) lands, *we* conquer.

The use of language like this, showing such earnest devotion to the cause of Clovis in the subject of a rival monarch, well illustrates the tendency of the Frankish king's conversion to loosen the bonds of loyalty in the neighbouring states, and to facilitate the spread of his dominion over the whole of Gaul. In fact, the Frankish kingdom, having become Catholic, was like the magnetic mountain of Oriental fable, which drew to itself all the iron nails of the ships which approached it, and so caused them to sink in hopeless dissolution. Seeing this obvious result of the conversion of the Frank, some historians, especially in the last century, were disposed to look upon that conversion as a mere hypocritical pretence. Later critics[4] have shown that this is not an accurate account of the matter. Doubtless the motives which induced Clovis to accept baptism and to profess faith in the Crucified One were of the meanest, poorest, and most unspiritual kind. Few men have ever been further from that which Christ called "the Kingdom of Heaven" than this grasping and brutal Frankish chief, to whom robbery, falsehood, murder were, after his baptism, as much as before it (perhaps even more than before it), the ordinary steps in the ladder of his elevation.

But the rough barbaric soul had in its dim fashion a faith that the God of the Christians was the mightiest God, and that it would go well with those who submitted to him. In his rude style he made imaginary bargains with the Most High: "so much reverence to 'Clotilda's God,' so many offerings at the shrine of St. Martin, so much land to the church of St. Genovefa, on condition that I shall beat down

4. Especially Dahn (*Urgeschichte der germanischen Völker*, iii., 61).

my enemies before me and extend my dominions from the Seine to the Pyrenees." This is the kind of calculation which the missionaries in our own day are only too well accustomed to hear from the lips of barbarous potentates like those of Uganda and Fiji. A conversion thus effected brings no honour to any church, and the utter selfishness and even profanity of the transaction disgusts the devout souls of every communion. Still the conversion of Clovis was not in its essence and origin a hypocritical scheme for obtaining the support of the Catholic clergy in Gaul, how clearly so ever the new convert may have soon perceived that from that support he would "suck no small advantage."

The first of his Arian neighbours whom Clovis struck at was the Burgundian, Gundobad. In the year 500 he beseiged Dijon with a large army. Gundobad called on his brother Godegisel, who reigned at Geneva, for help, but that brother was secretly in league with Clovis, and at a critical moment joined the invaders, who were for a time completely successful. Gundobad was driven into exile and Godegisel accepting the position of a tributary ally of his powerful Frankish friend, ruled over the whole Burgundian kingdom. His rule however seems not to have been heartily accepted by the Burgundian people. The exiled Gundobad returned with a few followers, who daily increased in number; he found himself strong enough to besiege Godegisel in Vienne; he at length entered the city through the blow-hole of an aqueduct, slew his brother with his own hand, and put his chief adherents to death "with exquisite torments." The Frankish troops who garrisoned Vienne were taken prisoners, but honourably treated and sent to Toulouse to be guarded by Alaric the Visigoth, who had probably assisted the enterprise of Gundobad.

The inactivity of Clovis during this counter-revolution in Burgundy is not easily explained. Either there was some great explosion of Burgundian national feeling against the Franks, which for the time made further interference dangerous, or Gundobad, having added his brother's dominions to his own, was now too strong for Clovis to meddle with, or, which seems on the whole the most probable supposition, Gundobad himself, secretly inclining towards the Catholic cause, had made peace with Clovis through the mediation of the clergy, and came back to Vienne to rule thenceforward as a dependent ally, though not an avowed tributary, of Clovis and the Franks. We shall soon have occasion to observe that in the crisis of its fortunes the confederacy of Arian states could not count on the co-operation of Gundobad.

To form such a confederacy and to league together all the old-er Arian monarchies against this one aspiring Catholic state, which threatened to absorb them all, was now the main purpose of Theo-doric. He seems, however, to have remained meanwhile on terms of courtesy and apparent harmony with his powerful brother-in-law.

He congratulated him on a second victorious campaign against the Alamanni (about 503 or 504), and he took some trouble to comply with a request, which Clovis had made to him, to find out a skilful harper who might be sent to his court. The letter[5] which relates to this transaction is a curious specimen of Cassiodorus' style. It is addressed to the young philosopher Boëthius, a man whose varied accomplish-ments adorned the middle period of the reign of Theodoric, and whose tragical death was to bring sadness over its close. To this man, whose knowledge of the musical art was pre-eminent in his generation, Cas-siodorus addresses one of the longest letters in his collection (it would occupy about six pages of an ordinary *octavo*), only one or two sentences of which relate to the business in hand. The letter begins:

> Since the king of the Franks, attracted by the fame of our ban-quets, has with earnest prayers besought us to send him a harper (*citharœdus*), our only hope of executing his commission lies in you, whom we know to be accomplished in musical learning. For it will be easy for you to choose a well-skilled man, having yourself been able to attain to that high and abstruse study.

Then follow a string of reflections on the soothing power of music, a description of the five "modes"[6] (Dorian, Phrygian, Aeolian, Ionian, and Lydian) and of the diapason; instances of the power of music drawn from the Scriptures and from heathen mythology, a discussion on the harmony of the spheres, and a doubt whether the enjoyment of this "astral music" be rightly placed among the delights of heaven. At length the marvellous state-paper draws to a close:

> But since we have made this pleasing digression[7] (because it is always agreeable to talk about learning with learned men) let your wisdom choose out for us the best harper of the day, for the purpose that we have mentioned. Herein will you accom-plish a task somewhat like that of Orpheus, when he with sweet

---

5. *Var.*, ii., 40.
6. Toni.
7. "*Voluptuosa digressio*"

sounds tamed the fierce hearts of savage creatures. The thanks which we owe you will be expressed by liberal compensation, for you obey our rule, and to the utmost of your power render it illustrious by your attainments.

Evidently the court of Theodoric was regarded as a centre of light and civilisation by his Teutonic neighbours, the lords of the new king-doms to the north of him. King Gundobad desired to become the possessor of a *clepsydra* or water-clock, such as had long been used in Athens and Rome, to regulate the time allotted to the orators in public debates. He also wished to obtain an accurately graduated sun-dial. For both he made request to Theodoric, and again[8] the universal genius Boëthius was applied to, Cassiodorus writes him, in his master's name, a letter which gives us some interesting information as to the past career of Boëthius, and then proceeds to give a specification of the required machines, in language so magnificent as to be, at any rate to modern mechanicians, hopelessly unintelligible.

Then a shorter letter, to accompany the clock and dial, is written to King Gundobad. This letter, which is written in a slightly conde-scending tone, says that the tie of affinity between the two kings makes it right that Gundobad should receive benefits from Theodoric:

Let Burgundy under your sway learn to examine the most curious objects, and to praise the inventions of the ancients. Through you she is laying aside her old barbarian tastes, and while she admires the prudence of her king she rightly desires the works of wise men of old. Let her mark out the different intervals of the day by her actions: let her in the most fitting manner assign the occupation of each hour. This is to lead the true human life, as distinguished from that of the brutes, who know the flight of time only by the cravings of their appetites.

A time, however, was approaching when this pleasant interchange of courtesies between the three sovereigns, Ostrogothic, Frankish, and Burgundian, was to be succeeded by the din of war. Alaric the Visig-oth, alarmed at the victorious progress of the Frankish king, sent a message to this effect:

If my brother is willing, let him consider my proposal that, by the favour of God, we should have an interview with one another.

---

8. Strictly speaking not "again" but "previously," for the letter about the water-clock precedes the letter about the harper.

143

Clovis accepted the offer, and the two kings met on an island in the Loire near Amboise.[9] But either no alliance could be formed, owing to religious differences, or the treaty so made was too weak for the strain which it had to bear, and it became manifest before long that war would soon break out between "Francia" and "Gothia."

Theodoric exerted himself strenuously to prevent the impending struggle, which, as he too surely foresaw, would bring only disaster to his Visigothic allies. He caused his eloquent secretary to write letters to Clovis, to Alaric, to Gundobad, to the neighbours of the Franks on their eastern border, the kings of the Heruli, the Warni, and the Thuringians. To Clovis he dilated on the horrors which war brings upon the inhabitants of the warring lands, who have a right to expect that the kinship of their lords will keep them at peace. A few paltry words were no sufficient cause of war between two such monarchs, and it was the act of a passionate and hot-headed man to be mobilising his troops while he was sending his first embassy. To Alaric he sent an earnest warning against engaging in war with Clovis:

> You are surrounded by an innumerable multitude of subjects, and you are proud of the remembrance of the defeat of Attila, but war is a terribly dangerous game, and you know not how the long peace may have softened the warlike fibre of your people.

He besought Gundobad to join with him in preserving peace between the combatants, to each of whom he had offered his arbitration.

> It behoves us old, men to moderate the wrath of the royal youths, who should reverence our age, though they are still in the flower of their hot youth.[10]

The kings of the barbarians were reminded of the friendship which

---

9. We have no date given us for this meeting, and the whole sequence of events between the Burgundian and Visigothic wars of Clovis (500-507) can only be stated conjecturally.

10. There is some difficulty in understanding this remark about the relative ages of the sovereigns If we put the date of the letters at 506 (and a later date is hardly possible, nor one more than two or three years earlier), though Gundobad might well be over sixty, Theodoric himself could be only fifty-two, while on the other hand the "regii juvenes," Clovis and Alaric, were about forty. But senex and juvenis are expressions often used with no great exactness; and I conjecture that the cares and struggles of Theodoric's early manhood had made him an old man before his time.

Alaric's father, Euric, had shown them in old days, and invited to join in a "League of Peace," in order to check the lawless aggressions of Clovis, which threatened danger to all.

The diplomatic action of Theodoric was powerless to avert the war; possibly even it may have stimulated Clovis to strike rapidly before a hostile coalition could be formed against him.

At an assembly of his nation (perhaps the "Camp of March") in the early part of 507, he impetuously declared:

> I take it grievously amiss that these Arians should hold so large a part of Gaul. Let us go and overcome them with God's help, and bring the land into subjection to us.

The saying pleased the whole multitude, and the collected army marched southward to the Loire. On their way they passed through the territory owned by the monastery of St. Martin of Tours, the greatest saint of Gaul. Here the king commanded them to abstain religiously from all depredations, taking only grass for their horses, and water from the streams. One of the soldiers, finding a quantity of hay in the possession of a peasant, took it from him, arguing that hay was grass, and so came within the permitted exception. He was, however, at once cut down with a sword, the king exclaiming. "What hope shall we have of victory if we offend the blessed Martin?" Having first prayed for a sign, Clovis sent his messengers with gifts to the great basilica of Tours, and behold! when these messengers set foot in the sacred building, the choristers were singing an antiphon, taken from the 18th Psalm: "*Thou hast girded me with strength unto the battle, thou hast subdued under me those that rose up against me.*"

Meanwhile, Alaric, taken at unawares, short of men and short of money, was endeavouring to remedy the latter deficiency by a depreciation of the currency. To swell his slender battalions he evidently looked to his father-in-law, Theodoric, whose peace-making letter had ended with these words: "We look upon your enemy as the common enemy of all. Whoever strives against you will rightly have to deal with me, as a foe." Yet notwithstanding this assurance, no Ostrogothic troops came at this time to the help of the Visigoths. In the great dearth of historical material, our account of these transactions has to be made up from scattered and fragmentary notices, which do not enable us to explain this strange inaction of so true-hearted an ally. It is not imputed to him as a fault by any contemporary authority, and it seems reasonable to suppose that not the will, but the power, to help his menaced son-in-law was wanting.

One alarming change in the situation had revealed itself since Theodoric ordered his secretary to write the letters recommending an anti-Frankish confederacy of kings. Gundobad the Burgundian was now the declared ally of Clovis, and promised himself a share of the spoil. So powerful an enemy on the flank, threatening the communications of the two Gothic states, may very probably have been the reason why no timely succour was sent from Ravenna to Toulouse.

Clovis and his Frankish host, hungering for the spoil, pressed forwards, and succeeded, apparently without opposition, in crossing the broad river Loire. Alaric had taken up a strong position at the Campus Vogladensis (*Vouillé: dep. Vienne*), about ten miles from Poitiers. Here he wished to remain on the defensive till the expected succours from Theodoric could arrive, but his soldiers, confident in their power to beat the Franks unassisted, began to revile their king's over-caution and his father-in-law's delay, and forced Alaric to fight.[11]

The Goths began hurling their missile weapons, but the daring Franks rushed in upon them and commenced a hand-to-hand encounter, in which they were completely victorious. The Goths turned to flee, and Clovis, riding up to where Alaric was fighting, slew him with his own hand. He himself had immediately afterwards a narrow escape from two of the enemy, who, coming suddenly upon him, thrust their long spears at him, one on each side. The strength of his coat of mail, however, and the speed of his horse saved him from a disaster which might possibly even then have turned the tide of victory.

The result of this battle was the complete overthrow of the Visigothic kingdom of Toulouse. In a certain sense it survived, and for two centuries played a great part in Europe as the Spanish kingdom of Toledo, but, as competitors for dominion in Gaul, the Visigoths henceforward disappear from history. There seems to have been a certain want of toughness in the Visigothic fibre, a tendency to rashness combined with a tendency to panic, which made it possible for their enemies to achieve a complete triumph over them in a single battle. (376) Athanaric staked his all on one battle with the Huns, and lost, by the rivers of Bessarabia. (507) Alaric II., as we have seen, staked his all on one battle with the Franks, and lost, on the Campus Vogladensis. (701) Two centuries later Roderic staked his all upon one battle with

---

11. This statement as to the battle being forced on, contrary to the wishes of Alaric, rests only on the authority of Procopius, not a contemporary author, and not very well informed as to the events of this campaign.

the Moors, and lost, at Xeres de la Frontera.

All through the year 507 the allied forces of Franks and Burgundians seem to have poured over the south-west and south of Gaul, an-
nexing Angoulème, Saintonge, Auvergne, and Gascony to the dominions of Clovis, and Provence to the dominions of Gundobad. Only
the strong city of Aries, and perhaps the fortress of Carcassonne (that
most interesting relic of the early Middle Ages, which still shows the
handiwork of Visigothic kings in its walls), still held out for the son
of Alaric.

In 508 the long delayed forces of Theodoric appeared upon the
scene under his brave general, Tulum, and dealt some severe blows at
the allied Frankish and Burgundian armies. In 509 another army, under Duke Mammo, crossed the Cottian Alps near Briançon, laid waste
part of Dauphiné, and probably compelled a large detachment of the
Burgundian army to return for the defence of their homes. And lastly,
in 510, Theodoric's general, Ibbas, inflicted a crushing defeat on the
allied armies, leaving, it is said, thirty thousand Franks dead upon the
field. The number is probably much exaggerated (as these historical
bulletins are apt to be), but there can be no doubt that a great and
important victory was won by the troops of Theodoric.

The immediate result of this victory was the raising of the siege of
Aries, whose valiant defenders had held out against storm and blockade, famine and treachery within, Franks and Burgundians without,
for the space of two years and a half. Ultimately, and perhaps before
many months had passed, the victory of Ibbas led to a cessation of
hostilities, if not to a formal treaty of peace, between the three powers
which disputed the possession of Gaul. The terms practically arranged
were these. Clovis remained in possession of far the largest part of
Alaric's dominions, Aquitaine nearly up to the roots of the Pyrenees,
and so much of Languedoc (including Toulouse, the late capital of the
Visigoths) as lay west of the mountains of the Cevennes.

Theodoric obtained the rest of Languedoc and Provence, the first
province being deemed to be a part of the Visigothic, the second of
the Ostrogothic, dominions, Gundobad obtained nothing, but lost
some towns on his southern frontier—a fitting reward for his tortu-
ous and shifty policy.

In the meantime something like civil war had been waged on the
other side of the Pyrenees for the Spanish portion of the Visigothic
inheritance. Alaric, slain on the field of Vouillé, had left two sons, one
Amalaric, his legitimate heir and the grandson of Theodoric, but still a

child, the other a young man, but of illegitimate birth, named Gesalic. This latter was, on the death of his father, proclaimed king by some fraction of the Visigothic people. Had Gesalic shown courage and skill in winning back the lost inheritance of his father, Theodoric, whose own descent was not legitimate according to strict church law, would not, perhaps, have interfered with his claim to the succession.

But the young man was as weak and cowardly as his birth was base, and the strenuous efforts of Theodoric, seconded probably by many of the Visigoths who had first acclaimed him as king, were directed to getting rid of this futile pretender. Gesalic, defeated by Gundobad at Narbonne (which, for a time, became the possession of the Burgundians), fled over the Pyrenees to Barcelona, and from thence across the sea to Carthage.

Thrasamund, king of the Vandals, aided him with money and promised him support, being probably deceived by the glozing tongue of Gesalic, and looking upon him simply as a brave young Visigoth battling for his rightful inheritance with the Franks. A correspondence followed between Ravenna and Carthage, in which Theodoric bitterly complained of the protection given by his brother-in-law to an intriguer and a rebel; and, on the receipt of Theodoric's letter, Thrasamund at once disclaimed all further intention of helping the pretender and sent rich presents to his offended kinsman, which Theodoric graciously returned.

Gesalic again appeared in Barcelona, still doubtless wearing the insignia of kingship, but was defeated by the same Duke Ibbas who had raised the siege of Aries, and, fleeing into Gaul, probably in order to claim the protection of the enemy of his house, King Gundobad, he was overtaken by the soldiers of Theodoric near the River Durance, and was put to death by his captors. Thus there remained but one undisputed heir to what was left of the great Visigothic kingdom, the little child Amalaric, Theodoric's grandson. He was brought up in Spain, but, apparently with the full consent of the Visigothic people, his grandsire assumed the reins of government, ruling in his own name but with a tacit understanding that Amalaric and no other should succeed him.

(510-525) There was thus for fifteen years a combination of states which Europe has not witnessed before or since, though Charles V. and some of his descendants were not far from achieving it. All of Italy and all of Spain (except the north-west corner, which was held by the Suevi) obeyed the rule of Theodoric, and the fair regions of Provence

and Languedoc,[12] acknowledging the same master, were the ligament that united them.

Of the character of the government of Theodoric in Spain, history tells us scarcely anything; but there is reason to think that it was as wise and beneficent as his government of Italy, its chief fault being probably the undue share of power which was grasped by the Ostrogothic minister Theudis, whom Theodoric had appointed as guardian to his grandson, and who, having married a wealthy Spanish lady, assumed a semi-royal state, and became at last so mighty that Theodoric himself did not dare to insist upon the recall which he had veiled under the courteous semblance of an invitation to his palace at Ravenna.

Thus then the policy of Theodoric towards his kinsmen and co-religionists in Gaul had failed, but it had not been a hopeless failure. He had missed, probably through no fault of his own, through the rashness of Alaric and the treachery of Gundobad, the right moment for saving the kingdom of Toulouse from shipwreck, but he had vindicated in adversity the honour of the Gothic name, and he had succeeded in saving a considerable part of the cargo which the stately vessel had carried.

COIN OF THE GOTHIC KINGDOM IN ITALY.

---

12. East of the Cevennes.

CHAPTER 11

Anastasius

In order to complete our survey of the foreign policy of the great Ostrogoth, we must now consider the relations which existed between him and the majestic personage who, though he had probably never set foot in Italy, was yet always known in the common speech of men as "The Roman Emperor." It has been already said that Zeno, the sovereign who bore this title when Theodoric started for Italy, died before his final victory, and that it was his successor, Anastasius, with whom the tedious negotiations were conducted which ended (497) in a recognition, perhaps a somewhat grudging recognition, by the emperor of the right of the Ostrogothic king to rule in Italy.

Anastasius, who was Theodoric's contemporary during twenty-five years of his reign, was already past sixty when the widowed Empress Ariadne chose him for her husband and her emperor, and he had attained the age of eighty-eight when his harassed life came to a close. A man of tall stature and noble presence, a wise administrator of the finances of the Empire, and therefore one who both lightened taxation and accumulated treasure, a sovereign who chose his servants well and brought his only considerable war, that with Persia, to a successful issue, Anastasius would seem to be an emperor of whom both his own subjects and posterity should speak favourably.

Unfortunately, however, for his fame he became entangled in that most wearisome of theological debates, which is known as the Monophysite controversy. In this controversy he took an unpopular side; he became embroiled with the Roman *pontiff*, and estranged from his own patriarch of Constantinople. Opposition and the weariness of age soured a naturally sweet temper, and he was guilty of some harsh proceedings towards his ecclesiastical opponents. Even worse than his harshness (which did not, even on the representations of his enemies,

amount to cruelty) was a certain want of absolute truthfulness, which made it difficult for a beaten foe to trust his promises of forgiveness, and thus caused the fire of civil discord, once kindled, to smoulder on almost interminably. The religious party to which he belonged had probably the majority of the aristocracy of Constantinople on its side, but the mob and the monks were generally against Anastasius, and some scenes very humiliating to the Imperial dignity were the consequence of this antagonism.

(511) Once, when he had resolved on the deposition of the orthodox patriarch of Constantinople, Macedonius, so great a tempest of popular and theological fury raged through the city, that he ordered the great gates of his palace to be barred and the ships to be made ready at what is now called Seraglio Point, intending to seek safety in flight. A humiliating reconciliation with the patriarch, the order for whose banishment he rescinded, saved him from this necessity. The citizens and the soldiers poured through the streets shouting triumphantly: "Our father is yet with us!" and the storm for the time abated. But the emperor had only appeared to yield, and some months later he stealthily but successfully carried into effect his design for the banishment of Macedonius. Again, the next year, a religious faction-fight disgraced the capital of the Empire.

(511) The addition of the words "Who wast crucified for us" to the chorus of the *Te Deum*, "*Holy, Holy, Holy, Lord God Almighty,*" goaded the orthodox but fanatical mob to madness. For three days such scenes as London saw during Lord George Gordon's "No Popery" riots were enacted in the streets of Constantinople. The palaces of the heterodox ministers were burned, their deaths were eagerly demanded, the head of a monk, who was supposed to be responsible for the heretical addition to the hymn, was carried round the city on a pole, while the murderers shouted: "Behold the head of an enemy to the Trinity!" Then the statues of the emperor were thrown down, an act of insurrection which corresponded to the building of barricades in the revolutions of Paris, and loud voices began to call for the proclamation of a popular general as Augustus.

Anastasius this time dreamed not of flight, but took his seat in the *podium*[1] at the hippodrome, the great place of public meeting for the citizens of Constantinople. Thither, too, streamed the excited mob, fresh from their work of murder and pillage, shouting with hoarse voices the line of the *Te Deum* in its orthodox form. A suppliant, with-

1. The Imperial box.

151

out his diadem, without his purple robe, the white-haired Anastasius, eighty-two years of age, sat meekly on his throne, and bade the criers declare that he was ready to lay down the burden of the Empire if the citizens would decide who should assume it in his stead. The humiliation was accepted, the clamorous mob were not really of one mind as to the election of a successor, and Anastasius was permitted still to reign and to reassume the diadem, which has not often encircled a wearier or more uneasy head.

Such an emperor as this, at war with a large part of his subjects, and suspected of heresy by the great body of the Catholic clergy, was a much less formidable opponent for Theodoric than the young and warlike Clovis, with his rude energy, and his unquestioning if somewhat truculent orthodoxy. Moreover, at this time, independently of these special causes of strife, there was a chronic schism between the *see* of Rome and the *see* of Constantinople (precursor of that great schism which, three centuries later, finally divided the Eastern and Western churches), and this schism, though it did not as yet lead to the actual excommunication of Anastasius,[2] caused him to be looked upon with coldness and suspicion by the successive Popes of Rome, and made the rule of Theodoric, avowed Arian as he was, but anxious to hold the balance evenly between rival churches, far more acceptable at the Lateran than that of the schismatic partisan Anastasius.

For some years after the embassy of Festus (497) and the consequent recognition of Theodoric by the emperor, there appears to have been peace, if no great cordiality, between the courts of Ravenna and Constantinople. But a war in which Theodoric found himself engaged with the Gepidæ (504), taking him back as it did into his old unwelcome nearness to the Danube, led to the actual outbreak of hostilities between the two states, hostilities, however, which were but of short duration.

The great city of Sirmium on the Save, the ruins of which may still be seen about eighty miles west of Belgrade, had once belonged to the Western Empire and had been rightly looked upon as one of the bulwarks of Italy. To anyone who studies the configuration of the great Alpine chain, which parts off the Italian peninsula from the rest of Europe, it will be manifest that it is in the north-east that that mountain barrier is the weakest. The Maritime, Pennine, and Cottian

---

2. By order of Pope Hormisdas the name of Anastasius was solemnly "erased from the diptychs" in 519; that is, he was virtually excommunicated after his death, but I do not find that he was formally excommunicated by the Pope in his life-time.

Alps, which soar above the plains of Piedmont and Western Lombardy, afford scarcely any passes below the snow-line practicable for an invading army. Great generals, like Hannibal and Napoleon, have indeed crossed them, but the pride which they have taken in the achievement is the best proof of its difficulty.

Modern engineering science has carried its zigzag roads up to their high crests, has thrown its bridges across their ravines, has defended the traveller by its massive galleries from their avalanches, and in these later days has even bored its tunnels for miles through the heart of the mountains; but all these are works done obviously in defiance of Nature, and if Europe relapsed into a state of barbarism, the eternal snow and the eternal silence would soon reassert their supremacy over the frail handiwork of man. Quite different from this is the aspect of the mountains on the north-eastern border of Italy. The countries which we now call Venetia and Istria are parted from their northern neighbours by ranges (chiefly that known as the Julian Alps) which are indeed of bold and striking outline, but which are not what we generally understand by "Alpine" in their character, and which often do not rise to a greater elevation than four thousand feet.

Therefore it was from this quarter of the horizon, from the Pannonian (or in modern language, Austrian) countries bordering on the Middle Danube, that all the greatest invaders in the fifth and sixth centuries, Alaric, Attila, Alboin, bore down upon Italy. And for this reason it was truly said by an orator[3] who was recounting the praises of Theodoric in connection with this war:

> The city of the Sirmians was of old the frontier of Italy, upon which emperors and senators kept watch, lest from thence the stored up fury of the neighbouring nations should pour over the Roman Commonwealth.

This city of Sirmium, however, and the surrounding territory had now been for many years divorced from Italy. In Theodoric's boyhood it is possible that his own barbarian countrymen, occupying as they did the province of Pannonia, lorded it in the streets of Sirmium, which was properly a Pannonian city. Since the Ostrogoths evacuated the province (473), the Gepidæ, as we have seen, had entered it, and it was a king of the Gepidæ, Traustila, who sought to bar Theodoric's march into Italy, and who sustained at the hands of the Ostrogothic king the crushing defeat by the Hiulca Palus (488). Traustila's son,

---

3. Ennodius.

Trasaric, had asked for Theodoric's help against a rival claimant to the throne, and had, perhaps, promised to hand over possession of Sirmium in return for that assistance.

Theodoric, who, as king of "the Hesperian realm," felt that it was a point of honour to recover possession of "the frontier city of Italy," gave the desired help, but failed to receive the promised recompense. When Trasaric's breach of faith was manifest, Theodoric sent an army (504) composed of the flower of the Gothic youth, commanded by a general named Pitzias, into the valley of the Save. The Gepidæ, though reinforced by some of the Bulgarians (who about thirty years before this time had made their first appearance in the country which now bears their name), were completely defeated by Pitzias. Trasaric's mother, the widow of Theodoric's old enemy, Traustila, fell into the hands of the invaders; Trasaric was expelled from that corner of Pannonia, and Sirmium, still apparently a great and even opulent city, notwithstanding the ravages of the barbarians, submitted, probably with joy, to the rule of Theodoric, under which she felt herself once more united to the Roman Commonwealth.

We have still (in the *Various Letters* of Cassiodorus) two letters relating to this annexation of Sirmium. In the first, addressed to Count Colossæus, that "Illustrious" official is informed that he is appointed to the governorship of Pannonia Sirmiensis, a former habitation of the Goths. This province is now to extend a welcome to her old Roman lords, even as she gladly obeyed her Ostrogothic rulers. Surrounded by the wild anarchy of the barbarous nations, the new governor is to exhibit the justice of the Goths, "a nation so happily situated in the midst of praise, that they could accept the wisdom of the Romans and yet hold fast the valour of the barbarians." He is to shield the poor from oppression, and his highest merit will be to establish in the hearts of the inhabitants of the land the love of peace and order.

To the barbarians and Romans settled in Pannonia the secretary of Theodoric writes, informing them that he has appointed as their governor a man mighty in name (Colossæus) and mighty in deeds. They must refrain from acts of violence and from redressing their supposed wrongs by main force. Having got an upright judge, they must use him as the arbiter of their differences. What is the use to man of his tongue, if his armed hand is to settle his cause, or how can peace be maintained if men take to fighting in a civilised state? They are therefore to imitate the example of "our Goths," who do not shrink from battles abroad, but who have learned to exhibit peaceable moderation at home.

The recovery of Sirmium from the Gepidæ, though doubtless the subject of congratulation in Italy, was viewed with much displeasure at Constantinople. Whether the part of Pannonia in which it was included belonged in strictness to the Eastern or Western Empire, is a question that has been a good deal discussed and upon which we have perhaps not sufficient materials for coming to a conclusion. The boundary line between east and west had undoubtedly fluctuated a good deal in the fourth and fifth centuries, and the fact that there were not, as viewed by a Roman statesman, two Empires at all, but only one great World-Empire, which for the sake of convenience was administered by two emperors, one dwelling at Ravenna or Milan and the other at Constantinople, was probably the reason why that boundary was not defined as strictly as it would have been between two independent kingdoms.

Moreover, through the greater part of the fifth century, when Huns and Ostrogoths, Rugians and Gepidæ were roaming over these countries of the Middle Danube, any claim of either the Eastern or Western emperor to rule in these lands must have been so purely theoretical that it probably seemed hardly worthwhile to spend time in defining it. But now that the actual ruler of Italy, and that ruler a strong and capable barbarian like Theodoric, was holding the great city of Sirmium, and was sending his governors to civilise and subdue the inhabitants of what is now called the "Austrian Military Frontier," the emperor who reigned at Constantinople was not unlikely to find his neighbourhood unpleasant.

It was doubtless in consequence of the jealousy, arising from the conquest of Sirmium, that war soon broke out between the two powers. Upper Mœsia (in modern geography Servia) was undoubtedly part of the Eastern Empire, yet it is there that we next find the Gothic troops engaged in war. (505) Mundo, the Hun, a descendant of Attila, was in league with Theodoric, but at enmity with the Empire, and was wandering with a band of freebooters through the half desolate lands south of the Danube. Sabinian, the son of the general of the same name, who twenty-six years before had fought with Theodoric in Macedonia, was ordered by Anastasius to exterminate this disorderly Hun. With 10,000 men (among whom there were some Bulgarian *fœderati*), and with a long train of waggons containing great store of provisions, he marched from the Balkans down the valley of the Morava.

Mundo, in despair and already thinking of surrender, called on his Ostrogothic ally for aid, and Pitzias, marching rapidly with an army of 2,500 young and warlike Goths (2,000 infantry and 500 cavalry), reached Horrea Margi,[4] the place where Mundo was besieged, in time to prevent his surrender. Notwithstanding the enthusiasm of the Gothic troops, the battle was most stubbornly contested, especially by the fierce Bulgarians, but in the end Pitzias obtained a complete victory. We may state this fact with confidence, as it is recorded in the chronicles of an official of the Eastern Empire.[5] He says of Sabinian: "Having joined battle at Horrea Margi, and many of his soldiers having been slain in this conflict and drowned in the river Margus (*Morava*), having also lost all his wagons, he fled with a few followers to the fortress which is called Nato. In this lamentable war so promising an army fell, that, speaking after the manner of men, its loss could never be repaired."

Without any general campaign, the quarrel between the Goths and the Empire seems to have smouldered on for three years longer. In his chronicle for the year 508, the same Byzantine official who has just been quoted, says very honestly: "Romanus Count of the Domestics and Rusticus Count of the Scholarii,[6] with 100 armed ships and as many cutters, carrying 8,000 soldiers, went forth to ravage the shores of Italy, and proceeded as far as the most ancient city of Tarentum. Having recrossed the sea they reported to Anastasius Cæsar this inglorious victory, which in piratical fashion Romans had snatched from their fellow-Romans."

These words of the chronicler show to what extent Theodoric's kingdom was looked upon as still forming part of the Roman Empire, and they also point to the difficulty of the position of Anastasius, who, whatever might be his cause of quarrel with Theodoric, could only enforce his complaints against him by resorting to acts which in the eyes of his subjects wore the unholy appearance of a civil war.

Though we are not precisely informed when or how hostilities were brought to a close, it seems probable that soon after this raid, about the year 509, peace, unbroken for the rest of Theodoric's reign, was re-established between Ravenna and Byzantium. The Epistle which stands in the forefront of the *Various Letters* of Cassiodorus was

---

4. *Morava Hissar*, about half-way between Nisch and Belgrade.
5. Marcellinus Comes. Strangely enough he makes no mention of the Goths as assisting Mundo.
6. Both these terms denote what we should call "household troops."

probably written on this occasion.

Most clement emperor, (says Theodoric, or rather Cassiodorus speaking in his name), there ought to be peace between us since there is no real occasion for animosity. Every kingdom should desire tranquillity, since under it the people flourish and the common good is secured. Tranquillity is the comely mother of all useful arts; she multiplies the race of men as they perish and are renewed; she expands our powers, she softens our manners, and he who is a stranger to her sway grows up in ignorance of all these blessings. Therefore, most pious prince, it redounds to your glory that we should now seek harmony with your government, as we have ever felt love for your person.

For you are the fairest ornament of all realms, the safeguard and defence of the world; to whom all other rulers rightly look up with reverence, inasmuch as they recognise that there is in you something which exists nowhere else. But we pre-eminently thus regard you, since by Divine help it was in your Republic that we learned the art of ruling the Romans with justice. Our kingdom is an imitation of yours, which is the mould of all good purposes, the only model of Empire, Just in so far as we follow you do we surpass all other nations.

You have often exhorted me to love the Senate, to accept cordially the legislation of the emperors, to weld together all the members of Italy. Then, if you wish thus to form my character by your counsels, how can you exclude me from your august peace? I may plead, too, affection for the venerable city of Rome, from which none can separate themselves who prize that unity which belongs to the Roman name.

We have therefore thought fit to direct the two ambassadors who are the bearers of this letter to visit your most Serene Piety, that the transparency of peace between us, which from various causes hath been of late somewhat clouded, may be restored to its former brightness by the removal of all contentions. For we think that you, like ourselves, cannot endure that any trace of discord should remain between two Republics which, under the older princes, ever formed but one body, and which ought not merely to be joined together by a languid sentiment of affection, but strenuously to help one another with their mutually imparted strength.

157

Let there be always one will, one thought in the Roman kingdom. . . . Wherefore, proffering the honourable expression of our salutation, we beg with humble mind that you will not even for a time withdraw from us the most glorious charity of your mildness, which *I* should have a right to hope for even if it were not granted to others.[7]

Other matters we have left to be suggested to your piety verbally by the bearers of this letter, that on the one hand this epistolary speech of ours may not become too prolix, and on the other that nothing may be omitted which would tend to our common advantage.

The letter which I have attempted thus to bring before the reader is one which almost defies accurate translation. It is an exceedingly diplomatic document, full of courtesy, yet committing the writer to nothing definite. The very badness of his style enables Cassiodorus to envelop his meaning in a cloud of words from which the *quæstor* of Anastasius perhaps found it as hard to extract a definite meaning then, as a perplexed translator finds it hard to render it into intelligible English now. It is certainly difficult to acquit Cassiodorus of the charge of a deficient sense of humour, when we find him putting into the mouth of his master, who had so often marched up and down through Thrace, ravaging and burning, these solemn praises of "Tranquillity."

And when we read the fulsome flattery which is lavished on Anastasius, the almost obsequious humbleness with which the great Ostrogoth, who was certainly the stronger monarch of the two, prays for a renewal of his friendship, we may perhaps suspect either that the "*illiteratus Rex*" did not comprehend the full meaning of the document to which he attached his signature, or that Cassiodorus himself, in his later years, when, after the death of his master, he republished his *Various Letters*, somewhat modified their diction so as to make them more Roman, more diplomatic, more slavishly subservient to the Emperor, than Theodoric himself would ever have permitted.

One other act of this emperor must be noticed, as illustrating the subject of the last chapter. When Clovis returned in triumph from the Visigothic war (508) he found messengers awaiting him from Anastasius, who brought to him some documents from the Imperial chancery which are somewhat obscurely described as "*Codicils* of the Consulship." Then, in the church of St. Martin at Tours he was robed

---

7. The change from We to I, which here occurs in the original, is puzzling.

in a purple tunic and *chlamys*, and placed apparently on his own head some semblance of the Imperial diadem. At the porch of the basilica he mounted his horse and rode slowly through the streets of the city to the other chief church, scattering largesse of gold and silver to the shouting multitude. "From that day," we are told, "he was saluted as Consul and Augustus."

The name of Clovis does not, like that of Theodoric, appear in the *Fasti* of Imperial Rome, and what the precise nature of the consulship conferred by the "codicils" may have been, it is not easy to discover.[8] But there is no doubt that the authority which Clovis up to this time had exercised by the mere right of the stronger, over great part of Gaul, was confirmed and legitimised by this spontaneous act of the Augustus at Constantinople, nor that this eager recognition of the royalty of the slayer of Alaric was meant in some degree as a demonstration of hostility against Alaric's father-in-law, with whom Anastasius had not then been reconciled.

The coalition of Eastern emperor and Frankish king boded no good to Italy. Perhaps could the eye of Anastasius have pierced through the mists of seven future centuries, could he have foreseen the insults, the extortions, the cruelties which a Roman emperor at Constantinople was to endure at the hands of "Frankish" invaders,[9] he would not have been so eager in his worship of the new sun which was rising over Gaul from out of the marshes of the Scheldt.

The remainder of the life of Clovis seems to have been chiefly spent in removing the royal competitors who were obstacles to his undisputed sway over the Franks. Doubtless these were kings of a poor and barbarous type, with narrower and less statesmanlike views than those of the founder of the Merovingian dynasty; but the means employed to remove them were hardly such as we should have expected from the eldest Son of the Church, from him who had worn the white robe of a catechumen in the baptistery at Rheims. His most formidable competitor was Sigebert, king of the Ripuarian Franks, that is the Franks dwelling on both banks of the Rhine between Maintz and Koln, in the forest of the Ardennes and along the valley of the Moselle.

---

8. Perhaps the simplest explanation is that Clovis was not "*Consul ordinarius*," but "*Consul suffectus*." Junghans suggests that he was *Proconsul* of one or more of the Gaulish provinces, and Gaudenzi, accepting this idea, is inclined to call him *Proconsul* of Narbonese Gaul.
9. In the Fourth Crusade, 1203.

But Sigebert, who had sent a body of warriors to help the Salian king in his war against the Visigoths, was now growing old, and among these barbarous peoples age and bodily infirmity were often considered as to some extent disqualifications for kingship. Clovis accordingly sent messengers to Cloderic, the son of Sigebert, saying: "Behold thy father has grown old and is lame on his feet. If he were to die, his kingdom should be thine and we would be thy friends." Cloderic yielded to the temptation, and when his father went forth from Köln on a hunting expedition in the beech-forests of Hesse, assassins employed by Cloderic stole upon him in his tent, as he was taking his noon-tide slumber, and slew him. The deed being done, Cloderic sent messengers to Clovis saying:

"My father is dead and his treasures are mine. Send me thy messengers to whom I may confide such portion of the treasure as thou mayest desire."

"Thanks," said Clovis, "I will send my messengers, and do thou show them all that thou hast, yet thou thyself shalt still possess all." When the messengers of Clovis arrived at the palace of the Ripuanan, Cloderic showed them all the royal hoard.

"And here," said he, pointing to a chest, "my father used to keep his gold coins of the Empire." (*In hanc arcellolam solitus erat pater meus numismata auri congerere.*)

"Plunge thy hand in," said the messenger, "and search them down to the very bottom." The king stooped low to plunge his hand into the coins, and while he stooped the messenger lifted high his battle-axe and clove his skull.

"Thus," says the pious Gregory, who tells the story, "did the unworthy son fall into the pit which he had digged for his own father."

When Clovis heard that both father and son were slain, he came to the same place (probably Colonia) where all these things had come to pass and called together a great assembly of the Ripuarian people.

Hear, (he said), what hath happened. While I was quietly sailing down the Scheldt, Cloderic, my cousin's son, practised against his father's life, giving forth that I wished him slain, and when he was fleeing through the beech-forests he sent robbers against him, by whom he was murdered. Then Cloderic himself, when he was displaying his treasures, was slain by someone, I know not whom. But in all these things I am free from blame. For I cannot shed the blood of my relations: that were an unholy thing to do. But since these events have so happened, I offer you my advice if it seem good to you to accept it. Turn you to me that you may be under my defence.

Then they, when they heard these things, shouted approval and clashed their spears upon their shields in sign of assent, and raising Clovis on a buckler proclaimed him their king. And he receiving the kingdom and the treasures of Sigebert added the Ripuanans to the number of his subjects.

"For," concludes Gregory, bishop of Tours, to whom we owe the story of this enlargement of the dominions of his hero, "God was daily laying low the enemies of Clovis under his hand and increasing his kingdom, because he walked before him with a right heart and did those things which were pleasing in his eyes."

This ideal champion of orthodoxy in the sixth century then proceeded to clear the ground of the little Salian kings, his nearer relatives and perhaps more dangerous competitors. Chararic had failed to help him in his early days against Syagrius. He was deposed: the long hair of the Merovingians was shorn away from his head and from his son's head, and they were consecrated as priest and deacon in the Catholic Church. Chararic wept and wailed over his humiliation, but his son, to cheer him, said, alluding to the loss of their locks: "The wood is green, and the leaves may yet grow again. Would that he might quickly perish who has done these things!" The words were reported to Clovis, who ordered both father and son to be put to death, and added their hoards to his treasure, their warriors to his host.

Chararic had not gone forth to the battle against Syagrius, but Ragnachar of Cambray had given Clovis effectual help in that crisis of his early fortunes. However Ragnachar, by his dissolute life and his preposterous fondness for an evil counsellor named Farro, had given great offence to the proud Franks, his subjects. Just as James I. said of the forfeited estates of Raleigh: "I maun hae the land, I maun hae it for Carr," so Ragnachar said whenever anyone offered him a present, or whenever a choice dish was brought to table: "This will do for me and Farro." Clovis learned and fomented the secret discontent. He sent to the disaffected nobles amulets and baldrics of copper-gilt—which they in their simplicity took for gold,—inviting them to betray their master. The secret bargain being struck, Clovis then moved his army towards Cambray.

The anxious Ragnachar sent scouts to discover the strength of the advancing host. "How many are they?" said he on their return.

"Quite enough for thee and Farro," was the discouraging and taunting reply: and in fact the soldiers of Ragnachar seem to have been beaten as soon as the battle was set in array. With his hands bound behind his back, Ragnachar and his brother Richiar were brought into the presence of Clovis.

"Shame on thee," said the indignant king, "for humiliating our race by suffering thy hands to be bound. It had been better for thee to die— thus," and the great battle-axe descended on his head. Then turning to Richiar, he said: "If thou hadst helped thy brother, he would not have been bound"; and his skull too was cloven with the battle-axe.

Before many days the traitorous chiefs discovered the base metal in the ornaments which had purchased their treason, and complained of the fraud. "Good enough gold," said Clovis, "for men who were willing to betray their lord to death"; and the traitors, trembling for their lives under his frown and fierce rebuke, were glad to leave the matter undiscussed.

Thus in all his arguments with the weaker creatures around him the Frankish king was always right. It was always they, not he, who had befouled the stream. In this, shall I say, shameless plausibility of wrong, the founder of the Frankish monarchy was a worthy prototype of Louis XIV. and of Napoleon.

Having slain these and many other kings, and extended his dominions over the whole of Gaul, he once, in an assembly of his nobles, lamented his solitary estate. "Alas, I am but a stranger and a pilgrim, and have no kith or kin who could help me if adversity came upon me." But this he said, not in real grief for their death, but in guile, in order that if there were any forgotten relative lurking anywhere he might come forth and be killed. None, however, was found to answer to the invitation.[10]

Like all his family, Clovis was short-lived, though not so conspicuously short-lived as many of his descendants. He died at forty-five, in the year 511, five years after the Battle of the Campus Vogladensis. He was buried (511) in the Church of the Holy Apostles at Paris, and his kingdom, consolidated with so much labour and at the price of so many crimes, was partitioned among his four sons. The aged

---

10. We are reminded of the well-known story of Marshal Narvaez on his death-bed. "My son," said the confessor, "it is necessary that you should with all your heart grant forgiveness to your enemies."
"Ah, that is easy," said the dying man, "I have shot them all."

Emperor Anastasius survived his Frankish ally seven years, and died in the eighty-ninth year of his age, 8th July, 518. His death was sudden, and some later writers averred that it was caused by a thunderstorm, of which he had always had a peculiar and superstitious fear. Others declared that he was inadvertently buried alive, that he was heard to cry out in his coffin, and that when it was opened some days after, he was found to have gnawed his arm. But these facts are not known to earlier and more authentic historians, and the invention of them seems to be only a rhetorical way of putting the fact that he died at enmity with the Holy See.

COPPER COIN OF ANASTASIUS FORTY *NUMMI.*

CHAPTER 12

Rome and Ravenna

The death of Anastasius was followed by changes in the attitude towards one another of pope and emperor, which embittered the closing years of Theodoric and caused his sun to set in clouds. But before we occupy ourselves with these transactions, we may consider a little more carefully the relations between Theodoric and his subjects in the happier days, the early and middle portion of his reign, and for this purpose we will first of all hear what the chroniclers have to tell us of a memorable visit to Rome which he paid in the eighth year after his accession, that year which, according to our present chronology, is marked as the five hundredth after the birth of Christ.[1]

Rome had been for more than two centuries strangely neglected by the rulers who in her name lorded it over the civilised world. Ever since Diocletian's reconstruction of the Empire, it had been a rare event for an Augustus to be seen within her walls. Even the emperor who had Italy for his portion generally resided at Milan or Ravenna rather than on the banks of the Tiber. Constantine was but a hasty visitor before he went eastward to build his marvellous New Rome beside the Bosphorus. His son Constantius in middle life paid one memorable visit(357).

Thirty years later Theodosius followed his example. His son Honorius celebrated there(403) his doubtful triumph over Alaric, and his grandson, Valentinian III., was standing in the Roman Campus Martius when he fell under the daggers of the avengers of Aëtius. But the fact that these visits are so pointedly mentioned shows the extreme

---

1. The chronology now in use, invented by the monk Dionysius Exiguus, a friend of Cassiodorus, was not adopted till some years after the death of Theodoric. Consequently, 500 *a.d.* would be known in Rome only as 1252 *a.u.c.* (from the foundation of the city), and would have no special interest attaching to it.

rarity of their occurrence; nor was any great alteration wrought herein by Theodoric, for this visit to Rome, which we are now about to consider, and which lasted for six months, seems to have been the only one that he ever paid in the course of his reign of thirty-three years.

He came at an opportune time, when there was a lull in the strife, amounting almost to civil war, caused by a disputed Papal election. Two years before, two bodies of clergy had met on the same day (22nd. November) in different churches, in order to elect the successor to a deceased pope. The larger number, assembled in the mother-church, the Lateran, elected a deacon of Sardinian extraction, named Symmachus. The smaller but apparently more aristocratic body, backed by the favour of the majority of the Senate and supported by the delegates of the emperor, met in the church now called by the name of S. Maria Maggiore and voted for the arch-presbyter Laurentius.

The effect of this contested election was to throw Rome into confusion. Parties of armed men who favoured the cause of one or the other candidate paraded the city, and all the streets were filled with riot and bloodshed. It seemed as if the days of Marius and Sulla were come back again, though it would have been impossible to explain to either Marius or Sulla what was the nature of the contest, a dispute as to the right to be considered successor to a fisherman of Bethsaida. When the anarchy was becoming intolerable, the Senate, clergy, and people determined to invoke the mediation of Theodoric, thus furnishing the highest testimony to the reputation for fairness and impartiality which had been earned by the Arian king. Both the rival bishops repaired to Ravenna, and having laid the case before the king, heard his answer. "Whichsoever candidate was first chosen, if he also received the majority of votes, shall be deemed duly elected." Both qualifications were united in Symmachus, who was therefore for a time recognised as lawful Pope even by Laurentius himself.

The disturbances broke out again later on; charges, probably false charges, of gross immorality were brought against Symmachus, who fled from Rome, returned, was tried by a synod, and acquitted. It was not till after nearly six years had elapsed and six synods had been held, that Laurentius and his party gave up the contest and finally acquiesced in the legitimacy of the claim of Symmachus to the Popedom.

But most of these troubles were still to come: there was a lull in the storm, and it seemed as if the king's wise and righteous judgment had settled the succession to the Papal chair, when in the year 500 Theodoric visited Rome, seeing for the first time, in full middle life, the city whose name he had doubtless often heard with a child's wonder and awe in his father's palace by the Platten See. His first visit was paid to the great *basilica* of St. Peter, outside the walls, where he performed his devotions with all the outward signs of reverence which would have been exhibited by the most pious Catholic.[2]

Before he entered the gates of the city he was welcomed by the Senate and people of Rome, who poured forth to meet him with every indication of joy. Borne along by the jubilant throng, he reached the Senate-house, which still stood in its majesty overlooking the Roman Forum. Here, in some *portico* attached to the Senate-house, which bore the name of the Golden Palm, he delivered an oration to the people. The accent of the speech may not have been faultless,[3] the style was assuredly not Ciceronian, but the matter was worthy of the enthusiastic acclamations with which it was received. Recognising the continuity of his government with that of the emperors who had preceded him, he promised that with God's help he would keep inviolate all that the Roman princes in the past had ordained for their people. So might a Norman or Angevin king, anxious to reassure his Saxon subjects, swear to observe all the laws of the good King Edward the Confessor.

This speech of Theodoric's at the Golden Palm was listened to by an obscure African monk, whose emotions on the occasion are described to us by his biographer. Fulgentius, the grandson of a senator of Carthage, had forsaken what seemed a promising official career, and had accepted the solitude and the hardships of a monastic life, at a time when, owing to the severe persecution of the Catholics by the Vandal kings, there was no prospect of anything but ignominy, exile, and perhaps death for every eminent confessor of the Catholic faith. Fulgentius and his friends had suffered many outrages at the hands of Numidian freebooters and Vandal officers, and they meditated a flight into Egypt, where they might practise a yet more rigid monastic rule undisturbed by the civil power. In his search after a suitable resting-place for his community, Fulgentius, who was in the thirty-third year of his age, had visited Sicily, and now had reached Rome in this same summer of 500, which was made memorable by Theodoric's visit.

---

2. *Et occurrit Beato Petro devotissimus ac si Catholicus* (*Anon. Valesii*, 65).3. It is possible that historians somewhat underrate the degree of Theodoric's acquaintance with Latin as a spoken language. There was a great deal of Latin used in the Pannonian and Mesian regions, in which his childhood and youth were passed; and some, though certainly not so much, at Constantinople, where he spent his boyhood.

He found, (we are told), the greatest joy in this city, truly called 'the head of the world,' both the Senate and people of Rome testifying their gladness at the presence of Theodoric the King. Wherefore the blessed Fulgentius, to whom the world had long been crucified, after he had visited with reverence the shrines of the martyrs and saluted with humble deference as many of the servants of God as he could in so short a time be introduced to, stood in that place which is called Palma Aurea while Theodoric was making his harangue. There, as he gazed upon the nobles of the Roman Senate marshalled in their various ranks and adorned with comely dignity, and as he heard with chaste ears the favouring shouts of the people, he had a chance of knowing what the boastful pomp of this world resembles.

Yet he looked not willingly upon aught in this gorgeous spectacle, nor was his heart seduced to take any pleasure in these worldly vanities, but rather kindled thereby to a more vehement desire for Jerusalem above. And thus with edifying discourse did he ever admonish the brethren who were present: 'How fair must be that heavenly Jerusalem, if the earthly Rome be thus magnificent! And if in this world such honour is paid to the lovers of vanity, what honour and glory shall be bestowed on the Saints who behold the Eternal Reality.' With many such words as these did the blessed Fulgentius debate with them in a profitable manner all that day, and now with his whole heart earnestly desiring to behold his monastery again, he sailed swiftly to Africa, touching at Sardinia, and presented himself to his monks, who, in the excess of their joy, could scarcely believe that the blessed Fulgentius was indeed returned.

Besides his promises of good government according to the old laws of Empire, Theodoric recognised the duty which, according to long-established usage, devolved upon the supreme ruler to provide "*panem et circenses*"[4] for the citizens of Rome. The elaborate machinery, part of the crowned Socialism of the Empire, by which a certain number of loaves of bread had been distributed to the poorer householders of the city, had probably broken down in the death-agony of the Cæsars of the West, and had not been again set going by Odovacar. We are told that Theodoric now distributed as rations "to the people of Rome and to the poor" 120,000 *modii* of corn yearly.

---

4. Bread and circus-shows.

As this represents only 30,000 bushels, and as in the flourishing days of the Empire no fewer than 200,000 citizens used to present themselves, probably once or twice a week, to receive their rations, it is evident that (if the chronicler's numbers are correct) we have here no attempt to revive the wholesale distribution of corn to the citizens— an expenditure with which the finances of Theodoric's kingdom were probably quite unable to cope. What was now done was more strictly a measure of "out-door relief" for the absolutely destitute classes, and was therefore a more legitimate employment of the energies of the State than the socialistic attempt to feed a whole people, which had preceded it.

At the same time that he granted these *annonæ*, Theodoric also set aside, from the proceeds of a certain wine-tax, two hundred pounds of gold (£8,000) yearly for the restoration of the Imperial dwellings on the Palatine, and for the repair of the walls of Rome. Little did he foresee that a time would come when those walls, battered and breached as they were, would be all too strong for the fortunes of the Gothic warriors who would dash themselves vainly against their ramparts.

It was now thirty years since Theodoric, returning from his exile at Constantinople, had been hailed by his Gothic countrymen as a partner of his father's throne. In memory of that event, from which he was separated by so many years of toil and triumph, so many battles, so many marches, so many weary negotiations with emperors and kings, Theodoric celebrated his Tricennalia at Rome. On this occasion the gigantic Flavian amphitheatre—the colosseum as we generally call it—seems not to have been opened to the people. The old murderous fights with gladiators which once dyed its pavement with human blood had been for a century suppressed by the influence of the church, and the costly shows of wild beasts which were the permitted substitute would perhaps have taxed too heavily the still feeble finances of the State.

But to the Circus Maximus all the citizens crowded in order to see the chariot-races which were run there, and which recalled the brilliant festivities of the Empire. The circus, oval in form, notwithstanding its name, was situated in the long valley between the Palatine and Aventine Hills. High above, on the north-east, rose the palaces of the Cæsars already mouldering to decay, but one of which had probably been furbished up to make it a fitting residence for the king of the Goths and Romans. On the south-west the solemn Aventme still perhaps showed side by side the decaying temples of the gods and the mansions of the holy Roman matrons who, under the preaching of St. Jerome, had made their sumptuous palaces the homes of monastic self-denial. In the long ellipse between the two hills the citizens of Rome were ranged, not too many now in the dwindled state of the city to find elbow-room for all. A shout of applause went up from senators and people as the Gothic king, surrounded by a brilliant throng of courtiers, moved majestically to his seat in the Imperial *podium*.

At one end of the circus were twelve portals (*ostia*), behind which the eager charioteers were waiting. In the middle of it there rose the long platform called the *spina*, at either end of which stood an obelisk brought from Egypt by an emperor. (One of these obelisks now adorns the *Piazza del Popolo*, and the other the square in front of the Lateran.) At a signal from the king the races began. Whether the first heat would be between *bigæ* or *quadrigæ* (two-horse or four-horse chariots), we cannot say; but, of one kind or the other, twelve chariots bounded forth from the *ostia* the moment that the rope which had hitherto confined them was let fall. Seven times they careered round and round the long *spina*, of course with eager struggles to get the inside turn, and perhaps with a not infrequent fall when a too eager charioteer, in his desire to accomplish this, struck against the protecting kerbstone.

As each circuit was completed by the foremost chariot, a steward of the races placed a great wooden egg in a conspicuous place upon the *spina* to mark the score; and keen was the excitement when, in a match between two well-known rivals, six eggs announced to the spectators that the seventh, the deciding circuit, had begun. The entire course thus traversed seven times in each direction made a race of between three and four miles, and each heat would probably occupy nearly a quarter of an hour.[5] The number of heats (*missus*) was usually four and twenty, and we may therefore imagine Theodoric and his people occupying the best part of a summer day in watching the galloping steeds, the shouting, lashing drivers, and the fast-flashing chariot wheels.

At Rome, as at Constantinople, though not in quite so exaggerated a degree, partisanship with the charioteers was more than a passing

---

5. I take this calculation from Friedlander (*Sittengeschichte Roms*, II., 329), but I cannot find the precise figures on which he bases his calculation We know the length of the Circus, but of course for our purpose the length of the *spina* round which the chariots careered is the important factor.

fancy; it was a deep and abiding passion with the multitude, and it sometimes went very near to actual madness. Four colours, the Blue and the Green, the White and the Red, were worn respectively by the drivers, who served each of the four joint-stock companies (as we should call them) that catered for the taste of the race-loving multitude. Red and White had had their day of glory and still won a fair proportion of races, but the keenest and most terrible competition was between Blue and Green. At Constantinople, a generation later than the time which we have now reached, the undue favour which an emperor (Justinian.) was accused (532) of showing to the Blues caused an insurrection which wrapped the city in flames and nearly cost that emperor his throne.

No such disastrous consequences resulted from circus-partisanship in Rome: but even in Rome that partisanship was very bitter, and, in the view of a philosopher, supremely ridiculous. As the sage Cassiodorus remarked: "In these beyond all other shows, men's minds are hurried into excitement, without any regard to a fitting sobriety of character. The Green charioteer flashes by: part of the people is in despair. The Blue gets a lead: a larger part of the city is in misery. The populace cheer frantically when they have gained nothing; they are cut to the heart when they have received no loss; and they plunge with as much eagerness into these empty contests as if the whole welfare of their imperilled country depended upon them." In two other letters Theodoric is obliged seriously to chide the Roman Senate for its irascible temper in dealing with one of the factions of the circus.

A patrician and a consul, so it was alleged, had truculently assaulted the Green party, and one man had lost his life in the fray. The king ordered that the matter should be enquired into by two officials of "Illustrious" rank, who had special jurisdiction in cases wherein nobles of high position were concerned. He then replied to a counter-accusation which had been brought by the senators against the mob for assailing them with rude clamours in the hippodrome. "You must distinguish," says the king, "between deliberate insolence and the festive impertinences of a place of public amusement. It is not exactly a congregation of Catos that comes together at the circus.

The place excuses some excesses. And moreover you must remember that these insulting cries generally proceed from the beaten party: and therefore you need not complain of clamour which is the result of a victory that you earnestly desired." Again the king had to warn the senators not to bring disgrace on their good name and do violence to public order by allowing their menials to embroil themselves with the mob of the hippodrome. Any slave accused of having shed the blood of a free-born citizen was to be at once given up to justice; or else his master was to pay a fine of £400, and to incur the severe displeasure of the king.

And do not you, O senators, be too strict in marking every idle word which the mob may utter in the midst of the general rejoicing. If any insult which requires special notice should be offered you, bring it before the *Prefect* of the City. This is far wiser and safer than taking the law into your own hands.

The festivities which celebrated Theodoric's visit to the Eternal City were perhaps somewhat discordantly interrupted by the discovery of a conspiracy against him, set on foot by a certain Count Odoin, about whom we have no other information, but the form of whose name at once suggests that he was of Gothic, not Roman, extraction. It is possible that this conspiracy indicates the discontent of the old Gothic nobility with the increasing tendency to copy Roman civilisation and to assume Imperial prerogatives which they observed in the king who had once been little more than chief among a band of comrades. But we have not sufficient information as to this conspiracy to enable us to fix its true place in the history of Theodoric, nor can we even say with confidence that it was directed against the king and not against one of his ministers. The result alone is certain. Odoin's treachery was discovered and he was beheaded in the Sessorian palace, a building which probably stood upon the patrimony of Constantine, hard by the southern wall of Rome, and near to the spot where we now see the Church of Santa Croce.

At the request of the people, the words of Theodoric's harangue on his entrance into the city were engraved on a brazen tablet, which was fixed in a place of public resort, perhaps the Roman *forum*. Even so did the *Joyeuse Entrée* of a Burgundian duke into Brussels confirm and commemorate the privileges of his good subjects the citizens of Brabant. Upon the whole, there can be little doubt that the half-year which Theodoric spent in Rome was really a time of joyfulness both to prince and people, and that the tiles which are still occasionally turned up by the spade in Rome, bearing the inscription "*Domino Nostro Theodorico Felix Roma*," were not merely the work of official flatterers, but did truly express the joy of a well-governed nation. After six months Theodoric returned to that city, which, during the last thirty years of his life, he probably regarded as his home—Ravenna by the Adriatic,—and there he delighted the heart of his subjects by the pageants which celebrated the marriage of his niece Amalaberga with Hermanfrid, the king of the distant Thuringians. This young prince, whom Theodoric had adopted as his "son by right of arms" [6] had sent to his future kinsman a team of cream-coloured horses of a rare breed,[7] and Theodoric sent in return horses, swords and shields, and other instruments of war, but, as he said, "the greatest requital that we make is joining you in marriage to a woman of such surpassing beauty as our niece."

The later fortunes of the Ostrogothic princess who thus migrated from Ravenna to the banks of the Elbe were not happy. A proud and ambitious woman, she is said to have stimulated her husband to make himself, by fratricide and civil war, sole king of the Thuringians. The help of one of the sons of Clovis had been unwisely invoked for this operation. So long as the Ostrogothic hero lived, Thuringia was safe under his protection, but soon after his death dissensions arose between Franks and Thuringians; a claim of payment was made for the ill-requited services of the former. Thuringia was invaded, (531) her king defeated, and after a while treacherously slain. Amalaberga took refuge with her kindred at Ravenna, and after the collapse of their fortunes retired to Constantinople, where her son entered the Imperial service. In after years that son, "Amalafrid the Goth," was not the least famous of the generals of Justinian. The broad lands between the Elbe and the Danube, over which the Thuringians had wandered, were added to the dominions of the Franks and became part of the mighty kingdom of Austrasia.

I have had occasion many times in the preceding pages to write the name of Ravenna, the residence of most of the sovereigns of the

---

6. *Filius per arma.*
7. Perhaps it might be safe to call these horses cobs; but let Cassiodorus describe their points. They were "horses of a silvery colour, as nuptial horses ought to be. Their chests and thighs are adorned in a becoming manner with spheres of flesh. Their ribs are expanded to a certain breadth; their bellies are short and narrow. Their heads have a likeness to the stag's, and they imitate the swiftness of that animal. These horses are gentle from their extreme plumpness; very swift, for all their bigness, pleasant to look upon, yet more pleasant to ride. For they have gentle paces and do not fatigue their riders with insane curvettings. To ride them is rest rather than labour; and being broken in to a delightfully steady pace, they have great staying power and lasting activity." These sleek and easy-paced cobs are not at all the ideal present from a rough barbarian of the North to his "father in arms."

sinking Empire, and now the home of Theodoric. Let me attempt in a few paragraphs to give some faint idea of the impression which this city, a boulder-stone left by the ice drift of the dissolving Empire amid the green fields of modern civilisation, produces on the mind of a traveller.

Ravenna stands in a great alluvial plain between the Apennines, the Adriatic, and the Po. The fine mud, which has been for centuries poured over the land by the streams descending from the mountains, has now silted up her harbour, and Classis, the maritime suburb of Ravenna, which, in the days of Odovacar and Theodoric, was a busy sea port on the Adriatic, now consists of one desolate church—magnificent in its desolation—and two or three farm-buildings standing in the midst of a lonely and fever-haunted rice-swamp. Between the city and the sea stretches for miles the glorious pine-forest, now alas! cruelly maimed by the hands of nature and of man, by the frost of one severe winter and by the spades of the builders of a railway, but still preserving some traces of its ancient beauty. Here it was that Theodoric pitched his camp when for three weary years he blockaded his rival's last stronghold, and here by the deep trench (*fossatum*), which he had dug to guard that camp, he fought the last and not the least deadly of his fights, when Odovacar made his desperate sortie from the famine-stricken town.

Memories of a gentler kind, but still not wanting in sadness, now cluster round the solemn avenues of the Pineta. There we still seem to see Dante wandering, framing his lay of the "*selva oscura*," through which lay his path to the unseen world, and ever looking in vain for the arrival of the messenger who should summon him back to ungrateful Florence. There, in Boccaccio's story, a maiden's hapless ghost is forever pursued through the woods by "the spectre-huntsman," Guido Cavalcanti, whom her cruelty had driven to suicide. And there, in our fathers' days, rode Byron, like Dante, an exile, if self-exiled, from his country, and feeding on bitter remembrances of past praise and present blame, both too lightly bestowed by his countrymen.

We leave the pine-wood and the desolate-looking rice-fields, we cross over the sluggish streams—Ronco and Montone—and we stand in the streets of historic Ravenna. Our first thoughts are all of disappointment. There is none of the trim beauty of a modern city, nor, as we at first think, is there any of the endless picturesqueness of a well-preserved mediæval city. We look in vain for any building like Giotto's Campanile at Florence, for any space like that noble, crescent-shaped

173

PINE FOREST, RAVENNA

Forum, full of memories of the Middle Ages, the *Piazzo del Campo* of Siena. We see some strange but not altogether beautiful bell-towers and one or two brown cupolas breaking the sky-line, but that seems to be all, and our first feeling as I have said, is one of disappointment.

But when we enter the churches, if we have leisure to study, them, if we can let their spirit mingle with our spirits, if we can quietly ask them what they have to tell us of the past, all disappointment vanishes. For Ravenna is to those who will study her attentively a very Pompeii of the fifth century, telling us as much concerning those years of the falling Empire and the rising mediæval church as Pompeii can tell us of the social life of the Romans in the days of triumphant paganism.

Not that the record is by any means perfect. Many leaves have been torn out of the book by the childish conceit of recent centuries, which vainly imagined that they could write something instead, which any mortal would now care to read. The destroying hand of the so-called *Renaissance* has passed over these churches, defacing sometimes the chancel, sometimes the nave. One of the most interesting of the churches of Ravenna[8] has "the cupola disfigured by wretched paintings which mislead the eye in following the lines of the building." Another[9] has its apse covered with those gilt spangles and clouds and cherubs which were the eighteenth century's ideal of impressive religious art.

The Duomo, which should have been one of the most interesting of all the monuments of Ravenna, was almost entirely rebuilt in the last century, and is now scarcely worth visiting. Still, enough remains in the un-restored churches of Ravenna to captivate the attention of every student of history and every lover of early Christian art. It is only necessary to shut our eyes to the vapid and tasteless work of recent embellishers, as we should close our ears to the whispers of vulgar gossipers while listening to some noble and entrancing piece of sacred music.

Thus concentrating our attention on that which is really interesting and venerable in these churches, while we admire their long colonnades, their skilful use of ancient columns—some of which may probably have adorned the temples of Olympian deities in the days of the emperors,—and the exceedingly rich and beautiful new forms of capitals, of a design quite unknown to Vitruvius, which the genius

8. S. Vitale. The quotation is from Prof. Freeman, *Historical and Architectural Sketches*, p. 53.
9. S. Apollinare Dentro.

of Romanesque artists has invented, we find that our chief interest is derived from the mosaics with which these churches were once so lavishly adorned. Mosaic, as is well-known, is the most permanent of all the processes of decorative art.

Fresco must fade sooner or later, and where there is any tendency to damp, it fades with cruel rapidity. Oil painting on canvas changes its tone in the long course of years, and the boundary line between cleaning and repainting is difficult to observe. But the fragments out of which the mosaic picture is formed, having been already passed through the fire, will keep their colour for centuries, we might probably say for millenniums. Damp injures them not, except by lessening the cement with which they are fastened to the wall, and therefore when restoration of a mosaic picture becomes necessary, a really conscientious restorer can always reproduce the picture with precisely the same form and colour which it had when the last stone was inserted by the original artist.

And thus, when we visit Ravenna, we have the satisfaction of feeling that we are (in many cases) looking upon the very same picture which was gazed upon by the contemporaries of Theodoric. Portraits of Theodoric himself, unfortunately we have none; but we have two absolutely contemporary portraits of Justinian, the overturner of his kingdom, and one of Justinian's wife, the celebrated Theodora. These pictures, it is interesting to remember, were considerably older when Cimabue found Giotto in the sheepfolds drawing sheep upon a tile, than any picture of Cimabue's or Giotto's is at the present time.

Let us enter the church which is now called "S. Apollinare within the Walls," but which in the time of Theodoric was called the Church of S. Martin, often with the addition "de Cælo Aureo," on account of the beautiful gilded ceiling which distinguished it from the other basilicas of Ravenna. This church was built by order of Theodoric, who apparently intended it to be his own royal chapel. Probably, therefore, the great Ostrogoth many a time saw "the Divine mysteries" celebrated here by bishops and priests of the Arian communion. Two long colonnades fill the nave of the church. The columns are classical, with Corinthian capitals, and are perhaps brought from some older building.

A peculiarity of the architecture consists in the high abacus—a frustum of an inverted pyramid—which is interposed between the capital of the column and the arch that springs from it, as if to give greater height than the columns alone would afford. Such in its main features was the Church of "St. Martin of the Golden Heaven," when Theodoric worshipped under its gorgeous roof. But its chief adornment, the feature which makes more impression on the beholder than anything else in Ravenna, was added after Theodoric's death, yet not so long after but that it may be suitably alluded to here as a specimen of the style of decoration which his eyes must have been wont to look upon.

About the year 560, after the downfall of the Gothic monarchy, Agnellus, the Catholic Bishop of Ravenna, "reconciled" this church, that is, re-consecrated it for the performance of worship by orthodox priests, and in doing so adorned the attics of the nave immediately above the colonnades with two remarkable mosaic *friezes*, each representing a long procession.

On the north wall of the church we behold a procession of Virgin Martyrs. They are twenty-four in number, a little larger than life, and are chiefly those maidens who suffered in the terrible persecution of Diocletian. The place from which they start is a seaport town with ships entering the harbour, domes and columns and arcades showing over the walls of the city. An inscription tells us that we have here represented the city of Classis, the seaport of Ravenna. By the time that we have reached the last figure in this long procession we are almost at the east end of the nave. Here we see the Virgin-mother throned in glory with the infant Jesus on her lap, and two angels on each side of her. But between the procession and the throne is interposed the group of the three Wise Men, in bright-coloured raiment, with tiara-like crowns upon their heads, stooping forward as if with eager haste[10] to present their various oblations to the Divine Child.

On the right, or south wall of the church, a similar procession of martyred men, twenty-six in number, seems to move along, in all the majesty of suffering, bearing their crowns of martyrdom as offerings to the Redeemer. The Christ is here not an infant but a full-grown man, the Man of Sorrows, His head encircled with a nimbus, and two angels are standing on either side. The martyr-procession starts from a building, with pediment above and three arches resting upon pillars below. The intervals between the pillars are partly filled with curtains looped up in a curious fashion and with bright purple spots upon them. An inscription on this building tells us that it is PALATIUM,

---

10. So Milton in his *Ode on the Nativity*: "*See how from far along the Eastern road, The star-led wizards haste with odours sweet. Oh run, present them with thy humble ode, And lay it lowly at His blessed feet.*"

INTERIOR OF BASILICA, IN RAVENNA.

that is Theodoric's palace at Ravenna.

In both these processions the representation is, of course, far from the perfection of art. Both the faces and the figures have a certain stiffness, partly due to the very nature of mosaic-work. There is also a sort of child-like simplicity in the treatment, especially of the female figures, which an unsympathetic critic would call grotesque. But, I think, most beholders feel that there is something indescribably solemn in these two great mosaic pictures in S. Apollinare Dentro. From the glaring, commonplace Italian town with its police-notices and its proclamation of the number of votes given to the government of Vittorio Emmanuele, you step into the grateful shade of the church and find yourself transported into the sixth century after Christ.

You are looking on the faces of the men and maidens who suffered death with torture rather than deny their Lord. For thirteen centuries those two processions have seemed to be moving on upon the walls of the *basilica*, and another ceaseless procession of worshippers, Goths, Byzantines, Lombards, Franks, Italians, has been in reality moving on beneath them to the grave. And then you remind yourself that when the artist sketched those figures on the walls, he was separated by no longer interval than three long lives would have bridged over, from the days of the persecution itself, that there were still men living on the earth who worshipped the Olympian Jupiter, and that the name of Mohammed, son of Abdallah, was unknown in the world. So, as you gaze, the telescope of the historic imagination does its work, and the far-off centuries become near.

One or two other Arian churches built during Theodoric's reign in the northern suburb of the city have now entirely disappeared. There still remains, however, the church which Theodoric seems to have built as the cathedral of the Arian community, while leaving the old metropolitan church (Ecclesia Ursiana, now the Duomo) as the cathedral of the Catholics. This Arian cathedral was dedicated to St. Theodore, but has in later ages been better known as the church of the Holy Spirit. Tasteless restoration has robbed it of the mosaics which it doubtless once possessed, but it has preserved its fine colonnade consisting of fourteen columns of dark green marble with Corinthian capitals, whose somewhat unequal height seems to show that they, like so many of their sisters, have been brought from some other building, where they have once perhaps served other gods.

Through the courtyard of the Church of San Spirito, we approach a little octagonal building known both as the Oratory of S. Maria in

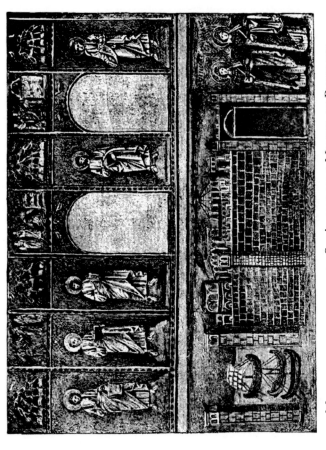

MOSAIC IN THE CHURCH OF ST. APOLLINARE NUOVO AT RAVENNA.

Cosmedia and as the Arian Baptistery. The great octagonal font, which once stood in the centre of the building, has disappeared, but we can easily reconstruct it in our imaginations from the similar one which still remains in the Catholic Baptistery. The interest of this building consists in the mosaics of its cupola. On the disk, in the centre, is represented the Baptism of Christ. The Saviour stands, immersed up to His loins, in the Jordan, whose water flowing past Him is depicted with a quaint realism. The Baptist stands on His left side and holds one hand over His head.

On the right of the Saviour stands an old man, who is generally said to represent the River-god, and the reed in his hand, the urn, from which water gushes, under his arms, certainly seem to favour this supposition. But in order to avoid so strange a medley of Christianity and heathenism it has been suggested that the figure may be meant for Moses, and in confirmation of this theory some keen-eyed beholders have thought they perceived the symbolical horned rays proceeding from each side of the old man's forehead.

Round this central disk are seen the figures of the twelve Apostles. They are divided into two bands of six each, who seem marching, with crowns in their hands, towards a throne covered with a veil and a cushion, on which rests a cross blazing with jewels. St. Peter stands on the right of the throne, St. Paul on the left; and these two Apostles carry instead of crowns, the one the usual keys, and the other two rolls of parchment. The interest of these figures, though they have something of the stern majesty of early mosaic-work, is somewhat lessened by the fact that they have undergone considerable restoration. It is suggested, I know not whether on sufficient grounds, that the figures of the Apostles were added when the Baptistery was "reconciled" to the Catholic worship after the overthrow of the Gothic dominion.

Two more buildings at Ravenna which are connected with the name of Theodoric require to be noticed by us,—his palace and his tomb. The story of his tomb, however, will be best told when his reign is ended. As for the palace, which once occupied a large space in the eastern quarter of the city, we have seen that there is a representation of it in mosaic on the walls of S. Apollinare Dentro. Closely adjoining that church, and facing the modern Corso Garibaldi, is a wall about five and twenty feet high, built of square brick-tiles, which has in its upper storey one large and six small arched recesses, the arches resting on columns. Only the front is ancient—it is admitted that the building behind it is modern. Low down in the wall, so low that the citizens of

PROCESSION OF MARTYRS
(MOSAIC FROM ST. APOLLINARE NUOVO AT RAVENNA.)

Ravenna, in passing, brush it with their sleeves, is a bath-shaped vessel of porphyry, which in the days of archaeological ignorance used to be shown to strangers as "the coffin of Theodoric," but the fact is that its history and its purpose are entirely unknown.

This shell of a building is called in the Ravenna guide-books "the Palace of Theodoric." Experts are not yet agreed on the question whether its architectural features justify us in referring it to the sixth century, though all agree that it does not belong to a much later age.[11] It does not agree with the representation of the *Palatium* in the Church of S. Apollinare Dentro, and if it have anything whatever to do with it, it is probably not the main front, nor even any very important feature of the spacious palace, which, as we are told by the local historians,[12] and learn from inscriptions, was surrounded with porticoes, adorned with the most precious mosaics, divided into several *triclinia*, surmounted by a tower which was considered one of the most magnificent of the king's buildings, and surrounded with pleasant and fruitful gardens, planted on ground which had been reclaimed from the morass.[13]

But practically almost all the monuments of the Ostrogothic hero except his tomb and the three churches already described, have vanished from Ravenna. Would that we could have seen the great mosaic which once adorned the pediment of his palace. There Theodoric stood, clad in mail, with spear and shield. On his left was a female figure representing the city of Rome, also with a spear in her hand and her head armed with a helmet, while towards his right Ravenna seemed speeding with one foot on the land and the other on the sea. How this great mosaic perished is not made clear to us. But there was also an equestrian statue of Theodoric raised on a pyramid six cubits high. Horse and rider were both of brass, "covered with yellow gold," and the king here too had his buckler on his left arm, while the right,

---

11. Gally Knight (*Ecclesiastical Architecture of Italy*, i., 7) seems to accept it without hesitation as belonging to the age of Theodoric. Freeman (*Historical, etc., Sketches*, p. 47) expresses considerable doubt: "The works of Theodoric are Roman; this palace is not Roman but Romanesque, though undoubtedly a very early form of Romanesque."

12. Agnellus and others, as quoted by Corrado Ricci, *Ravenna ei suoi Dintorni*, p. 139. I cannot verify all Ricci's quotations, but take the result of them on his authority.

13. An inscription quoted by Ricci tells us this: *Rex Theodoricuvs Favente Deo Et Bello Gloriosvs Et Otio. Fabriciis Svis Amœna Conivi(n)gens Sterili Palvde Siccata Hos Hortos Svavi Pomorvm Fœcvnditate Ditavit.*

extended, pointed a lance at an invisible foe.

This statue was carried off from Ravenna, probably by the Frankish Emperor Charles, to adorn his capital at Aachen, and it was still to be seen there when Agnellus wrote his ecclesiastical history of Ravenna, three hundred years after the death of Theodoric.

COIN OF THE GOTHIC KINGDOM IN ITALY.

PALACE OF THEODORIC, RAVENNA.
(SIDE VIEW).

CHAPTER 13

Boëthius

Hithero the career of Theodoric has been one of almost unbroken prosperity, and the reader who has followed his history has perhaps grown somewhat weary of the monotonous repetition of the praises of his mildness and his equity. Unfortunately he will be thus wearied no longer. The sun of the great Ostrogoth set in sorrow, and what was worse than in sorrow, in deeds of hasty wrath and cruel injustice, which lost him the hearts of the majority of his subjects and which have dimmed his fair fame with posterity.

Many causes combined to sadden and depress the king's heart, as he felt old age creeping upon him. Providence had not blessed him with a son; and while his younger rival, Clovis, left four martial sons to defend (and also to partition) his newly formed kingdom, Theodoric's daughter Amalasuentha was the only child born of his marriage with Clovis' sister.

In order to provide himself with a male heir (for the customs of the Goths did not favour, if they did not actually exclude, female sovereignty), Theodoric summoned to his court a distant relative, a young man named Eutharic, descended from the mighty Hermanric, who was at the time living in Spain. Eutharic, who was well reported of for bodily vigour and for statesmanlike ability, came to the Ostrogothic court, married Amalasuentha (515), four years afterwards received the honour of a consulship, which he held along with the Emperor Justin, and exhibited games and combats of wild beasts to the populace of Rome and Ravenna on a scale of unsurpassed magnificence. But he died, probably soon after his consulship, leaving two children—a boy and a girl,—and thus Theodoric's hope of bequeathing his crown to a mature and masculine heir was disappointed. Still, however, he would not propose a female ruler to his old Gothic comrades; and the little grandson, Athalaric, though under ten years of age, was solemnly presented by him to an assembly of Gothic counts and the nobles of the nation as their king.

The proclamation of Athalaric was made when the king felt that he should shortly depart this life, probably in the summer of 526. I have mentioned it here in order to complete my statement as to the succession to the throne, but we will now return to an earlier period to the events which immediately followed Eutharic's consulship. Coming as he did from Spain, the Visigothic lords of which were still an aristocracy of bitter Arians in the midst of a cowed but Catholic Roman population, Eutharic, who, as we are expressly told, "was too harsh and hostile to the Catholic faith," may have to some extent swayed the mind of his father-in-law away from its calm balance of even-handed justice between the rival Churches. But the state of affairs at Constantinople exercised a yet more powerful influence. Anastasius, who, though no Arian, had during his long reign been always in an attitude of hostility towards the Papal See, was now dead, and had been succeeded by Justin.

This man, a soldier of fortune, who had as a lad tramped down from the Macedonian highlands into the capital, with a wallet of biscuit over his shoulder for his only property, had risen, by his soldierly qualities, to the position of Count of the Guardsmen, and by a judicious distribution of gold among the soldiers—gold which was not his own, but had been entrusted to him for safe-keeping,—he won for himself the diadem, and for his nephew,[1] as it turned out, the opportunity of making his name forever memorable in history. Justin was absolutely illiterate—the story about the stencilled signature is told of him as well as of Theodoric,—but he was strictly orthodox, and his heart was set on a reconciliation with the Roman See. This measure was also viewed with favour by the majority of the populace of Constantinople, with whom the heterodoxy of Anastasius had become decidedly unpopular.

Thus the negotiations for a settlement of the dispute went prosperously forward. The *anathemas* which were insisted upon by the Roman *pontiff* were soon conceded, the names of Zeno, of Anastasius, and of five Patriarchs of Constantinople who had dared to dissent from the Roman See were struck out of the *Diptychs* (or lists of those men, living or dead, whom the Church regarded as belonging to her communion); and thus the first great schism between the Eastern and

---

1. Justinian.

Western Churches—a schism which had lasted for thirty-five years—was ended.

It was probably foreseen by the statesmen of Ravenna that this reconciliation between pope and emperor, a reconciliation which had been celebrated by the enthusiastic shout of the multitude in the great church of the Divine Wisdom at Constantinople, would sooner or later bring trouble to Theodoric's Arian fellow-worshippers. In point of fact, however, an interval of nearly six years elapsed before any actual persecution of the Arians of the Empire was attempted. The first cause of alienation between the Ostrogothic king and his Catholic subjects seems to have arisen in connection with the Jews. Theodoric, on account of some fear of invasion by the barbarians beyond the Alps, was dwelling at Verona. That city, the scene of his most desperate battle with Odovacar, commanding as it does the valley of the Adige and the road by the Brenner Pass into the Tyrol, was probably looked upon by Theodoric as the key of north-eastern Italy, and when there was any danger of invasion he preferred to hold his court there rather than in the safer but less convenient Ravenna.

There too he may probably have often received the ambassadors of the Northern nations, who went back to their homes with those stories of the might and majesty of the Ostrogothic king which made "Dietrich of Bern" (Theodoric of Verona) a name of wonder and a theme of romance to many generations of German minstrels. While Theodoric was dwelling in the city of the Adige, tidings came to him, apparently from his son-in-law Eutharic, whom he had left in charge at Ravenna, that the whole city was in an uproar. The Jews, of whom there was evidently a considerable number, were accused of having made sport of the Christian rite of baptism by throwing one another into one of the two muddy rivers of Ravenna, and also, in some way not described to us, to have mocked at the supper of the Lord.[2] The Christian populace of the city were excited to such madness by these rumours that they broke out into rioting, which neither the Gothic vicegerent, Eutharic, nor their own bishop, Peter III., was able to quell, and which did not cease till all the Jewish synagogues of the city were laid in ashes.

When tidings of these events were brought to Verona by the Grand Chamberlain Triwan (or Trigguilla) who, as an Arian, was suspected of favouring the Jews, and when the Hebrews came themselves to invoke

2. The passage of the *Anonymus Valesii* which describes these events is so corrupt that it is hardly possible to make sense of it.

VIEW OF MODERN CONSTANTINOPLE (AS AT TIME OF FIRST PUBLICATION)

the justice of the king, Theodoric's righteous indignation was kindled against these flagrant violations of *civilitas*. It was not, indeed, the first time that his intervention had been claimed on behalf of the persecuted children of Israel. At Milan and at Genoa they had already appealed to him against the vexations of their neighbours, and at Rome the mob, excited by some idle story of harsh punishments inflicted by the Jews on their Christian servants, had burned their synagogue in the Trastevere to the ground. The protection claimed had always been freely conceded. Theodoric, while expressing or permitting Cassiodorus to express his pious wonder that a race which wilfully shut itself out from the eternal rest of Heaven should care for quietness on earth, was strong in declaring that for the sake of *civilitas* justice was to be secured even for the wanderers from the right religious path, and that no one should be forced to believe in Christianity against his will.

Nor was this willingness to protect the Jews from popular fanaticism peculiar to Theodoric. Always, so long as the Goths, either the Western or Eastern branch, remained Arian, the Jews found favour in their eyes, and Jacob had rest under the shadow of the sons of Odin. Now, therefore, the king sent an edict addressed to Eutharic and Bishop Peter, ordaining that a pecuniary contribution should be levied on all the Christian citizens of Ravenna, out of which the synagogues should be rebuilt, and that those who were not able to pay their share of this contribution should be flogged through the streets, the crier going behind them and in a loud voice proclaiming their offence. The order was doubtless obeyed, but from that day there was a secret spirit of rebellion in the hearts of the Roman citizens of Ravenna.

From this time onward occasions of difference between Theodoric and his Roman subjects were frequently arising. For some reason which is not explained to us, he ordered the Catholic church of St. Stephen in the suburbs of Verona to be destroyed. Then came suspicion, the child of rancour. An order was put forth forbidding the inhabitants of Roman origin to wear any arms, and this prohibition extended even to pocket-knives. In the excited state of men's minds earth and heaven seemed to them to be full of portents. There were earthquakes; there was a comet with a fiery tail which blazed for fifteen days; a poor Gothic woman lay down under a *portico* near Theodoric's palace at Ravenna and gave birth (so we are assured) to four dragons, two of which, having one head between them, were captured, while the other two, sailing away eastward through the clouds, were seen to fall headlong into the sea.

More important than these old wives' fables was the changed attitude and the wavering loyalty of the Roman Senate. From the remarks made in an earlier chapter,[3] it will be clear that a conscientious Roman citizen might truly feel that he owed a divided allegiance to the Ostrogoth, his ruler *de facto*, and to the Augustus at Constantinople, his sovereign *de jure*. Through the years of religious schism this conflict of duties had slumbered, but now, with the enthusiastic reconciliation between the see of Rome and the throne of Constantinople, it awoke; and in that age when, as has been already said, religion was nationality, an orthodox Eastern emperor seemed a much more fitting object of homage than an Arian Italian king.

There were two men, united by the ties of kindred, who seemed marked out by character and position as the leaders of a patriotic party in the Senate, if such a party could be formed. These men were Boëthius and his father-in-law Symmachus, both Roman nobles of the great and ancient Anician *gens*. Boëthius, whose name we have already met with as the skilful mechanic who was requested to construct a water-clock and a sun-dial for the king of the Burgundians, was a man of great and varied accomplishments—philosopher, theologian, musician, and mathematician. He had translated thirty books of Aristotle into Latin for the benefit of his countrymen; his treatise on Music was for many centuries the authoritative exposition of the science of harmony. He had held the high honour of the consulship in 510; twelve years later he had the yet higher honour of seeing his two sons, Symmachus and Boëthius, though mere lads, arrayed in the *trabea* of the consul.

Symmachus the other leader of the patriotic party in the Roman Senate had memories of illustrious ancestors behind him. A century before, another Symmachus had been the standard-bearer of the old Pagan party, and had delivered two great orations in order to prevent the Christian emperors from removing the venerable Altar of Victory from the Senate-house. Now, his descendant and namesake was an equally firm adherent of Christianity, a friend and counsellor of Popes, a man who was willing to encounter obloquy and even death in behalf of Nicene orthodoxy. He had been consul so long ago as in the reign of Odovacar, he had been an "Illustrious" *Prefect* of the City under Theodoric; he was now Patrician and Chief of the Senate (*Caput Senatus*).

The last two titles conferred honour rather than power; the head-

3. See chapter 9.

191

ship of the Senate especially being generally held by the oldest, and if not by the oldest, by the most esteemed and venerated member of that body. Such was Symmachus, a man full of years and honours, a historian, an orator, and a generous contributor of some portion of his vast wealth for the adornment of his native city.

Boëthius, left an orphan in childhood, had enjoyed the wise training of his guardian Symmachus. When he came to man's estate he married that guardian's daughter Rusticiana. Though there was the difference of a generation between them, a close friendship united the old and the middle-aged senators, and the young consuls sprung from this alliance, who were the hope of their blended lines, bore, as we have seen, the names of both father and grandfather.

Up to the year 523, Boëthius appears to have enjoyed to the full the favour of Theodoric. From a chapter of his autobiography[4] we learn that he had already often opposed the ministers of the crown when he found them to be unjust and rapacious men.

How often (says he), have I met the rush of Cunigast, when coming open-mouthed to devour the substance of the poor! How often have I baffled the all but completed schemes of injustice prepared by the chamberlain Trigguilla! How often have I interposed my influence to protect the unhappy men whom the unpunished avarice of the barbarians was worrying with infinite calumnies! Paulinus, a man of consular rank, whose wealth the hungry dogs of the palace had already devoured in fancy, I dragged as it were out of their very jaws.

But all these acts of righteous remonstrance against official tyranny, though from the names given they seem to have been chiefly directed against Gothic ministers, had not forfeited for Boëthius the favour of his sovereign. The proof of this is furnished by the almost unexampled honour conferred upon him—certainly with Theodoric's consent—by the elevation of his two sons to the consulship. The exultant father, from his place in the Senate, expressed his thanks to Theodoric in an oration of panegyric, which is now no longer extant, but was considered by contemporaries a masterpiece of brilliant rhetoric.

So far all had gone well with the fortunes of Boëthius; but now, perhaps about the middle of 523, there came a great and calamitous change. We must revert for a few minutes to the family circumstances of Theodoric, in order to understand the influences which were em-

---

4. Contained in the *Consolation of Philosophy*.

bittering his spirit against his Catholic—that is to say, his Roman—subjects. The year before, his grandson Segeric, the Burgundian, had been treacherously assassinated by order of his father, King Sigismund, who had become a convert to the orthodox creed, and after the death of Theodoric's daughter had married a Catholic woman of low origin. In the year 523 itself, Thrasamund, king of the Vandals, died and was succeeded by his cousin Hilderic, son of one of the most ferocious persecutors of the Catholic Church, but himself a convert to her creed.

Notwithstanding an oath which Hilderic had sworn to his predecessor on his death-bed, never to use his royal power for the restoration of the churches to the Catholics, Hilderic had recalled the bishops of the orthodox party and was in all things reversing the bitter persecuting policy of his ancestors, Amalafrida, the sister of Theodoric and widow of Thrasamund, who had been for nearly twenty years queen of the Vandals, passionately resented this undoing of her dead husband's work and put herself at the head of a party of insurgents, who called in the aid of the Moorish barbarians, but who were, notwithstanding that aid, defeated by the soldiers of Hilderic at Capsa. Amalafrida herself was taken captive and shut up in prison, probably about the middle of 523.

Thus everywhere the Arian League, of which Theodoric had been the head, and which had practically given him the hegemony of Teutonic Europe, was breaking down; and in its collapse disaster and violent death were coming upon the members of Theodoric's own family. If Eutharic himself, as seems probable, had died before this time, and was no longer at the king's side to whisper distrust of the Catholics at every step, and to put the worst construction on the actions of every patriotic Roman, yet even Eutharic's death increased the difficulties of Theodoric's position, and his doubts as to the future fortunes of a dynasty which would be represented at his death only by a woman and a child. And these difficulties and doubts bred in him not depression, but an irascible and suspicious temper, which had hitherto been altogether foreign to his calm and noble nature.

Such was the state of things at the court of Ravenna when, in the summer or early autumn of 523, Cyprian, reporter in the King's Court, accused the Patrician Albinus of sending letters to the Emperor Justin hostile to the royal rule of Theodoric. Of the character and history of Albinus, notwithstanding his eminent station, we know but little. He was not only Patrician, but *Illustris*—that is, in modern phraseology, he had held an office of cabinet-rank. On the occasion of some quarrel between the factions of the circus, Theodoric had graciously ordered him to assume the patronage of the Green Faction, and to conduct the election of a pantomimic performer for that party. He had also received permission to erect workshops overlooking the *forum* on its northern side, on condition that his buildings did not in any way interfere with public convenience or the beauty of the city.

Evidently he was a man of wealth and high position, one of the great nobles of Rome, but perhaps one who, up to this time, had not taken any very prominent part in public affairs. His accuser, Cyprian, still apparently a young man, was also a Roman nobleman. His father had been consul, and he himself held at this time the post of *referendar-ius* (or, as I have translated it, reporter) in the King's Court of Appeal. His ordinary duty was to ascertain from the suitor what was the nature of his plea, to state it to the king, and then to draw up the document, which contained the king's judgement. It was an arduous office to ascertain from the flurried and often trembling suitor, in the midst of the hubbub of the court, the precise nature of his complaint, and a responsible one to express the king's judgment, neither less nor more, in the written decree. There was evidently great scope for corrupt conduct in both capacities, if the *referendarius* was open to bribes; and in the "Formula," by which these officers were appointed, some stress is laid on the necessity of their keeping a pure conscience in the exercise of their functions. Cyprian seems to have been a man of nimble and subtle intellect, who excelled in his statement of a case.

So well was this done by him, from the two opposite points of view, that plaintiff and defendant in turn were charmed to hear each his own version of the case so admirably presented to the king. Of later years, Theodoric, weary of sitting in state in the crowded hall of justice, had often tried his cases on horseback. Riding forth into the forest he had ordered Cyprian to accompany him, and to state in his own lively and pleasing style the "for" and "against" of the various causes that came before him on appeal. Even, we are told, when Theodoric was roused to anger by the manifest injustice of the plea that was thus presented, he could not help being charmed by the graceful manner in which the young *referendarius*, the temporary asserter of the claim, brought it under his notice.

Thus trained to subtle eloquence, Cyprian had been recently sent on an embassy to Constantinople, and had there shown himself in the word-fence a match for the keenest of the Greeks. Lately returned, as it should seem, from this embassy, he came forward in the Roman Senate and accused the Patrician Albinus of outstepping the bounds of loyalty to the Ostrogothic king in the letters which he had addressed to the Byzantine Emperor.

In this accusation was Cyprian acting the part of an honest man or of a base informer? The times were difficult: the relations of a Roman Senator to emperor and king were, as I have striven to show, intricate and ill-defined; it was hard for even good men to know on which side preponderated the obligations of loyalty, of honour, and of patriotism. On the one hand Cyprian may have been a true and faithful servant of Theodoric, who had in his embassy at Constantinople discovered the threads of a treasonable intrigue, and who would not see his master betrayed even by Romans without denouncing their treason.

As a real patriot he may have seen that the days of purely Roman rule in Italy were over, that there must be some sort of amalgamation with these new Teutonic conquerors, who evidently had the empire of the world before them, that it would be better and happier, and in a certain sense more truly Roman, for Italy to be ruled by a heroic "King of the Goths and Romans" than for her to sink into a mere province ruled by *exarchs* and *logothetes* from corrupt and distant Constantinople. This is one possible view of Cyprian's character and purposes. On the other hand, he may have been a slippery adventurer, intent on carving out his own fortune by whatever means, and willing to make the dead bodies of the noblest of his countrymen stepping-stones of his own ambition. In his secret heart he may have cared nothing for the noble old Goth, his master, with whom he had so often ridden in the pine-wood; nothing, too, for the great name of Rome, the city in which his father had once sat as consul.

Long accustomed to state both sides of a case with equal dexterity, and without any belief in either, this nimble-tongued advocate, who had already found that Greece had nothing to teach him that was new, may have had in his inmost soul no belief in God, in country, or in duty, but in Cyprian alone. Both views are possible; we have before us only the passionate invectives of his foes and the stereotyped commendations of his virtues penned by his official superiors, and I will not attempt to decide between them.

When Cyprian brought his charge of disloyalty against Albinus, the accused patrician, who was called into the presence of the king, at once denied the accusation. An angry debate probably followed, in the course of which Boëthius claimed to speak The attention of all men was naturally fixed upon him, for by the king's favour, the same favour which in the preceding year had raised his two sons to the consulship, he was now filling the great place of Master of the Offices.[5]

"False," said Boëthius in loud, impassioned tones, "is the accusation of Cyprian; but whatever Albinus did, I and the whole Senate of Rome, with one purpose, did the same. The charge is false, O King Theodoric."

The interposition of Boëthius was due to a noble and generous impulse, but it was not perhaps wise, in view of all that had passed, and without in any way helping Albinus, it involved Boëthius in his ruin. Cyprian, thus challenged, included the Master of the Offices in his accusation, and certain persons, not Goths, but Romans and men of senatorial rank, Opilio (the brother of Cyprian), Basilius, and Gaudentius, came forward and laid information against Boëthius.

Here the reader will naturally ask, "Of what did these informers accuse him?" but to that question it is not possible to give a satisfactory answer. He himself in his meditations on his trial says:

Of what crime is it that I am accused? I am said to have desired the safety of the Senate. 'In what way?' you may ask. I am accused of having prevented an informer from producing certain documents in order to prove the Senate guilty of high treason. Shall I deny the charge? But I did wish for the safety of the Senate and shall never cease to wish for it, nor, though they have abandoned me, can I consider it a crime to have desired the safety of that venerable order. That posterity may know the truth and the real sequence of events, I have drawn up a written memorandum concerning the whole affair.

For, as for these forged letters upon which is founded the accusation against me of having hoped for Roman freedom, why should I say anything about them? Their falsehood would have been made manifest, if I could have used the confession of the informers themselves, which in all such affairs is admitted to have the greatest weight. As for Roman freedom, what hope is left to us of attaining that? Would that there were any such hope. Had the king questioned me, I would have answered in the words Canius, when he was questioned by the Emperor Caligula as to his complicity in a conspiracy formed against him. If I, said he, had known, thou shouldest never have known.

---

5. See chapter 9.

These words, coupled with some bitter statements as to the tainted character of the informers against him, men oppressed by debt and accused of peculation, constitute the only statement of his case by Boëthius which is now available. The memorandum so carefully prepared in the long hours of his imprisonment has not reached posterity. Would that it might even yet be found in the library of some monastery, or lurking as a palimpsest under the dull commentary of some mediæval divine! It could hardly fail to throw a brilliant, if not uncoloured light on the politics of Italy in the sixth century. But, trying as we best may to spell out the truth of the affair from the passionate complaints of the prisoner, I think we may discern that there had been some correspondence on political affairs between the Senate and the Emperor Justin, correspondence which was perfectly regular and proper if the emperor was still to them "*Dominus Noster*" (our Lord and Master), but which was kept from the knowledge of "the King of the Goths and Romans," and which, when he heard of it, he was sure to resent as an act of treachery to himself.

That Boëthius, the Master of the Offices under Theodoric, should have connived at this correspondence, naturally exasperated the master who had so lately heaped favours on this disloyal servant. But in addition to this he used the power which he wielded as Master of the Offices, that is, head of the whole Civil Service of Italy, to prevent some documents which would have compromised the safety of the Senate from coming to the knowledge of Theodoric. All this was dangerous and doubtful work, and though we may find it hard to condemn Boëthius, drawn as he was in opposite directions by the claims of historic patriotism and by those of official duty, we can hardly wonder that Theodoric, who felt his throne and his dynasty menaced, should have judged with some severity the minister who had thus betrayed his confidence.

The political charge against Boëthius was blended with one of another kind, to us almost unintelligible, a charge of sacrilege and necromancy. At least this seems to be the only possible explanation of the following words written by him: "My accusers saw that the charge 'of desiring the safety of the Senate' was no crime but rather a merit; and therefore, in order to darken it by the mixture of some kind of wickedness, they falsely declared that ambition for office had led me to pollute my conscience with sacrilege. But Philosophy had chased from my breast all desire of worldly greatness, and under the eyes of her who had daily instilled into my mind the Pythagorean maxim

'Follow God,' there was no place for sacrilege. Nor was it likely that I should seek the guardianship of the meanest of spirits when Divine Philosophy had formed and moulded me into the likeness of God. The friendship of my father-in-law, the venerable Symmachus, ought alone to have shielded me from the suspicion of such a crime. But alas! it was my very love for Philosophy that exposed me to this accusation, and they thought that I was of kin to sorcerers because I was steeped in philosophic teachings."

The only reasonable explanation that we can offer of these words is that mediæval superstition was already beginning to cast her shadow over Europe, that already great mechanical skill, such as Boëthius was reputed to possess when his king asked him to manufacture the water-clock and the sun-dial, caused its possessor to be suspected of unholy familiarity with the Evil One; perhaps also that astronomy, which was evidently the favourite study of Boëthius, was perilously near to astrology, and that his zeal in its pursuit may have exposed him to some of the penalties which the Theodosian code itself, the law-book of Imperial Rome, denounced against "the mathematicians."

This seems to be all that can now be done towards re-writing the lost indictment under which Boëthius was accused. The trial was conducted with an outrageous disregard of the forms of justice. It took place in the Senate-house at Rome; Boëthius was apparently languishing in prison at Pavia, where he had been arrested along with Albinus.[6] Thus at a distance of more than four hundred miles from his accusers and his judges was the life of this noble Roman, unheard and undefended, sworn away on obscure and preposterous charges by a process which was the mere mockery of a trial. He was sentenced to death and the confiscation of his property; and the judges whose trembling lips pronounced the monstrous sentence were the very senators whose cause he had tried to serve.

This thought, the remembrance of this base ingratitude, planted the sharpest sting of all in the breast of the condemned patriot. It is evident that the Senate themselves were in desperate fear of the newly awakened wrath of Theodoric, and the fact that they found Boëthius guilty cannot be considered as in any degree increasing the probability of the truth of the charges made against him. But it does perhaps

---

6. Boëthius complains thus: "Now, at a distance of nearly five hundred miles, unheard and undefended, I have been condemned to death and proscription for my too enthusiastic love to the Senate." Pavia, where he seems to have been first confined, was, according to the Antonine Itinerary, 455 Roman miles from the capital.

somewhat lessen his reputation for far-seeing statesmanship, since it shows how thoroughly base and worthless was the body for whose sake he sacrificed his loyalty to the new dynasty, how utterly unfit the Senate would have been to take its old place as ruler of Italy, if Byzantine emperor and Ostrogothic king could have been blotted out of the political firmament.

Boëthius seems to have spent some months in prison after his trial, and was perhaps transferred from Pavia to "the *ager Calventianus*," a few miles from Milan. There at any rate he was confined when the messenger of death sent by Theodoric found him. There is some doubt as to the mode of execution adopted. One pretty good contemporary authority says that he was beheaded, but the writer whom I have chiefly followed, who was almost a contemporary, but a credulous one, says that torture was applied, that a cord was twisted round his forehead till his eyes started from their sockets, and that finally in the midst of his torments he received the *coup de grâce* from a club.

In the interval which elapsed between the condemnation and the death of this noble man, who died verily as a martyr for the great memories of Rome, he had time to compose a book which exercised a powerful influence on many of the most heroic spirits of the Middle Ages. This book, the well-known, if not now often read, *Consolation of Philosophy*, was translated into English by King Alfred and by Geoffrey Chaucer, was imitated by Sir Thomas More (whose history in some respects resembles that of Boëthius), and was translated into every tongue and found in every convent library of mediæval Europe. There is a great charm, the charm of sadness, about many of its pages, and it may be considered from one point of view as the swan's song of the dying Roman world and the dying Greek philosophy, or from another, as the Book of Job of the new mediæval world which was to be born from the death of Rome. For like the Book of Job, the *Consolation* is chiefly occupied with a discussion of the eternal mystery why a Righteous and Almighty Ruler of the world permits bad men to flourish and increase, while the righteous are crushed beneath their feet: and, as in the Book of Job, so here, the question is not, probably because it cannot be, fully answered.

It is the consolation of philosophy, not of religion, or at any rate not of revealed religion, which is here administered. So marked is the silence of Boëthius on all those arguments, which a discussion of this kind inevitably suggests to the mind of a believer in the Crucified One, that scholars long supposed that he was not even by profession a Christian. A manuscript which has been lately discovered[7] seems to prove beyond a doubt that Boëthius was a Christian, and wrote orthodox treatises on disputed points of theology; but for some reason or other he fell back on his early philosophical studies, rather than on his formal and conventional Christianity, when he found himself in the deep waters of adversity and imminent death. He represents himself in the *Consolation* as lying on his dungeon-couch, sick in body and sad at heart, and courting the Muses as companions of his solitude. They come at his call, but are soon unceremoniously dismissed by one nobler than themselves, who asserts an older and higher right to cheer her votary in the day of his calamity.

This is Philosophy, a woman of majestic stature, whose head seems to touch the skies, and who has undying youth and venerable age mysteriously blended in her countenance. Having dismissed the Muses, she sits by the bedside of Boëthius and looks with sad and earnest eyes into his face. She invites him to pour out his complaints; she sings to him songs first of pity and reproof, then of fortitude and hope; she reasons with him as to the instability of the gifts of Fortune, and strives to lead him to the contemplation of the *Summum Bonum*, which is God Himself, the knowledge of whom is the highest happiness. Then, in order a little to lighten his difficulties as to the permission of evil by the All-wise and Almighty One, she enters into a discussion of the relation between Divine Foreknowledge and Human Freewill, but this discussion, a thorny and difficult one, is not ended when the book comes to an abrupt conclusion, being probably interrupted by the arrival of the messengers of Theodoric, who brought the warrant for the writer's execution.

The *Consolation of Philosophy* is partly in prose, partly in verse. The prose is generally strong, clear, and comparatively pure in style, wonderfully superior to the vapid diffusiveness of Cassiodorus and most writers of the age. The interspersed poems are sometimes in hexameters, but more often in the shorter lines and more varied metres of Horace, and are to some extent founded upon the tragic choruses of Seneca. It is of course impossible in this place to give any adequate account of so important a work and one of such far-reaching influence as the *Consolation* but the following translation of one of the poems in which the prisoner makes his moan to the Almighty may give the reader some little idea of the style and matter of the treatise.

---

7. Called the *Anecdoton Holderi*, from the German scholar who has edited it.

The Harmony of the Natural World: The Discord of the Moral World.

Oh Thou who hast made this starry Whole,
Who hast fixed on high Thy throne;
Who biddest the Blue above us roll,
And whose sway the planets own!
At Thy bidding she turns, the changing Moon
To her Brother her full-fed fire,
Dimming the Stars with her light, which soon
Wanes, as she draws to him nigher.

Thou givest the word, and the westering Star,
The Hesper who watched o'er Night's upspringing,
Changing his course, shines eastward far,
Phosphor now, for the Sun's inbringing.

When the leaves fall fast, 'neath Autumn's blast,
Thou shortenest the reign of light.
In radiant June Thou scatterest soon
The fast-flown hours of night.
The leaves which fled from the cruel North
Are with Zephyr's breath returning,
And from seeds which the Bear saw dropped in earth
Springs the corn for the Dog-star's burning.

Thus all stands fast by Thine old decree,
Nothing wavers in Nature's plan:
In all her changes she bows to Thee:
Yea, all stands fast but Man.

Oh! why is the wheel of Fortune rolled,
While guilt Thy vengeance shuns?
Why sit the bad on their thrones of gold,
And trample Thine holy ones?
Why doth Virtue skulk where none may see
In the great world's corners dim?
And the just man mark the knave go free,
While the penalty falls on him?

No storm the perjurer's soul o'erwhelms,
Serene the false one stands:
He flatters, and Kings of mighty realms
Are as clay in his moulding hands.

Oh Ruler! look on these lives of ours,
Thus dashed on Fortune's sea.
Thou rulest the calm eternal Powers,
But thine handiwork, too, are we.
Ah! quell these waves with their tossings high;
Let them own Thy bound and ban:
And as Thou rulest the starry sky
Rule also the world of Man!

COPPER PIECE OF ATHALARIC. TEN NUMMI.
(HEAD OF JUSTINIAN—?)

CHAPTER 14

Heodoric's Tomb

The death of Boëthius[1] occurred probably about the middle of 524, and in the same year, as it would seem, Theodoric left Verona and returned to his old quarters at Ravenna. The danger from the barbarians on the northern frontier had apparently been averted, but a far greater danger, the hatred and the terror of his subjects of Roman origin, had entered his kingdom. It was probably during this same year 524 that the zeal of the orthodox Emperor Justin began to flame out against the Arians. Their churches were taken from them and given to the Catholics, and, as we hear that several Arians at this time embraced the Catholic faith, we may conjecture that the usual methods of conversion in that age, confiscation, imprisonment, and possibly torture, had been pretty freely employed.

These measures, coming close after the alleged conspiracy of the senators, or perhaps simultaneously with it, completed the exasperation of Theodoric, He sent for the Pope, John I., a Tuscan, who had been lately elevated to the Papal chair, and when the successor of St. Peter appeared at Ravenna commanded him, with some haughtiness in his tone, to proceed to Constantinople, to the Emperor Justin, and tell him that "he must in no wise attempt to win over those whom he calls heretics to the Catholic religion." The Pope is said to have made some protestations, distinguishing between his duty to God and his duty to his king, but nevertheless accepted a commission of some kind or other to treat with the emperor on the subject of mutual toleration between Catholics and Arians.

(525) He set forth at the head of a brilliant train, accompanied by Ecclesius, bishop of Ravenna, and Eusebius, bishop of Fano, by Sena-

---

1. Possibly of Albinus also, but he disappears from the story, according to the tantalising manner of the annalists from whom we get our information.

tor Theodorus, who had been consul in 505, by Senator Importunus, consul in 509, who was descended from the historic family of the Decii, and from whom his coevals expected deeds worthy of that illustrious name, by Senator Agapetus, who had been consul along with the Eastern emperor in 517, and by many other noblemen and bishops.

The visit of a pope to Constantinople, an event which had not occurred since the very earliest days of the new capital, created profound sensation in that city and was the very thing to cement that union between the papacy and the Empire which constituted Theodoric's greatest danger. The whole city poured forth with crosses and candles to meet the Pope and his companions at the twelfth milestone, and to testify with shouts their veneration for the Apostles Peter and Paul, whose representative they deemed that they saw before them. "Justinus Augustus," the fortunate farm-lad, before whom in his old age all the great ones of the earth prostrated themselves in reverence, now saluted the Vicar of St. Peter with the same gestures of adoration. The coronation of the emperor, who had already been for six years on the throne, was celebrated with the utmost magnificence, the Roman Pontiff himself placing the diadem on his head.

Then the Pope and all the senators with tears besought the emperor that their embassy might be acceptable in his sight. In the private interviews which were held, the Pope probably hinted to his orthodox ally the dangers which might result to the Catholic cause in Italy, if Theodoric, hitherto so tolerant a heretic, should be provoked to measures of retaliation on behalf of his church. There does seem to have been some modification of the persecuting edicts against the Arians, and at least some restoration of churches to the heretics, though certain Papal historians, unwilling to admit that a pope can have pleaded for any concession to misbelievers, endeavour to represent the Pope's mission as fruitless, while the Pope's person was greeted with enthusiastic reverence. But that which is upon the whole our best authority declares that "the Emperor Justin having met the Pope on his arrival as if he were St. Peter himself, and having heard his message, promised that he would comply with all his demands except that the converts who had given themselves to the Catholic faith could by no means be restored to the Arians."

This last exception does not seem an unreasonable one. Surely Theodoric could hardly have expected that Justin would exert his Imperial power in order to force any of his subjects back into what he deemed a deadly heresy. But for some cause or other, probably because he perceived the mistake which he had committed in giving to the world so striking a demonstration of the new alliance between emperor and Pope, Theodoric's ambassadors, on their return to Ravenna, found their master in a state of wrath bordering on frenzy. All, both Pope and senators, were cast into prison and there treated with harshness and cruelty. The Pope, who was probably an aged and delicate man, began to languish in his dungeon, and there he died on the 25th of May, 526.

In the meantime, while the papal embassy had been absent on its mission to Constantinople, Theodoric had perpetrated another crime under the influence of his maddening suspicions. Symmachus, father-in-law of Boëthius, the venerable head of the Senate, a man of saintly life and far advanced in years, had probably dared to show that he condemned as well as lamented the execution of his brilliant son-in-law. Against him, therefore, a charge, doubtless of treason, was brought by command of the king. To be accused was of course to be condemned, and Symmachus was put to death in one of the prisons at Ravenna.

After the deaths of these three men, Boëthius, Symmachus, and Pope John, all chance of peace between Theodoric and his subjects, and what was worse, all chance of peace between Theodoric and his nobler and truer self was over, and there was nothing left him but to die in misery and remorse. It was probably in these summer days of 526 that (as before stated) he presented his young grandson Athalaric to his faithful Goths as their king. An edict was issued—and the faithful groaned when they saw that it bore the counter-signature of a Jewish treasury-clerk—that on Sunday the 30th of August all the Catholic churches of Italy should be handed over to the Arians. But this tremendous religious revolution was not to be accomplished, nor was an insurrection of the Catholics to be required in order to arrest it. The edict was published on Wednesday the 26th of August. On the following day the king was attacked by diarrhoea, and after three days of violent pain he died on the 30th of August, the very day on which the churches were to have been handed over to the heretics and ninety-seven days after the death of the Pope.[2]

---

2. The disease and death, of Theodoric are thus described by the chief contemporary authority, the *Anonymous Valesii*: "*Sed qui non patitur fideles cultores suos ab alienigenis opprimi, mox intulit in eum sententiam Arrii, auctoris religionis ejus: fluxum ventris incurrit, et dum intra triduo evacuatus fuisset, eodem die, quo se gaudebat ecclesias invadere, simul regnum et animam amisit.*"

There is certainly something in this account of Theodoric's death which suggests the idea of arsenical poisoning. No hint of this kind is given by any of the analysts, but they are all hostile to Theodoric and disposed to see in his rapid illness and most opportune death a Divine judgment for his meditated persecution of the church. On the other hand it is impossible to read the account of his strange incoherent deeds and words during the last three years of his life, without suspecting that his brain was diseased and that he was not fully responsible for his actions. As bearing on this question it is worthwhile to quote the story of his death given by a Greek historian[3] who wrote twenty-four years after his death. It is, perhaps, only an idle tale, but it shows the kind of stories which were current among the citizens of Ravenna as to the last days of their great king.

> When Theodoric was dining, a few days after the death of Symmachus and Boëthius,[4] the servants placed on the table a large fish's head. This seemed to Theodoric to be the head of Symmachus, newly slain. The teeth seemed to gnaw the lower lip, the eyes glared at him with wrath and frenzy, the dead man appeared, to threaten him with utmost vengeance. Terrified by this amazing portent and chilled to the bone with fear, he hastily sought his couch, where, having ordered the servants to pile bed-clothes upon him, he slept awhile. Then sending for Elpidius, the physician, he related all that had happened to him, and wept for his sins against Symmachus and Boëthius. And with these tears and with bitter lamentations for the tragedy in which he had taken part, he soon afterwards died, this being the first and last injustice which he had committed against any of his subjects. And it proceeded from his not carefully sifting, as he was wont to do, the evidence on which a capital charge was grounded.

This story of Procopius, if it have any foundation at all, seems to show that Theodoric's last days were passed in delirium, and might suggest a doubt whether in the heart-break of these later years he had not endeavoured to drown his sorrows in wine. But it is interesting to see that the Greek historian, though writing from a somewhat hos-

---

3. Procopius. He was present with Belisarius in Ravenna in 540, and wrote his history of the Gothic war (first three books) probably in 550.
4. This is, of course, an error. Theodoric's death was about two years after that of Boëthius, and many months after that of Symmachus.

tile point of view, recognises emphatically the justice of Theodoric's ordinary administration, and considers the execution of Symmachus and Boëthius (we ought to add the imprisonment of the Pope and his co-ambassadors) as the one tyrannical series of acts which marred the otherwise fair fame of a patriot-king.

The tomb of Theodoric still stands, a noble monument of the art of the sixth century, outside the walls of the north-east corner of Ravenna. This edifice, which belongs to the same class of sepulchral buildings as the tomb of Hadrian (now better known as the Castle of S. Angelo), is built of squared marble stones, and consists of two storeys, the lower one a decagon, the upper one circular. The roof is composed of one enormous block of Istrian marble 33 feet in diameter, 3 feet in height, and weighing, it is said, nearly 300 tons. It is a marvel and a mystery how, with the comparatively rude engineering appliances of that age, so ponderous a mass can have been transported from such a distance and raised to such a height.[5] At equal intervals round the outside of this shallow, dome-like roof, twelve stone brackets are attached to it. They are now marked with the names of eight Apostles and of the four Evangelists. One conjecture as to their destination is that they were originally crowned with statues, perhaps of these Apostles and Evangelists; another, to me not very probable, is, that the ropes used (if any were used) in lifting the mighty *monolith* to its place were passed through these, which would thus be the handles of the dome.

This mausoleum, which is generally called *La Rotonda* by the citizens of Ravenna, was used in the Middle Ages as the choir of the Church of S. Maria della Rotonda, and divine service was celebrated in it by the monks of an adjoining monastery. It is now a "public monument" and there are few traces left of its ecclesiastical employment. The basement, as I have seen it, is often filled with water, exuding from the marshy soil: the upper storey is abandoned to gloom and silence.

Of Theodoric himself, whose body, according to tradition, was once deposited in a porphyry vase in the upper storey of the mausoleum, there is now no vestige in the great pile which in his own life-time he raised as his intended sepulchre. Nor is this any recent spoliation. Agnellus, bishop of Ravenna, writing in the days of Charlemagne, says that the body of Theodoric was not in the mausoleum,

---

5. The mausoleum of Theodoric was a work that excited the admiration of his contemporaries. The *Anonymous Valesii* writes "*Se autem vivo fecit sibi monumentum ex lapide quadrato, miræ magnitudinis opus, et saxum ingens quod superponeret inquisivit.*"

THE TOMB OF THEODRIC, RAVENNA.

and had been, as he thought, cast forth out of its sepulchre,[6] and the wonderful porphyry vase in which it had been enclosed placed at the door of the neighbouring monastery. A recent enquirer[7] has connected these somewhat ambiguous words of Agnellus with a childish story told by Pope Gregory the Great, who wrote some seventy years after the death of Theodoric.

According to this story, a holy hermit, who lived in the island of Lipari, on the day and hour of Theodoric's death saw him, with bound hands and garments disarranged, dragged up the volcano of Stromboli by his two victims Symmachus and Pope John, and hurled by them into the fire-vomiting crater. What more likely, it is suggested, than that the monks of the adjoining monastery should seize the opportunity of some crisis in the troubled history of Ravenna to cast out the body of Theodoric from its resting-place, and so, to the ignorant people, give point to Pope Gregory's edifying narrative as to the disposal of his soul?

A discovery, which was made some forty years ago in the neighbourhood of Ravenna, may possibly throw some light on these mysterious words of Bishop Agnellus: "As it seems to me, he was cast forth out of his sepulchre." In May, 1854, the labourers employed in widening the bed of the Canale Corsini (now the only navigable water-way between Ravenna and the sea) came, at the depth of about five feet beneath the sea-level, on some *tumuli*, evidently sepulchral in their character, made of bricks laid edgeways. Near one of these *tumuli*, but lying apart by itself, was a golden *cuirass* adorned with precious stones. The rascally labourers, when they caught sight of their treasure, feigned to see nothing, promptly covered it up again, and returned at nightfall to divide the spoil. A little piece of gold which was found lying on the ground caused enquiries to be set on foot; the labourers were arrested, but unfortunately the greater part of the booty had already been cast into the melting-pot.

A few pieces were, however, recovered, and are now in the museum at Ravenna, where they figure in the catalogue as part of the armour of Odovacar. This is, however, a mere conjecture, and another, at least equally probable conjecture, is that the *cuirass* of gold once covered the breast of Theodoric. The spot where it was found is about one hundred and fifty yards from the Rotonda, and if the monks had for any

---

6. "*Sed ut mihi videtur, ex sepulcro projectus est, et ipsa urna, ubi jacuit, ex lapide pirfiretico valde mirabilis ante ipsius monasterii aditum posita est.*"

7. Corrado Ricci, *Della Corazzo d'Oro*, in *Cronologio Ravennate*, 1879.

reason decided to pillage the sepulchre of its precious deposit, this was a not improbable place where they might hide it for a time. Certainly the self-denial which they showed in not stripping the body of its costly covering is somewhat surprising, but possibly the conspirators were few in number and the chances of war may have removed them, before they had an opportunity to disinter the body a second time and strip it of its *cuirass*, which moreover could not have been easily disposed of without exciting suspicion.

One little circumstance which seems somewhat to confirm this theory, is the fact that there is an enrichment[8] running round the border of the *cuirass* very similar in character to a decoration of the cornice in Theodoric's tomb.

Whether this theory be correct or not, the indignity which was certainly at some time offered to the mortal remains of the great Ostrogothic king reminds us of the similar insults offered to the body of the great Puritan Protector, Cromwell, like Theodoric, was carried to his grave with all the conventional demonstrations of national mourning. He was dragged from it again and cast out "like an abominable branch" when the legitimate monarchy was restored, when "Church and King" were again in the ascendant, and when the stout soldiers, who had made him in all but the name king *de facto*, were obliged to bow their heads beneath the recovered might of the king *de jure*.

---

8. A "*meandro*," as it is called by Ricci.

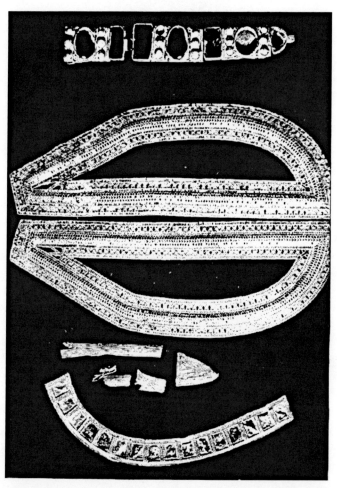

CUIRASS OF THEODORIC (?) IN THE MUSEUM AT RAVENNA

CHAPTER 15

Amalasuentha

Our special subject, the life of Theodoric, is ended, but so closely was the king identified with the people that the narration can hardly close without a sketch of the fortunes of the Ostrogothic nation during the generation which followed his death. I shall not attempt any detailed history of this period, but shall draw merely its broadest outlines.

Notwithstanding the melancholy and apparently threatening circumstances which attended the death of Theodoric, his descendants succeeded to his power without a contest. In Spain, his grandson, Amalaric, who had probably by this time attained his majority, was hailed as king of the Visigoths. In Italy, Athalaric, now barely ten years old, became the nominal ruler, the real powers being exercised by his widowed mother, Amalasuentha, who was guided more implicitly than her father had been by the counsel of Cassiodorus, and availed herself of his fertile pen for the proclamations in which she addressed the subjects of her son. In writing to the Roman Senate, Cassiodorus made his child-sovereign enlarge on the felicity of the country in which the accession of a new ruler could take place without war or sedition or loss of any kind to the republic.

On account of the unsurpassed glory of the Amal race, the promise of my youth has been preferred to the merits of all others. The chiefs, glorious in council and in war, have flocked to recognise me as king, so gladly that it seems like a Divine inspiration, and the kingdom has been changed as one changes a garment. The general consent of Goths and Romans has crowned one king, and they have confirmed their allegiance by an oath. You, though distant from my person, are as near

212

to me in heart as they, and I therefore call on you to follow their example. We all know that the most excellent fathers of the Senate love their king more fervently than other ranks of the state, in proportion to the greater benefits which they have received at his hand.

To the senators, who had witnessed the denunciation of Albinus, and who had been compelled with anguish of heart to vote the condemnation of Boëthius, this allusion to the great benefits which they had received from their Gothic sovereign might seem almost like mockery: yet there can be little doubt that the Senate did hail the accession of Athalaric with acclamations, and that Amalasuentha's administration of affairs was popular with the Roman inhabitants of Italy. It might well be so, for this princess, born under an Italian sky, and accustomed from her childhood to gaze upon the great works which Rome had constructed for the embellishment of the peninsula, was no Goth at heart, but enthusiastically, even unwisely, Roman. In religious matters we are almost surprised to find that she adhered to the Arian creed of her father and her husband, but all talk of persecution of the Catholics ceased, and no more was heard of the enforced cession of their churches to the Arians.

And in everything else but religion the sympathies of the new ruler were entirely on the side of the subject, not the dominant, nationality. As it had been said of old that "Captive Greece subdued her conquerors," so now was it with subject Italy and its Gothic mistress. A diligent student of Greek as well as of Latin literature, able to discourse with the ambassadors of Constantinople in well-turned Attic sentences, or to deliver a stately Latin oration to the messengers of the Senate, she could also, when the occasion required brevity, wrap herself in the robe of taciturnity which she inherited from her Teutonic ancestors, and with few, diplomatically chosen words, make the hearer feel his immeasurable inferiority to the "Lady of the Kingdoms." A woman with a mind thus richly stored with the literary treasure of Greece and Rome was likely to look with impatient scorn on the barren and barbarous annals of her people.

We in whose ears the notes of the Teutonic minstrelsy of the Middle Ages are still sounding, we who know that Shakespeare, Milton, Gœthe were all one day to arise from beneath the soil of Germanic literature, can hardly conceive how dreary and repulsive the national sagas, and even the every-day speech of her people, would seem in that day to a woman of great intellectual endowments, nor how strong would be the antagonism between culture and national patriotism in the heart of a princess like Amalasuentha.

Thus the position of things during the reign of the young Athalaric was strangely altered from that which had existed under his grandfather. The "King of the Goths and Romans" was under the sway of a mother who would make him virtually "King of the Romans," only leaving the Goths outside in moody isolation. Of course every step that Amalasuentha, in the enthusiasm of her love for things Roman, took towards the Roman Senate carried her farther from the traditions of her people, and lost her the love of some stern old Gothic warriors. And, moreover, with all her great intellectual endowments, it is clear that this highly cultivated, statuesque, and stately woman had little skill in reading character, little power in estimating the force of human motives. She had read (we may conjecture) Virgil and Sophocles, but she did not know what was in the heart of a child, and she knew not how long a scoundrel will wait for his revenge.

At the time that the Gothic kingdom was thus being administered by a child and a woman, the Roman Empire, which had seemed effete and decaying, was astonishing the world by its recovered and increasing vigour. Since the death of Theodosius (more than one hundred and thirty years before that of Theodoric) no great historic name had illustrated the annals of the Eastern Empire, But now, a year after the accession of Athalaric at Ravenna, the death of Justin, in the palace at Constantinople, (1st Aug., 527) brought upon the scene an emperor who, whatever his faults, however disastrous (as I hold it to have been) his influence on the general happiness of the human race, made for himself undoubtedly one of the very greatest names in the whole series from Julius to Palaeologus—the world-famous Emperor *Justinian*.

With Justinian's long wars on the eastern frontier of his Empire we have here no concern. He was matched there against a terrible rival, Chosroes Nushirvan, and at most succeeded (and that not always) in upholding the banner of Europe against triumphant Asia. His domestic affairs, his marriage with the actress Theodora, the strange ascendancy which she exerted over him through life, his magnificent buildings, the rebellion in Constantinople (springing out of the factions of the hippodrome) which had all but hurled him from his throne,—these also are all beyond our province. So too is his noblest title to immortality, the composition by his orders of that magnificent legal trilogy, the Code, the Digest, and the Institutes, which summed up whatever was most worthy of preservation in the labours of Roman lawyers for nine centuries in the past, and sent it forward for at least thirteen centuries into the future to ascertain the rights and to mould the institutions of men dwelling in lands of the very existence of which no Roman, from the first Julius to the last Constantine, ever dreamed. Justinian as legislator is as much out of our present focus as Justinian the antagonist of Persia.

But what we have here briefly to concern ourselves with is that marvellous display of renewed energy by which the Empire, under Justinian, made its presence felt in Western Europe and Africa. During the thirty-eight years of his reign the great world-kingdom, which for five generations had been losing province after province to the Barbarians, and which, when she had once lost a game had seemed never to have the heart to try her fortune again on the same battlefield, now sent out her fleets and her armies, apparently with the same confidence of success which had once animated her Scipios and her Sullas, again planted her victorious standards on the citadel of Carthage, made the New Carthage in Spain, Malaga, and distant Cadiz her own, and—what concerns our present subject more nearly—once more asserted the unrestricted dominion of the Roman Augustus over Italy "from the Alps to the Sea."

Let us beware of thinking of all these great changes as strange and precarious extensions of "the Byzantine Empire." To do so is to import the language of much later ages into the politics of the sixth century. However clearly we may now see that the relations thus established between Constantinople and the western shores of the Mediterranean were artificial, and destined not to endure, to Justinian and his contemporaries these were not "conquests by Constantinople," but "the recovery of Africa, Italy, and part of Spain for the Roman Republic."

The first of the Teutonic states to fall was the kingdom of the Vandals. Its ruin was certainly hastened by the estrangement between its royal house and that of the Ostrogoths. We left Theodoric's sister, the stately and somewhat domineering Amalafrida in prison at Carthage. Soon after her brother's death she was executed or murdered, by order of her cousin the Catholic reformer, Hilderic. This outrage was keenly resented by the court of Ravenna. Hostilities between the two states were apparently imminent, but probably Amalasuentha felt that war, whether successful or unsuccessful, would be too dangerous for the dynasty, and sullen alienation took the place of the preparation of fleets and armies.

215

JUSTINIAN AND HIS NOBLES, FROM THE MOSAICS AT RAVENNA.

In June, 531, five years after the accession of Athalaric, the elderly and effeminate Hilderic was deposed by his martial subjects who had long chafed under the rule of such a sovereign, and his cousin, the warlike Gelimer, ascended the throne. The deposition of Hilderic, followed for the present not by his death but by his close imprisonment, furnished the ambitious Justinian with a fair pretext for war, since Hilderic was not only the ally of the Empire, and a Catholic, but was descended on his mother's side from the great Theodosius and related to many of the Byzantine nobility. In spite of the opposition of the more cautious among his counsellors, Justinian decided to despatch an expedition for the conquest of Carthage, and about Midsummer, 533, a fleet of 500 ships, manned by 20,000 sailors and conveying 15,000 soldiers (10,000 infantry and 5,000 cavalry), sailed forth from the Bosphorus into the Sea of Marmora, bound for the Libyan waters.

At the head of the army was Belisarius, now about twenty-eight years of age, a man who came, like his Imperial master, from the highlands of Illyricum, but who, unlike that master, was probably of noble lineage. Three years before, he had won the battle of Daras, defeating the Persian general, whose army was nearly twice as numerous as his own, and he had already shown signs of that profound knowledge of the science, and that wonderful mastery of the art of war which he was afterwards to display in many a hard-fought campaign, and which entitled him to a place in the innermost circle of the greatest generals that the world has seen.

The voyage of the Imperial fleet was slow and tedious, and had the Vandal king been well served by his ambassadors there was ample time to have anticipated its attack. But Gelimer seems to have been quite ignorant of the projected expedition, and had actually sent off some of his best troops under the command of his brother, Tzazo, to suppress a rebellion which had broken out in Sardinia. Moreover, the estrangement between Vandals and Ostrogoths was a most fortunate event for the Imperial cause. In consequence of that estrangement Belisarius was able to land in Sicily to refresh his soldiers wearied with a long voyage, and to obtain accurate information as to the preparations, or rather no-preparations, of the enemy.

Early in September the army landed at the promontory of Caput-vada, about one hundred and thirty miles south-east of Carthage, and began their march towards the capital. They journeyed unopposed through friendly Catholic villages, and royal parks beautiful in verdure and abounding in luscious fruits, until, after eleven days, they arrived at the tenth milestone[1] from Carthage, and here came the shock of war. Gelimer had planned a combined attack on (13th Sept., 533) the Imperial army, by himself, operating on their rear, and his brother Ammatas making a vigorous sally from Carthage and attacking them in front. If the two attacks had been really simultaneous, it might have gone hardly with the Imperial army; but Ammatas came too soon to the field, was defeated and slain. Gelimer arriving later on in the day inflicted a partial defeat on the troops of Belisarius, but, coming to the spot where lay the dead body of his brother, he stayed so long to bewail and to bury him that Belisarius had time to rally his forces and to convert defeat into victory.

Gelimer fled to the open country. Belisarius pressed on and without further opposition entered the gates of Carthage, where he was received by the majority of the citizens, who spoke the Latin tongue, and professed the Catholic faith, with unconcealed rejoicing. Some Roman merchants who had been confined for many weeks in the dungeon were (15th Sept., 533) liberated by their anxious gaoler. But the Imperial victory came too late for the captive Hilderic, as he had been already put to death in prison by order of his successor. There was thus neither friend nor foe left to bar Justinian's claim to rule as Augustus over Africa.

Belisarius was accompanied in this, as in many subsequent expeditions, by his secretary and counsellor, the rhetorician Procopius, who has written the story of their wars in a style worthy of his hero-chief. He describes the sensations of surprise at their own good fortune, with which Belisarius and his suite found themselves at noon of the 15 th September, sitting in Gelimer's gorgeous banquet-hall, served by the Vandal's lackeys and partaking of the sumptuous repast which he had ordered to be prepared in celebration of his anticipated victory. At this point Procopius indulges in a strain of meditation which is not unusual with him:

We may see hereby how Fortune wantons in her pride, how she teaches us that she is mistress of all things, and that she will not suffer Man to have anything which he can call his own"

Though Carthage was taken, the war was not yet over. Tzazo, who, in the midst of his victories in Sardinia, heard of the ruin of his country, hastened home with a valiant and hitherto triumphant army, and joined his brother, Gelimer, on the plain of Bulla, in Numidia. When

---

1. *Ad Decimum.*

the two brothers met they clasped one another round the neck and for long could not loosen their hold, yet could they speak no word to each other, but wrung their hands and wept; and so did each one of the companions of Gelimer with some one of the officers of the army of Sardinia. But tears soon gave place to the longing for revenge, and the two armies, forming one strong and determined host, moved eastward to Tricamaron, about twenty miles distant from Carthage, and began a partial blockade of the capital.

On the 15 th December Belisarius met the Vandals in battle-array. The fight was more stubbornly contested than that of Ad Decimum; but Tzazo fell in the thickest of the battle, and again the impulsive nature of Gelimer was so moved by the sight of a brother's blood that he renounced the struggle for his crown and galloped away from the field.

Now the conquest of Africa was indeed completed, but Belisarius was set upon capturing the person of the fugitive king, as an ornament to his triumph and the pledge of victory. The tedious task was delegated to a Teutonic chief named Pharas, who for three months beleaguered the impregnable hill on the confines of Mauritania, on the summit of which was the fortress in which Gelimer had taken refuge. The incidents which marked his final surrender have been often described. He who had been of late the daintily-living lord of Africa found life hard indeed among the rough, half-savage Moors, who were partly his body-guard and partly his gaolers.

An ambassador sent by Pharas to exhort him to surrender and cast himself on the clemency of Justinian brought back his proud refusal to submit to one who had done him so much undeserved wrong, but brought back also a pathetic request that his courteous foe would grant him three things, a lyre, a sponge, and a loaf of bread. The loaf was to remind him of the taste of baked bread, which he had not eaten for months; the sponge was to bathe his eyes, weakened with continual tears; the lyre, to enable him to set to music an ode which he had composed on the subject of his misfortunes. A few days more passed by, and then came Gelimer's offer to surrender at discretion, trusting to the generosity of the emperor. What finally broke down his proud spirit was the sight of a delicately nurtured child, the son of one of his Vandal courtiers, fighting with a dirty little Moor for a half-baked piece of dough, which the two boys had pulled out of the ashes where it was baking.

Gelimer, whose reason was perhaps somewhat unhinged by his

hardships, gave a loud laugh—professedly at the instability of human greatness—when brought into the presence of Belisarius. He and his captors soon embarked for Constantinople, where they arrived probably about the middle of 534. It had thus taken less than a year to level with the ground the whole fabric of Vandal dominion, reared a century before by the terrible Gaiseric, and to reunite Africa to the Roman Republic. Belisarius received a splendid triumph, the chief figure of which was of course the captive Gelimer, who, with a purple robe on his shoulders, paced through the streets, shouting ever and *anon* in a melancholy voice, "Vanity of vanities, all is vanity."

When the procession reached the palace, Gelimer by constraint and Belisarius willingly prostrated themselves at the feet of "Justinianus Augustus." The promises on the faith of which the Vandal king had surrendered himself were well kept. He might have been raised to the dignity of patrician, if he would have renounced his Arian creed. As it was, he lived in honourable exile on the large estates in Galatia, which he had received from the bounty of the emperor.

In the same year (534) which witnessed the triumph of Belisarius over the conquered Vandals came the final overthrow of the Burgundian monarchy. In 523 Sigismund, the son-in-law of Theodoric, the convert to Catholicism who ordered the murder of his son, had been defeated in battle by the sons of Clovis, and together with his wife and two sons had been thrown down a deep well and so slain. Theodoric, incensed at the murder of his grandson, had taken part against Sigismund and obtained a large accession of territory in Dauphiné as the price of his alliance with the Franks. But a brother of Sigismund's, named Godamir, rallied the beaten Burgundians, defeated the Franks in a battle in which one of their kings was slain, and succeeded in maintaining for eleven years longer the independence of his nation. In the year 532, however, the Frankish kings again entered the valley of the Rhone with their desolating hosts, and in 534 they completed its conquest and added it to the great unwieldy monarchy over which they ruled in a kind of family partnership.

In Spain too the Frankish kings had achieved some successes, and at the cost of a descendant of Theodoric. Amalaric, king of the Visigoths, had married, probably after his grandfather's death, Clotilda, daughter of Clovis, and for a time seems to have pursued a tolerant policy towards the Catholics, but gradually drifted into a position of unreasoning and barbarous hostility towards them, hostility from which his own wife was not exempted. He caused filth to be cast at the devout Clotilda, when she was on her way to the Catholic *basilica*, nay, he even lifted his hand to strike her. The cowardly blow brought blood, and the drops of this blood, royal and Frankish, collected on a handkerchief and sent northward over the Pyrenees, brought the two brother-kings of the Franks into Spain (431).

Amalaric was defeated,[2] fled to Barcelona, and sought to escape thence by sea, probably to Italy; but his passage to the harbour was barred by his own mutinous soldiers, and he perished by a javelin hurled by one of them. The Franks returned, enriched with great booty, to their own land, and Theudis, the Ostrogothic noble, whose power had long overshadowed his master's, and who was accused by some of having caused the mutiny of his troops, succeeded to his throne.

So had the great Arian league and the network of family alliances, by which Theodoric had sought to guard it from the spoiler, passed away into nothingness: and thus did the Ostrogothic kingdom now stand alone and without allies before the rejuvenated Empire, flushed with victory, and possessing such a head as Justinian, such a terrible right arm as Belisarius. Not many months had elapsed from the battle of Tricamaron when the ambassadors of the Empire appeared at Ravenna to present those claims out of which Greek ingenuity would soon fashion a pretext for war. The town of Lilybæum, in Sicily had long ago been handed over by Theodoric to the Vandal king Thrasamund as part of Amalafrida's dowry. Apparently it had been recaptured by the Goths after the death of the Vandal queen, but Justinian urged that it was still the rightful possession of Gelimer, and therefore of himself, who now by the fortune of war was Gelimer's master.

Then there were certain Huns, deserters from the emperor's service, who had been allowed by the governor of Naples to enlist in the Gothic army. A Gothic general who had to conduct some warlike operations near Sirmium had crossed the Danube and sacked Gratiana, a city in Mœsia. All these grievances were rehearsed by the Imperial ambassador, who hinted, not obscurely, that war would follow if they were not redressed.

In fact, however, the real object of the embassy which came with this formal statement of grievances was to discuss a strange proposition which had been made by Amalasuentha, one for the understanding of which we must go back a few years (we are not told exactly

2. At Narbonne. The part of Languedoc called Septimania was still held by the Visigoths.

221

how many) to an event which illustrates the manner in which the Gothic princess conducted the education of her son. She wished, we are told, to have him brought up in all respects after the manner of the Romans, and forced him every day to go to the house of a grammarian to learn his lessons.

Moreover, she chose out three Gothic ancients, men of wisdom and of calm, reasonable temperament, and assigned these venerable persons to Athalaric as his constant companions. This manner of training the kingly boy did not at all suit the ideas of the Goths, the Roman historian says, "because they wished him to be trained in more barbaric style in order that they might have the more liberty for oppressing their subjects": a modern historian may suggest, "because they remembered their own childhood and knew what was in the heart of a boy," of which Amalasuentha, who was evidently elderly and wise in her cradle, had no conception.

One day, for some childish offence, the young king was slapped in the face by his mother, and thereupon, in a tempest of passionate tears, he burst out of the women's apartments and appeared sobbing in the men's hall of audience. All Gothic hearts were stirred when they saw the princely Amal thus mishandled, and the warriors began to hint the insulting suspicion that Amalasuentha wished to educate her child into his grave, that she might marry again and make her new husband king of the Goths and Romans. The nobles of the nation were gathered together, and seeking an audience with the princess, their spokesman thus addressed her:

O lady, you are not dealing justly by us, nor doing that which is expedient for the nation, in your way of educating your son. Letters and book-learning are very different from manly courage and fortitude, and to hand a lad over to the teaching of greybeards is generally the way to make him a coward and a *caitiff*. He who is to do daring deeds and win glory in the world must be emancipated from fear of the *pedagogue* and be practising martial exercises. Your father Theodoric would never suffer his Goths to send their sons to the grammarian-school, for he used to say: 'If they fear their teacher's strap now they will never look on sword or javelin without a shudder.' And he himself, who won the lordship of such wide lands, and died king of so fair a kingdom which he had not inherited from his fathers, knew nothing even by hearsay of this book-learning. Therefore, lady, you must say 'goodbye' to these *pedagogues*, and give Athalaric companions of his own age, who may grow up with him to manhood and make of him a valiant king after the pattern of the barbarians.

Amalasuentha listened with outward calmness to this harangue, and though filled with secret indignation recognised the people's voice to which she was forced to bow. The meek old men were removed from Athalaric's bedchamber; he was released from his daily attendance on the grammarian; and some young Gothic nobles were assigned to him as associates. But the rebound was too sudden. His barbarian comrades led astray the young king's heart after wine and women. His health began to be undermined by his excesses, and the surly ill-nature which he manifested towards his mother was a sure indication of the defenceless position in which she would find herself as soon as her son should assume the reins of government. Feeling these reins slipping from her grasp, she opened secret negotiations with Justinian to assure herself of his protection in case she should be driven from Italy by rebellion.

But in the meantime she singled out three of the Gothic nobles who had been prominent in the revolt against her authority and sent them, on one pretext or another connected with the defence of the realm, to widely separated towns on the extreme borders of Italy. Though severed, they still found means to hold mutual communications and to plot the downfall of the princess. Informed of this conspiracy, she freighted a vessel with forty thousand pounds' weight of gold (£1,6000,000) and sent it to Dyrrhachium, on the eastern shore of the Adriatic, to await her further orders. If things should go ill with her she would thus, in any event, have a line of retreat opened towards Constantinople and a comfortable subsistence assured to her in that capital.

Having taken these precautions, she gave a commission to some of her bravest and most devoted followers (for she evidently had a strong party in her favour) to seek out the three disaffected nobles in their various places of banishment and put them to death. Her henchmen obeyed her bidding; no popular tumult was excited; the sceptre seemed to be more firmly than ever grasped by the hand of the princess; the ship, without having discharged its cargo, was ordered back from Dyrrhachium, and there came a slight lull in the underground negotiations with Constantinople.

But another candidate for the favours of Justinian was also appearing in the royal family of the Goths. Theodahad, son of Amalfrida, and therefore nephew of Theodoric, was a man now pretty far advanced in middle life. He had received in his boyhood that literary and rhetorical training which Amalasuentha yearned to bestow on her son; he was well versed in the works of the Roman orators and could discourse learnedly on the dialogues of Plato. Unhappily, this varnish of intellectual culture covered a thoroughly vile and rotten character. He was averse to all the warlike employments of his forefathers, but his whole heart was set on robbery, under the form of civilisation, by means of extortion and chicane.

He had received from his uncle ample estates in the fertile province of Tuscany, but he was one who, as the common people said, "could not endure a neighbour," and, on one pretence or other, he was perpetually adding farm after farm and villa after villa to his enormous property. Already during his uncle's reign the grave pen of Cassiodorus had been twice employed to censure Theodahad's avarice, "a vulgar vice, which the kinsman of the king and a man of Amal blood is especially bound to avoid," and to complain that "you, who should have shown an example of glorious moderation, have caused the scandal of high-handed spoliation."

After Theodoric's death the process of unjust accumulation went on rapidly. From every part of Tuscany the cry went up that the provincials were being oppressed and their lands taken from them on no pretext whatever; and the counts of the Royal Patrimony had to complain that even the king's domain was suffering from Theodahad's depredations.

He was summoned to the *Comitatus* or King's Court, at Ravenna; his various acts of alleged spoliation were inquired into; their injustice was clearly proved, and he was compelled by Amalasuentha to restore the wrongfully appropriated lands.

It was perhaps before this process was actually begun, but after Theodahad was made aware that the clamour against him was growing louder and had reached the ears of his cousin, that he sought an interview with the Bishops of Ephesus and Philippi, who had come over to Italy on some ecclesiastical errand from the emperor to the Pope.

To these clerical ambassadors Theodahad made the extraordinary proposal that Justinian should buy of him the province of Tuscany for a certain large sum of money, to which was to be added the dignity of a senator of Constantinople. If this negotiation could be carried through, the diligent student of Plato and Cicero proposed to end his days in dignified retirement at the Eastern capital.

We may now return to the palace of Ravenna and be present at the audience granted, probably in the summer of 534, by Amalasuentha to Alexander, the ambassador of Justinian. To the demands for the surrender of Lilybæum and the complaints as to the enlistment of Hunnish deserters, Amalasuentha made, in public, a suitable and sprited reply:

> It was not the part of a great and courageous monarch to pick a quarrel with an orphaned king, too young to be accurately informed of what was going on in all parts of his dominions, about such paltry matters as the possession of Lilybæum, a barren and worthless rock of Sicily, about ten wild Huns who had sought refuge in Italy, and about the offence which the Gothic soldiers had, in their ignorance, committed against a friendly city in Mœsia.
>
> Justinian should look at the other side of the account, should remember the aid and comfort which his soldiers, on their expedition against the Vandals, had received from the friendly Ostrogoths in Sicily, and should ask himself whether without that aid he would ever have recovered possession of Africa. If Lilybæum did belong by right to the emperor it was not too great a reward for him to bestow on his young ally for such opportune assistance.

This was publicly the answer of Amalasuentha—a bold and determined refusal to surrender the rock of Lilybæum. In her private interview with the ambassador, she assured him that she was ready to fulfil her compact and to make arrangements for the transfer to the emperor of the whole of Italy.

When the two sets of ambassadors, civil and ecclesiastical, returned to Constantinople the emperor perceived that here were two negotiations to be carried on of the most delicate kind and requiring the presence of a master of diplomacy. He accordingly despatched to Ravenna a rhetorician named Peter, a man of considerable intellectual endowments—he was a historian as well as an orator—and one who had, eighteen years before, held the high office of consul. But it was apparently winter before Peter started on his journey, and when he arrived at Aulon (now Valona), just opposite Brindisi, he heard such

225

startling tidings as to the events which had occurred on the Italian side of the Adriatic, that he waited there and asked for further instructions from his master as to the course which he was to pursue in the existing position of affairs. (2nd Oct., 534.)

First of all came the death of the unhappy lad, Athalaric, in his eighteenth year, the victim of unwise strictness, followed by unwise licence, and of the barbarian's passion for swinish and sensual pleasures. When her son was dead, Amalasuentha, who had an instinctive feeling that the Goths would never submit to undisguised female sovereignty, took a strange and desperate resolution. She sent for Theodahad, now the only surviving male of the stock of Theodoric, and, fashioning her lips to a smile, began to apologise for the humiliating sentence which had issued against him from the King's Court.

She had known all along, she said, that her boy would die, and as he, Theodahad, would then be the one hope of Theodoric's line, she had wished to abate his unpopularity and set him straight with his future subjects by strictly enforcing their rights against him. Now all that was over: his record was clear and she was ready to invite him to become the partner of her throne;[3] but he must first swear the most solemn oaths that he would be satisfied with the name of royalty and that the actual power should remain, as it had done for nine years, in the hands of Amalasuentha.

Theodahad cheerfully swore tremendous oaths to the observance of this compact. Proclamations in the name of the two new sovereigns were put forth to all the Goths and Italians. In them Theodahad grovelled in admiration of the wisdom, the virtue, the eloquence of the noble lady who had raised him to so high a station and who had done him the inestimable favour of making him feel her justice before she bestowed upon him her grace. Few weeks, however, passed, before Amalasuentha was a prisoner, hurried away to a little lonely island in the Lake of Bolsena in Tuscany by order of the partner of her throne. Having taken this step, Theodahad began with craven apologies to excuse it to the Eastern Cæsar.

He had done no harm to Amalasuentha; he would do no harm to her, though she had been guilty of the most nefarious designs against him: he only sought to protect her from the vengeance of the kinsmen of the three Gothic nobles whom she had murdered.

An embassy composed of Roman Senators was ordered to carry

---

3. As colleague, not as husband; Theodahad's wife, Gudelina, was still living when he ascended the throne.

this tale to Justinian and to confirm it by a letter which, under duresse, had been wrung from the unfortunate princess in her prison.
When the ambassadors arrived at Constantinople one of them spoke
the words of the part which had been set down for him and declared
that Theodahad had done nothing against Amalasuentha of which any
reasonable complaint could be made; but the others, headed by the
brave Liberius, "a man of singularly high and noble nature, and of the
most watchful regard to truth," told the whole story exactly as it had
happened to the emperor. The result was a despatch to the ambassador
Peter enjoining him to find means of assuring Amalasuentha that Justinian would exert all his influence for her safety, and to inform Theodahad publicly, in presence of all his counsellors, that it was at his own
peril that he would touch a hair of the head of the Gothic queen.

Scarcely, however, had Peter touched the Italian shore—he had
not conveyed a letter to the prison nor uttered a word in the palace—
when the sad tragedy was ended. The relations of the three nobles,
who had "blood-feud" with the queen, and who were perhaps, according to the code of barbarian morality, justified in avenging their
death, made their way to Amalasuentha's island prison, and there, in
that desolate abode, the daughter of Theodoric met her death at their
hands, dying with all that stately dignity and cold self-possession with
which she had lived.

Justinian's ambassador at once proceeded to the King's Court, and
there, in the presence of all the Gothic nobles, denounced the foul
deed which they had permitted to be done, and declared that for this
there must be "truceless war" between the emperor and them. Theodahad, as stupid as he was vile, renewed his ridiculous protestations
that he had no part in the violence done to Amalasuentha, but had
heard of it with the utmost regret, and this although he had already
rewarded the murderers with signal tokens of his favour.

Thus, by the folly of the wise and the criminal audacity of the
coward, had a train been laid for the destruction of the Ostrogothic
kingdom. All the petty pretexts for war, the affair of Lilybæum, the
Hunnish deserters, the sack of Gratiana, faded into insignificance before this new and most righteous cause of quarrel. If Hilderic's deposition had been avenged by the capture of Carthage, with far more
justice might the death of the noble Amalasuentha be avenged by the
capture of Ravenna and of Rome.

In the great war which was soon to burst upon Italy Justinian
could figure not only as the protector of the provincials, not only as

the defender of the Catholics, but as the avenger of the blood of the daughter of Theodoric.

PIECE OF FORTY NUMMI OF THEODAHAD.
NUMMI (COPPER).

CHAPTER 16

Belisarius

The emperor's preparations for the Gothic war were soon made, and in the summer of 535 two armies were sent forth from Constantinople, one destined to act on the east and the other on the west of the Adriatic. When we think of the mighty armaments by means of which Pompey and Cæsar, or even Licinius and Constantine, had contended for the mastery of the Roman world, the forces entrusted to the generals of Justinian seem strangely small. We are not informed of the precise number of the army sent to Dalmatia, but the whole tenor of the narrative leads us to infer that it consisted of not more than 3,000 or 4,000 men. It fought with varying fortunes but with ultimate success. Salona, the Dalmatian capital, was taken by the Imperial army, wrested from them by the Goths, retaken by the Imperialists.

The Imperial general, a brave old barbarian named Mundus, fell dead by the side of his slaughtered son; but another general took his place, and being well supported by a naval expedition, succeeded, as has been said, in reconquering Salona, drove out the Gothic generals, and reincorporated Dalmatia with the Empire. This province, which had for many generations been treated almost as a part of Italy, was now for four centuries to be for the most part a dependency of Constantinople. The Dalmatian war was ended by the middle of 536.

But it was of course to the Italian expedition that the eyes of the spectators of the great drama were most eagerly turned. Here Belisarius commanded, peerless among the generals of his own age, and not surpassed by many of preceding or following ages. The force under his command consisted of only 7,500 men, the greater part of whom were of barbarian origin—Huns, Moors, Isaurians, Gepidse, Heruli, but they were welded together by that instinct of military discipline and that unbounded admiration for their great commander and con-

229

fidence in his success which is the surest herald of victory. Not only in nationality but in mode of fighting they were utterly unlike the armies with which republican Rome had won the sovereignty of the world. In those days it might have been truly said to the inhabitant of the seven-hilled city as Macaulay has imagined Capys saying to Romulus:

"Thine, Roman! is the pilum:
Roman! the sword is thine.
The even trench, the bristling mound,
The legion's ordered line"—

but now, centuries of fighting with barbarian foes, especially with the nimble squadrons of Persia, had completely changed the character of the Imperial tactics. It was to the deadly aim of his *Hippo-toxotai* (mounted bowmen) that Belisarius, in pondering over his victories, ascribed his antonishing success.

He said that at the beginning of his first great battle he had carefully studied the characteristic differences of each army, in order that he might prevent his little band from being over-borne by sheer force of numbers. The chief difference which he noted was that almost all the Roman (Imperialist) soldiers and their Hunnish allies were good *Hippo-toxotai*, while the Goths had none of them practised the art of shooting on horseback. Their cavalry fought only with javelins and swords, and their archers fought on foot covered by the horsemen. Thus till the battle became a hand-to-hand encounter the horsemen could make no reply to the arrows discharged at them from a distance, and were therefore easily thrown into disorder, while the foot-soldiers, though able to reply to the enemy's archers, could not stand against the charges of his horse.[1]

From this passage we can see what were the means by which Belisarius won his great victories. While the Goth, with his huge broadsword and great javelin, chafing for a hand-to-hand encounter with the foe, found himself mowed down by the arrows of a distant enemy, the nimble barbarian who called himself a Roman solder discharged his arrows at the cavalry, dashed in impetuous onset against the infantry, wheeled round, feigned flight, sent his arrows against the too eagerly advancing horsemen, in fact, by Parthian tactics won a Roman

1. Procophis, *De Bello Gotthico*, i, 27.

victory, or to use a more modern illustration, the *Hippo-toxotai* were the "Mounted Rifles" of the Imperial army.

The expedition under the command of Belisarius made its first attack on the Gothic kingdom in Sicily. Here the campaign was little more than a triumphant progress. In reliance on its professions of loyalty, Theodoric and his successors had left the wealthy and prosperous island almost bare of Gothic troops, and now the provincials, eager to form once more a part of the Eternal Roman Empire, opened the gates of city after city to the troops of Justinian; only at Palermo was a stout resistance made by the Gothic soldiers who garrisoned the city. The walls were strong, and that part of them which bordered on the harbour was thought to be so high and massive as not to need the defence of soldiers.

When unobserved by the foe, Belisarius hoisted up his men, seated in boats, to the yard-arms of his ships and made them clamber out of the boats on to the unguarded parapet. This daring manœuvre gave him the complete command of the Gothic position, and the garrison capitulated without delay. So was the whole island of Sicily won over to the realm of Justinian before the end of 535, and Belisarius, Consul for the year, rode through the streets of Syracuse on the last day of his term of office, scattering his *"donative"* to the shouting soldiers and citizens.

Operations in 536, the second year of the war, were suspended for some months by a military mutiny at Carthage, which called for the presence of Belisarius in Africa. But the mutineers quailed before the very name of their late commander. Carthage was delivered from the siege wherewith they were closely pressing it, a battle was won in the open field, and the rebellion though not yet finally crushed was sufficiently weakened for Belisarius to return to Sicily in the late spring of 536. He crossed the Straits of Messina, landed in Italy, was received by the provincials of Bruttii and Lucania with open arms, and met with no check to his progress till, probably in the early days of June, he stood with his army under the walls of the little town of Neapolis, which in our own days is represented by a successor ten times as large, the superbly situated city of Naples.

Here a strong Gothic garrison held the place for Theodahad and prevented the surrender which many of the citizens, especially those of the poorer class, would gladly have made. An orator, who was sent by the Neapolitans to plead their cause in the general's camp, vainly endeavoured to persuade Belisarius to march forward to Rome, leaving the fate of, Naples to be decided under the walls of the capital. The Imperial general could not leave so strong a place untaken in his rear, and though himself anxious enough to meet Theodahad, commenced the siege of the city. His land army was supported by the fleet which was anchored in the harbour, yet the operations of the siege languished, and after twenty days Belisarius seemed to be no nearer winning the prize of war than on the first day.

But just then one of his soldiers, a brave and active Isaurian mountaineer, reported that he had found a means of entering the empty aqueduct through which, till Belisarius severed the communication, water had been supplied to the city. The passage was narrow, and at one point the rock had to be filed away to allow the soldiers to pass, but all this was done without arousing the suspicions of the besieged, and one night Belisarius sent six hundred soldiers, headed by the Isaurian, into the aqueduct, having arranged with them the precise portion of the walls to which they were to rush as soon as they emerged into the city. The daring attempt succeeded. The soldiers found themselves in a large cavern with a narrow opening at the top, on the brink of which was a cottage. Some of the most active among them swarmed up the sides of the cave, found the cottage inhabited by one old woman who was easily frightened into silence, and let down a stout leather thong which they fastened to the stem of an olive-tree, and by which all their comrades mounted.

They rushed to that part of the walls beneath which Belisarius was standing, blew their trumpets, and assisted the besiegers to ascend. The Gothic garrison were taken prisoners and treated honourably by Belisarius. The city suffered some of the usual horrors of a sack from the wild Hunnish soldiers of the Empire, but these were somewhat mitigated, and the citizens who had been taken prisoners were restored to liberty, in compliance with the earnest entreaties of Belisarius.

The fall of Neapolis, to whose assistance no Gothic army had marched, and the unhindered conquest of Southern Italy crowned the already towering edifice of Theodahad's unpopularity. It is not likely that this selfish and unwarlike pedant—a "nithing," as they probably called him—had ever been aught but a most unwelcome necessity to the lion-hearted Ostrogoths, and for all but the families and friends of the three slain noblemen, the imprisonment and the permitted murder of his benefactress must have deepened dislike into horror. His dishonest intrigues with Constantinople were known to many, intrigues in which even after Amalasuentha's death he still offered himself and his crown for sale to the emperor, and the emperor, not-withstanding his brave words about a truceless war, seemed willing to pay the caitiff his price.

Some gleams of success which shone upon the Gothic arms in Dalmatia towards the end of 535 filled the feeble soul of Theodahad with presumptuous hope, and he broke off with arrogant faithlessness the negotiations which he had begun. Still, with all the gallant men under him longing to be employed, he struck not one blow for his crown and country, but shut himself up in his palace, seeking by the silliest auguries to ascertain the issue of the war. The most notable of these vaticinations was "the Augury of the Hogs," which he practised by the advice of a certain Jewish magician. He shut up in separate pens three batches of hogs, each batch consisting of ten. One batch was labelled "Romans" (meaning the Latin-speaking inhabitants of Italy), another "Goths," and the third "Soldiers of the Emperor."

They were all left for a certain number of days without food, and when the appointed day was come, and the pens were opened, all the "Gothic" hogs but two were found dead. The "Emperor's soldiers," with very few exceptions, were living; of the "Romans" half only were alive, and all had lost their bristles. Ridiculous as the manner of divination was, it furnished no inapt type of the miseries which the Gothic war was to bring upon all concerned in it, and not least upon that Latin population which was still so keen to open its gates to Belisarius.

But, as I have said, when Neapolis had fallen, the brave Gothic warriors felt that they had submitted too long to the rule of a das-tard like Theodahad. They met in arms, a nation-parliament, on the plain of Regeta, about forty-three miles from Rome in the direction of Terracina. Here there was plenty of grass for the pasture of their horses, and here, while the steeds grazed, the dismounted riders could deliberate as to the fortunes of the state. There was found to be an unanimous determination that Theodahad should be dethroned, and, instead of him, they raised on the shield, Witigis, a man somewhat past middle age, not of noble birth, who had distinguished himself by his deeds of valour thirty years before in the war of Sirmium.

As soon as Theodahad heard the tidings of his deposition, he sought to escape with all speed to Ravenna. The new king ordered a Goth named Optaris to pursue him and bring him back alive or dead. Optaris had his own wrongs to avenge, for he had lost a rich and beautiful bride through Theodahad's purchased interference on behalf

233

of another suitor. He followed him day and night, came up with him while still on the road, "made him lie down on the pavement, and cut his throat as a priest cuts the throat of a victim."[2] So did Theodahad perish, one of the meanest insects that ever crawled across the page of history.

Witigis, the new king of the Goths, had personal courage and some experience of battles, but he was no statesman and, as the event proved, no general. By his advice, the Goths committed the astounding blunder of abandoning Rome and concentrating their forces for defence in the north of Italy. It is true that a garrison of four thousand Goths was left in the city under the command of the brave veteran Leudaris, but, unsupported by any army in the field, this body of men was too small to hold so vast a city unless they were aided by the inhabitants. As for Witigis, he marched northward to Ravenna with the bulk of the Gothic army and there celebrated, not a victory, but a marriage. The only remaining scion of the race of Theodoric was a young girl named Matasuentha, the sister of Athalaric.

In some vain hope of consolidating his dynasty, Witigis divorced his wife and married this young princess. The marriage was, as might have been expected, an unhappy one. Matasuentha shared the Romanising tendencies of her mother, and her spirit revolted against the alleged reasons of state which gave her this elderly and low-born barbarian for a husband. In the darkest hour of the Gothic fortunes (540) Matasuentha was suspected of opening secret negotiations with the Imperial leaders, and even of seeking to aid the progress of their arms by crime.

By the end of November, 536, Belisarius, partly aided by the treachery of the Gothic general who commanded in Samnium, had recovered for the Empire all that part of the Italian peninsula which, till lately, formed the Kingdom of Naples. Pope Silverius, though he had sworn under duresse an oath of fealty to King Witigis, sent messengers offering to surrender the Eternal City, and the four thousand Goths, learning what negotiations were going forward, came to the conclusion that it was hopeless for them to attempt to defend the city against such a general as Belisarius and against the declared wish of the citizens. They accordingly marched out of Rome by a northern gate

2. There was perhaps an interval of some months during which Theodahad was in hiding. His deposition is fixed by one authority (Anastasius) to August, and his death, by another (Agnellus), to December, 536, but all our chronological details as to this part of the history are vague and uncertain.

as Belisarius entered it on the south.[3] The brave old Leudaris, refusing to abandon his trust, was taken prisoner, and sent, together with the keys of the city, to Justinian, most undoubted evidences of victory.

Belisarius took up his headquarters in the Pincian Palace (on that hill at the north of the city which is now the fashionable promenade of the Roman aristocracy), and from thence commanded a wide outlook over that part of the Campagna on which, as he knew, a besieging army would shortly encamp. He set to work with all speed to repair the walls of the city, which had been first erected by Aurelian and afterwards repaired by Honorius at dates respectively 260 and 130 years before the entry of Belisarius. Time and barbarian sieges had wrought much havoc on the line of defence, the work of repair had to be done in haste, and to this day some archaeologists think that it is possible to recognise the parts repaired by Belisarius through the rough style of the work and the heterogeneous nature of the materials employed in it. All through the winter months his ships were constantly arriving with cargoes of corn from Sicily, which were safely stored away in the great state-warehouses.

These preparations were viewed with dismay by the citizens, who had fondly imagined that their troubles were over when the Gothic soldiers marched forth by the Porta Flaminia; that any fighting which might follow would take place on some distant field, and that they would have nothing to do but calmly to await the issue of the combat. This, however, was by no means the general's idea of the right way of playing the game. He knew that the Goths immensely outnumbered his forces; he knew also that they were of old bad besiegers of cities, the work of siege requiring a degree of patience and scientific skill to which the barbarian nature could not attain; and his plan was to wear them down by compelling them to undertake a long and wearisome blockade before he tried conclusions with them in the open field. If the Roman clergy and people had known that this was in his thoughts, they would probably not have been so ready to welcome the eagles of the emperor into their city.

Some hint of the growing disaffection of the Roman people was carried to Ravenna and quickened the impatience of Witigis, who was now eager to retrieve the blunder which he had committed in the evacuation of Rome. He marched southward with a large army, which is represented to us as consisting of 150,000 men, and in the early days of March he was already at the other end of the Milvian

3. December, 536.

235

Bridge,[4] about two miles from Rome. Belisarius had meant to dispute the passage of the Tiber at this point. The fort on the Tuscan side of the river was garrisoned, and a large body of soldiers was encamped on the Roman side; but when the garrison of the fort saw the vast multitude of the enemy, who at sunset pitched their tents upon the plain, they despaired of making a successful resistance, and abandoning the fort under cover of the night, skulked off into the country districts of Latium. Thus one point of the game was thrown away.

Next morning the Goths finding their passage unopposed, marched quietly over the bridge and fell upon the Roman camp. A desperate battle followed, in which Belisarius, exposing himself more than a general should have done, did great deeds of valour. He was mounted on a noble steed, dark roan, with a white star on its forehead, which the barbarians, from that mark on its brow, called "Balan." Some Imperial soldiers who had deserted to the enemy knew the steed and his rider, and shouted to their comrades to aim all their darts at Balan. So the cry "Balan! Balan!" resounded through the Gothic ranks, and though only imperfectly understood by many of the utterers, had the effect of concentrating the fight round Belisarius and the dark-roan steed. The general was nobly protected by the picked troops which formed his guard. They fell by scores around him, but he himself, desperately fighting, received never a wound, though a thousand of the noblest Goths lay dead in the narrow space of ground where this Homeric combat had been going forward.

The Imperialists not merely withstood the Gothic onset, but drove their opponents back to their camp, which had been already erected on the Roman bank of the Tiber. Fresh troops, especially of cavalry, issuing forth from thence turned the tide of battle, and, overborne by irresistible numbers, Belisarius and his soldiers were soon in full flight towards Rome. When they arrived under the walls, with the barbarians so close behind them that they seemed to form one raging multitude, they found the gates closed against them by the panic-stricken garrison. Even Belisarius in vain shouted his orders to open the gates; in his gory face and dust-stained figure the defenders did not recognise their brilliant leader.

A halt was called, a desperate charge was made upon the pursuing Goths, who were already beginning to pour down into the fosse; they were pushed back some distance, not far, but far enough to enable the Imperialists to reform their ranks, to make the presence of the general

4. Now the Ponte Molle, (as at time of first pication).

known to the defenders on the walls, to have the gates opened, and in some sort of military order to enter the city. Thus the sun set on Rome beleaguered, the barbarians outside the city. Belisarius with his gallant band of soldiers thinned but not disheartened by the struggle, within its walls, and the citizens—

with terror dumb,
Or whispering with white lips, 'The foe, they come, they come!'

Of the great Siege of Rome, which began on that day, early in March, 537, and lasted a year and nine days, till March, 538, a siege perhaps the most memorable of all that "Roma Æterna" has seen and has groaned under, as part of the penalty of her undying greatness, it will be impossible here to give even a meagre outline. The events of those wonderful 374 days are chronicled almost with the graphic minuteness of a Kinglake by a man whom we may call the literary assessor of Belisarius, the rhetorician Procopius of Cæsarea. One or two incidents of the siege may be briefly noticed here, and then we must hasten onwards to its close.

Owing to the vast size of Rome not even the host of the Goths was able to accomplish a complete blockade of the city. They formed seven camps six on the left and one on the right bank of the Tiber, and they obstructed eight out of its four teen gates; but while the east and south sides of the city were thus pretty effectually blockaded, there were large spaces in the western circuit by which it was tolerably easy for Belisarius to receive reinforcements, to bring in occasional convoys of provisions, and to send away non-combatants who diminished his resisting power. One of the hardest blows dealt by the barbarians was their severance of the eleven great aqueducts from which Rome received its water.

This privation of an element so essential to the health and comfort of the Roman under the Empire (who resorted to the bath as a modern Italian resorts to the *café* or the music hall), was felt as a terrible blow by all classes, and wrought a lasting change, and not a beneficial one, in the habits of the citizens, and in the sanitary condition of Rome. It also seemed likely to have an injurious effect on the food supply of the city, since the mills in which corn was ground for the daily rations of the people were turned by water-power derived from the aqueduct of Trajan. Belisarius, however, always fertile in resource, a man who, had he lived in the nineteenth century, would assuredly have been a great engineer, contrived to make Father Tiber grind out the daily supply of flour for his Roman children. He moored two barges in the narrowest part of the stream, where the current was the strongest, put his mill-stones on board of them, and hung a water-wheel between them to turn his mills. These river water-mills continued to be used on the Tiber all through the Middle Ages, and even until they were superseded by the introduction of steam.

The Goths did not resign themselves to the slow languors of a blockade till they had made one vigorous and confident attempt at a storm. On the eighteenth day of the siege the terrified Romans saw from their windows the mighty armament approaching the city. A number of wooden towers as high as the walls, mounted on wheels, and drawn by the stout oxen of Etruria, moved menacingly forward amid the triumphant shouts of the barbarians, each of whom had a bundle of boughs and reeds under his arm ready to be thrown into the fosse, and so prepare a level surface upon which the terrible engines might approach the walls. To resist this attack Belisarius had prepared a large number of *balistæ* (gigantic cross-bows worked by machinery and discharging a short wedge-like bolt with such force as to break trees or stones) had planted on the walls, great slings, which the soldiers called Wild Asses (*onagri*), and had set in each gate the deadly machine known as the Wolf, and which was a kind of double portcullis, worked both from above and from below.

But though the Gothic host was approaching with its threatening towers close to the walls, Belisarius would not give the signal, and not a *balista*, nor a Wild Ass was allowed to hurl its missiles against the foe. He only laughed aloud, and bade the soldiers do nothing till he gave the word of command. To the citizens this seemed an evil jest, and they grumbled aloud at the impudence of the general who chose this moment of terrible suspense for merriment. But now when the Goths were close to the fosse, Belisarius lifted his bow, singled out a mail-clad chief, and sent an arrow through his neck, inflicting a deadly wound. A great shout of triumph rose from the Imperial soldiers as the proudly accoutred barbarian rolled in the dust. Another shot, another Gothic chief slain, and again a shout of triumph. Then the signal to shoot was given to the soldiers, and hundreds of bolts from Wild Ass and *balista* were hurtling through the air, aimed not at Gothic soldiers, but at the luckless oxen that drew the ponderous towers.

The beasts being slain, it was impossible for the Goths who were immediately under the walls and exposed to a deadly discharge of arrows from the battlements, to move their towers either backward or forward, and there they remained mere laughing-stocks in their huge immobility, till the end of the day, when they with all the rest of the Gothic enginery were given as a prey to the flames. Then men understood the meaning of the laughter of Belisarius as he watched the preparations of the barbarians and derided their childish simplicity in supposing that he would allow them calmly to move up their towers till they touched his wall, without using his artillery to cripple their advance.

Though the attack with the towers had thus failed there was still fierce fighting to be done on the south-east and north-west of the city. At the Prænestine Gate (*Porta Maggiore*), that noble structure which is formed out of the arcades of the Aqueducts, there was a desperate onslaught of the barbarians, which at one time seemed likely to be successful, but a sudden sortie of Belisarius taking them in their rear turned them to headlong flight. In the opposite quarter the Aurelian Gate was commanded by the mighty tomb-fortress then known as the Mausoleum of Hadrian, and now, in its dismantled and degraded state, as the castle of Sant'Angelo. Here the peculiar shape of the fortress prevented the defenders from using their *balistæ* with proper effect on the advancing foe, and when the besiegers were close under the walls the bolts from the engines flew over their heads. It seemed as if, after all, by the Aurelian Gate the barbarians would enter Rome, when, by a happy instinct, the garrison turned to the marble statues which surrounded the tomb, wrenched them from their bases, and rained down such a terrible shower of legs and arms and heads of gods and goddesses on their barbarian assailants that these soon fled in utter confusion.

The whole result of this great day of assault was to convince Witigis and his counsellors that the city could not be taken in that manner, and that the siege must be turned into a blockade. A general sally which Belisarius ordered, against his better judgment, in order to still the almost mutinous clamours of his troops, and which took place about the fiftieth day of the siege, proved almost as disastrous for the Romans as the assault had done for the Goths. It was manifest that this was not a struggle which could be ended by a single blow on either side. All the miseries of a long siege must be endured both by attackers and attacked, and the only question was on which side patience would first give way—whether the Romans under roofs, but short of provisions, or the Goths better fed, but encamped on the deadly Campagna, would be the first to succumb to hunger and disease.

Witigis had been in his day a brave soldier, but he evidently knew nothing of the art of war. He allowed Belisarius to disencumber himself of many useless consumers of food by sending the women, the children, and the slaves out of the city. His attention was disturbed by feigned attacks, when the reinforcements, which were tardily sent by Justinian, and the convoys of provisions, which had been collected by the wife of Belisarius, the martial Antonina, were to be brought within the walls. And, lastly, when at length, about the ninth month of the siege, he proposed a truce and the reopening of negotiations with Constantinople, he did not even insert in the conditions of the truce any limit to the quantity of supplies which under its cover the Imperialists might introduce into the city. Thus he played the game of his wily antagonist, and abandoned all the advantages—and they were not many—which the nine months of blockade had won for him.

The parleyings which preceded this truce have an especial interest for us, whose forefathers were at this very time engaged in making England their own. The Goths, after complaining that Justinian had broken the solemn compact made between Zeno and Theodoric as to the conquest of Italy from Odovacar, went on to propose terms of compromise. "They were willing," they said, "for the sake of peace to give up Sicily, that large and wealthy island, so important to a ruler who had now become master of Africa."

Belisarius answered with sarcastic courtesy:

Such great benefits should be repaid in kind. We will concede to the Goths the possession of the whole island of Britain, which is much larger than Sicily, and which was once possessed by the Romans as Sicily was once possessed by the Goths.

Of course that country, though much larger than Sicily, was one the possession of which was absolutely unimportant to the emperor and his general.

What mattered it, (they might well say), who owned that misty and poverty-stricken island. The oysters of Rutupiæ, some fine watch-dogs from Caledonia, a little lead from the Malvern Hills, and some cargoes of corn and wool—this was all that the Empire had ever gained from her troublesome conquest. Even in the world of mind Britain had done nothing more than give birth to one second-rate heretic.[5] The curse of poverty and of barbarous insignificance was upon her, and would remain upon

5. Pelagius.

her till the end of time.

The truce, as will be easily understood, brought no alleviation to the sufferings of the Goths, who were now almost more besieged than besiegers, and who were dying by thousands in the unhealthy Campagna. Before the end of March, 538, they broke up their encampment, and marched, in sullen gloom, northwards to defend Ravenna, which was already being threatened by the operations of a lieutenant of Belisarius. The 150,000 men who had hastened to Rome, dreading lest the Imperialists should escape before they could encompass the city, were reduced to but a small portion of that number, perhaps not many more than the 10,000 which, after all his reinforcements had been received, seems to have been the greatest number of actual soldiers serving under Belisarius in the defence of Rome.

I pass rapidly over the events of 538 and 539. The Imperial generals pressed northwards along the Flaminian Way. Urbino, Rimini, Osimo, and other cities in this region were taken by them. But the Goths fought hard, though they gave little proof of strategic skill; and once, when they recaptured the great city of Milan, it looked as though they might almost be about to turn the tide of conquest. Evidently they were far less demoralised by their past prosperity than the Vandals. Perhaps also the Roman population of Italy, who had met with far gentler and more righteous treatment from the Ostrogoths than their compeers in Africa had met with from the Vandals, and who were now suffering the horrors of famine, owing to the operations of the contending armies, assisted the operations of the Byzantine invaders less than the Roman provincials in Africa had done.

Whatever the cause, it was not till the early months of 540, nearly five years after the beginning of the war, that Belisarius and his army stood before the walls and among the rivers of Ravenna, almost the last stronghold of Witigis. Belisarius blockaded the city, and his blockade was a far more stringent one than that which Witigis had drawn around Rome. Still there was the ancient and well-founded reputation for impregnability of the great Adrian City, and, moreover, just at this time the ambassadors, sent by Witigis to Justinian, returned from Constantinople, bearing the emperor's consent to a compromise. Italy, south of the Po, was to revert to the Empire; north of that river, the Goths were still to hold it, and the royal treasure was to be equally divided between the two states. Belisarius called a council of war, and all his officers signed a written opinion "that the proposals of the emperor were excellent, and that no better terms could be obtained from the Barbarians."

This, however, was by no means the secret thought of Belisarius, who had set his heart on taking Witigis as a captive to Constantinople, and laying the keys of Ravenna at his master's feet. A strange proposition which came from the beleaguered city seemed to open the way to the accomplishment of his purpose. The Gothic nobles suggested that he, the great captain, whose might in war they had experienced, should become their leader, should mount the throne of Theodoric, and should be crowned "King of the Italians and Goths," the change in the order of the names indicating the subordinate position which the humbled barbarians were willing to assume. Belisarius seemed to acquiesce in the proposal (though his secretary assures us that he never harboured a thought of disloyalty to his master), and received the oath of the Gothic envoys for the surrender of the city, postponing his own coronation-oath to his new subjects till he could swear it in the presence of Witigis and all his nobles, for Witigis, too, was a consenting, nay, an eager, party to the transaction.

Thus, by an act of dissimulation, which brought some stain on his knightly honour (we are tempted to use the language of chivalry in speaking of these events), but which left no stain on his loyalty to the emperor of Rome, did Belisarius obtain possession of the impregnable Ravenna. He marched in, he and his veterans, into the famine-stricken city. When the Gothic women saw the little dark men filing past them through the streets, and contrasted them with their own long-limbed, flaxen-haired giants, they spat in the faces of their husbands, and said: "Are you men, to have allowed yourselves to be beaten by such manikins as these?"

Before the triumphal entry was finished the Goths had no doubt discovered that they were duped. No coronation oath was sworn. Belisarius, still the humble servant of Justinianus Augustus, did not allow himself to be raised on the shield and saluted as King of the Italians and Goths. The Gothic warriors were kindly treated, but dismissed to their farms between the Apennines and the Adriatic. Ravenna was again an Imperial city, and destined to remain so for two centuries. Witigis, with his wife and children, were carried captives to Constantinople where, before many years were over, the dethroned monarch died. His widow, Matasuentha, was soon remarried to Germanus, the nephew of Justinian, and thus the granddaughter of Theodoric obtained that position as a great lady of Byzantium which was far more

242

gratifying to her taste than the rude royalty of Ravenna.

There is one more personage whose subsequent fortunes must be briefly glanced at here. Cassiodorus, the minister of Theodoric and Amalasuentha, remained, as we regret to find, in the service of Theodahad when sole king and composed his stilted sentences at the bidding of Amalasuentha's murderer. Witigis also employed him to write his address to his subjects on ascending the throne. He does not seem to have taken any part in the siege of Rome, and before the tide of war rolled back upon Ravenna, he had withdrawn from public affairs. He retired to his native town, Squillace, high up on the Calabrian hills, and there founded a monastery and a hermitage in the superintendence of which his happy years glided on till he died, having nearly completed a century of life. His was one of the first and greatest of the literary monasteries which, by perpetuating copies of the Scriptures, and the Greek and Roman classics, have conferred so great a boon on posterity. When Ceolfrid, the abbot of Jarrow, would offer to the Holy Father at Rome a most priceless gift, he sent the far-famed Codex Amiatinus, a copy of the *Vulgate*, made by a disciple of Cassiodorus, if not by Cassiodorus himself.

GOLDEN *SOLIDUS*.
(JUSTIN I. AND JUSTINIAN)

CHAPTER 17

Totila

With the fall of Ravenna, and the captivity of King Witigis, it seemed as if the chapter of Ostrogothic dominion in Italy was ended. In fact, however, the war was prolonged for a further period of thirteen years, a time glorious for the Goths, disgraceful for the Empire, full of lamentation and woe for the unhappy country which was to be the prize of victory.

The departure of Belisarius, summoned to the East by his master in order to conduct another Persian war, left the newly won provinces on an in cline sloping downwards to anarchy. Of all the generals who remained behind, brave and capable men as some of them were, there was none who possessed the unquestioned ascendancy of Belisarius, either in genius or character. Each thought himself as good as the others: there was no subordination, no hearty co-operation towards a common end, but instead of these necessary conditions of success there was an eager emulation in the race towards wealth, and in this ignoble contest the unhappy "Roman," the Italian landholder, for whose sake, nominally, the Gothic war was undertaken, found himself pillaged and trampled upon as he had never been by the most brutal of the barbarians.

Nor were the military officers the only offenders. A swarm of civil servants flew westwards from Byzantium and lighted on the unhappy country. Their duty was to extort money by any and all means for their master, their pleasure to accumulate fortunes for themselves; but whether the *logothete* plundered for the emperor or for himself, the Italian tax-payer equally had the life-blood sucked from his veins. Even the soldiers by whom the marvellous victories of the last five years had been won, found themselves at the mercy of this hateful bureaucracy; arrears of pay left undischarged, fines inflicted, everything

244

done to force upon their embittered souls the reflection that they had served a mean and ungrateful master.

Of all these oppressors of Italy none was more justly abhorred than Alexander the Logothete. This man, who was placed at the head of the financial administration, and who seems by virtue of that position to have been practically supreme in all but military operations, had been lifted from a very humble sphere to eminence, from poverty to boundless wealth, but the one justification which he could always offer for his self-advancement was this, that no one else had been so successful as he in filling the coffers of his master. The soldiers were, by his proceedings against them, reduced to a poor, miserable, and despised remnant. The Roman inhabitants of Italy, especially the nobles, found that he hunted up with wonderful keenness and assiduity, and enforced with relentless sternness all the claims—and they were probably not a few—which the easy-tempered Gothic kings had suffered to lapse.

In their simplicity these nobles may have imagined that they could plead that they were serving the emperor by withholding contributions from the barbarian. Not so, however. Theodoric, now that his dynasty had been overthrown, became again a legitimate ruler, and Justinian as his heir would exact to the uttermost his unclaimed rights. The nature of the grasping logothete was well-known in his own country, and the Byzantines, using the old Greek weapon of satire against an unpopular ruler, called him "Alexander the Scissors," declaring that there was no one so clever as he in clipping the gold coins of the currency without impairing their roundness.

The result of all these oppressions and this misgovernment was to raise up in a marvellous manner the Gothic standard from the dust into which it had fallen. When Belisarius left Italy, only one city still remained to the Goths, the strong city of Ticinum, which is now known as Pavia, and which, from its magnificent position at the angle of the Ticino and the Po, was often in the early Middle Ages the last stronghold to be surrendered in northwestern Italy. Here had the Goths chosen one of their nobles, Ildibad, for their king, but the new king had but one thousand soldiers under him, and his might well seem a desperate cause. Before the end of 540, however, the departure of Belisarius, the wrangling among his successors, the oppressions of Alexander the Logothete, the disaffection of the ruined soldiery had completely changed the face of affairs.

An army of considerable size, consisting in great measure of deserters from the Imperial standard, obeyed the orders of Ildibad; he won a great pitched battle near Treviso over Vitalius, the best of the Imperial generals, and the whole of Italy north of the Po again owned the sway of the Gothic king.

Internal feuds delayed for a little time the revival of the strength of the barbarians. There was strife between Ildibad and the family of the deposed Witigis, and this strife led to Ildibad's assassination and to the election of an utterly incapable successor, Eraric the Rugian. But in the autumn of 541 all these domestic discords were at an end; Eraric had been slain, and the nephew of Ildibad was the universally recognised king of the Ostrogoths. This man, who was destined to reign for eleven years, twice to stand as conqueror within the walls of Rome, to bring back almost the whole of Italy under the dominion of his people, to be in a scarcely lower degree than Theodoric himself the hero and champion of the Ostrogothic race, was the young and gallant Totila.[1]

With true statesmanlike instinct the new king perceived that the cause of the past failure of the Goths lay in the alienated affections of the people of Italy. The greater misgovernment of the emperor's servants, the coldly calculating rapacity of Alexander the Scissors, and the arrogant injustice of the generals, terrible only to the weak, had given him a chance of winning back the love of the Italian people and of restoring that happy state of things which prevailed after the downfall of Odovacar, when all classes, nobles and peasants, Goths and Romans, joined in welcoming Theodoric as their king. Totila therefore kept a strong hand upon his soldiers, sternly repressed all plundering and outrage, and insisted on the peasants being paid for all the stores which the army needed on its march. One day a Roman inhabitant of Calabria came before him to complain of one of the king's life-guardsmen who had committed an outrage upon his daughter. The guardsman, not denying the charge, was at once put in ward.

Then the most influential nobles assembled at the king's tent, and besought him not to punish a brave and capable soldier for such an offence. Totila replied that he mourned as much as they could do over the necessity of taking away the life of one of his countrymen, but that the common good, the safety of the nation, required this sacrifice.

1. This is the form of the name which was known to the Greek writers, and which is now irrevocably accepted by history. It is clear, however, from his coins that the new king called himself Baduila, and we cannot certainly say that he ever accepted the other designation.

At the outset of the war they had all the wealth of Italy and countless brave hearts at their disposal, but all these advantages had availed them nothing because they had an unjust king, Theodahad, at their head. Now the Divine favour on their righteous cause seemed to be giving them the victory, but only by a continuance in righteous deeds could they hope to secure it. With these words he won over even the interceding Goths to his opinion. The guardsman was sentenced to death, and his goods were confiscated for the benefit of the maiden whom he had wronged.

At the same time that Totila showed himself thus gentle and just towards the Roman inhabitants, he skilfully conducted the war so as to wound the Empire in its tenderest part—finance. Justinian's aim, in Italy as in Africa, was to make the newly annexed territory pay its own expenses and hand over a good balance to the Imperial treasury. It was for this purpose that the *logothetes* had been let loose upon Italy—that the provincials had been maddened by the extortions of the tax-gatherer, that the soldiers had been driven to mutiny and defection. Now with his loyal and well disciplined troops, Totila moved over the country from the Alps to Calabria, quietly collecting the taxes claimed by the emperor and the rents due to the refugee landlords, and in this way, without oppressing the people, weakened the Imperial government and put himself in a position to pay liberally for the commissariat of his army. Thus the difficulties of the Imperial treasury increased. Justinian became more and more unwilling to loosen his purse-strings for the sake of a province which showed an ever-dwindling return.

The pay of the soldiers got more and more hopelessly into arrear. They deserted in increasing numbers to the standard of the brave and generous young king of the Goths. Hence, it came to pass, that in the spring of 544, when Totila had been only for two and a half years king, he had gained two pitched battles by land and one by sea, had taken Naples and Beneventum, could march freely from one end of Italy to the other, and in fact, with the exception of Ravenna, Rome, and a few other strongholds, had won back from the Empire the whole of that Italy which had been acquired with so much toil and so much bloodshed.

There was, of course, bitter disappointment in the council-chamber of Justinian at this issue of an enterprise which had seemed at first so successful. There was but one sentence on all men's lips— "Only Belisarius can recover Italy," and it was uttered so loudly and so universally, that the emperor could not but hear it. But Justinian, ever since the offer of the Western throne to Belisarius, seems to have looked upon him with jealousy as a possible rival, and (what was even more fatal to his interests at court), the Empress Theodora had come to regard him with dislike and suspicion, partly because of a domestic quarrel in which she had taken the part of his wife Antonina against him, and partly because when Justinian was lying plague-stricken and apparently at the point of death, Belisarius had discussed the question of the succession to the throne in a manner which the empress considered hostile to her interests.

For these reasons the great general had been for some years in disgrace. A large part of his property was taken away from him, and some of it was handed over to Antonina, with whom he had been ordered to reconcile himself on the most humbling terms: his great military household, containing many men of servile origin, whom he had trained to such deeds of valour that it was a common saying, "One household alone has destroyed the kingdom of Theodoric," was broken up, and those brave men who would willingly have died for their chief, were portioned out by lot among the other generals and the eunuchs of the palace.

Still, in deference to the unanimous opinion of his counsellors, Justinian decided once more to avail himself of the services of Belisarius for the reconquest of Italy. But his unquenched jealousy of his great general's fame, and the almost bankrupt condition of the Imperial exchequer converged to the same point, and caused Justinian, while entrusting Belisarius with the command, to couple with it the monstrous stipulation that he was not to ask for any money for the war. And this, though it was clear to all men that the want of money and the consequent desertion of the Imperial standard by whole companies of grumbling barbarians, had been one main cause of the amazing success of Totila. Thus crippled by his master, and having his own spirit broken by Imperial ingratitude and domestic unhappiness, Belisarius, in the whole course of his second command in Italy, which lasted for five years—(544-549) did nothing, or I should rather say only one thing, worthy of his former reputation.

This is the judgement which his former friend and admirer, Procopius, passes on this period of his life. "Thus then," (in 549) "Belisarius departed to Byzantium without glory, having been for five years in Italy, but having never been strong enough to make a regular march by land in all that time, but having flitted about from one fortress on the coast to another, and so left the enemy free to capture Rome and almost every other place which they attacked."

Notwithstanding this harsh sentence, it was in connection with the Siege of Rome that the old Belisarius, the man of infinite resource and courageous dexterity, once more revealed himself, and while we gladly let all the other events of these five tedious years glide into oblivion, it is worth while devoting a few pages to the Second and Third Gothic Sieges of Rome.

Totila had quite determined not to repeat the mistake of Witigis, by dashing his army to pieces against the walls of Rome, but, for all that, he could not feel his recovery of Italy to be complete so long as the Eternal City defied his power. He therefore slowly tightened his grasp on the city, capturing one town after another in its neighbourhood and watching the roads to prevent convoys of provisions from entering it. He was on good terms with the peasants of the surrounding country, paid liberally for all the provisions required by his army (far smaller than that of Witigis), and kept his soldiers in good heart and in high health, while the unhappy citizens were seeing the great enemy—Famine—slowly approach nearer and nearer to their homes.

Within the city there was now no such provident and resourceful general as Belisarius. Bessas, the commandant, himself an Ostrogoth of Mœsia by birth, was a brave man, but coarse, selfish, and unfeeling. Intent only on filling his own coffers by selling the corn which he had stored up in his warehouses at a famine-price to the citizens, he was not touched by the increasing misery around him, and made no effectual attempt to break the net which Totila had drawn round Rome. Belisarius himself, "flitting from point to point of the coast," had come to Portus eighteen miles from Rome, at the mouth of the Tiber. It was no want of good-will on his part that prevented him from bringing his provision-ships up the river to the help of the famished city, but about four miles above Portus Totila had placed a strong boom of timber, protected in front by an iron chain and guarded by two towers, one at each end of the bridge which was above the boom.

Belisarius made his preparations for destroying the boom: a floating tower as high as the bridge placed on two barges, a large vessel filled with "Greek fire" at the top of the tower, soldiers below to hew the boom in pieces and sever the chain, a long train of merchantmen behind laden with provisions for the hungry Romans, and manned by archers who poured a deadly volley of arrows on the defenders of the bridge. All went well with his design up to a certain point. The chain was severed, the Goths fell fast under the arrows from the ships, the vessel of "Greek fire" was hurled upon one of the forts, which was soon wrapped in flames. With might and main the Imperial soldiers began to hack at the boom, and it seemed as if in a few minutes the corn-laden vessels would be sailing up the Tiber, bringing glad relief to the starving citizens.

But just at that moment a horseman galloped up to Belisarius with the unwelcome tidings—"Isaac is taken prisoner." Isaac the Armenian was Belisarius' second in command, whom he had left at Portus in charge of his stores, his munitions of war, and most important of all, the now reconciled Antonina. In spite of Belisarius' strict injunction to act solely on the defensive, Isaac, watching from afar the successful movements of his chief, had sallied forth to attack the Gothic garrison at Ostia on the opposite bank of the river. His defeat and consequent capture were events of little moment in themselves, but all-important as arresting the victorious career of Belisarius. For to the anxious soul of the general the capture of Isaac seemed to mean the capture of Portus, the cutting off of his army from their base of operations, the captivity of his beloved Antonina. He gave the signal for retreat; the attempt to provision Rome had failed; the Imperial army returned to Portus. When he found what it was that had really happened, and by what a combination of folly and ill luck he had been prevented from winning a splendid victory, his annoyance was so great that combined with the unwholesome air of the Campagna it threw him into a fever which brought him near to death and prevented him for some months from taking any part in the war.

Meanwhile dire famine bore sway in the beleaguered city. Wheat was sold for £22 a quarter, and the greater part of the citizens were thankful to live on coarse bread made of bran, which was doled out to them by Bessas at a quarter of the price of wheat. Before long even this bran became a luxury beyond their power to purchase. Dogs and mice provided them with their only meals of flesh, but the staple article of food was nettles. With blackened skin and drawn faces, mere ghosts of their former selves, the once proud and prosperous citizens of Rome wandered about the waste places where these nettles grew, and often one of them would be found dead with hunger, his strength having suddenly failed him while attempting to gather his wretched meal.

At length this misery was suddenly ended. Some Isaurian soldiers who were guarding the Asinarian Gate in the south-east of the city made overtures to the Gothic soldiers for the betrayal of their post.

These Isaurians were probably part of the former garrison of Naples whom Totila had treated with great generosity after the surrender of that city. They remembered the kindness then shown them; they were weary of the siege, and disgusted with the selfish avarice of their generals, and they soon came to terms with the besiegers.

Four of the bravest Goths being hoisted over the walls at night by the friendly Isaurians, ran round to the Asinarian Gate, battered its bolts and bars to pieces, and let in their waiting comrades. Unopposed, the Gothic army marched in,[1] unresisting, the Imperial troops marched out by the Flaminian Gate. The play was precisely the same that had been enacted ten years before when Belisarius won the city from Leudaris, but with the parts reversed. What Witigis with his one hundred and fifty thousand Goths had failed to accomplish, an army of not more than a tenth of that number[2] had accomplished under Totila. Bessas and the other generals fled headlong with the rest of the crowd that pressed out of the Flaminian Gate, and the treasure, accumulated with such brutal disregard of human suffering, fell into the hands of the besiegers.

At first murder and plunder raged unchecked through the streets of the city, the exasperation which had been caused by the events of the long siege having made every Gothic heart bitter against Rome and Romans. But after sixty citizens had been slain, Totila, who had gone to St. Peter's to offer up his prayers and thanksgivings, listened to the intercession of the deacon Pelagius[3] and commanded that slaughter should cease. But there were only five hundred citizens left in Rome to receive the benefit of the amnesty, so great had been the depopulation of the city by war and famine.[4]

And now had come a fateful moment in the history of Roma Æterna. A conqueror stood within her walls, not in mere joyousness of heart like Alaric, pleased with the exploit of bringing to her knees the mistress of the world, not intent on vulgar plans of plunder like Gaiseric, but nourishing a deep and deadly hatred against that false and

---

1. 17th December, 546.
2. Apparently, but we do not seem to have a precise statement of the numbers of Totila's army at this time.
3. Pelagius was at this time, owing to the absence of Pope Vigilius on a journey to Constantinople, the most influential ecclesiastic in Rome, and eight years later he succeeded Vigilius in the Papal Chair.
4. At a certain point of the siege the non-combatants had been sent out of the city by Bessas, but the number of those who passed safely through the lines of the besiegers was not great.

251

ungrateful city, and, by the ghosts of a hundred and fifty thousand of his countrymen who had died before her untaken walls, beckoned on a memorable revenge. Totila would spare, as he had promised, the lives of the trembling citizens, but he had determined that Rome herself should perish. The walls should be dismantled, the public buildings burned to the ground, and sheep should graze again over the seven hills of the city as they had grazed thirteen hundred years before, when Romulus and Remus were suckled by the wolf.

From this purpose, however, he was moved by the intercession of Belisarius, who, from his couch of fever, wrote a spirit-stirring letter to Totila, pleading for Rome, greatest and most glorious of all cities that the sun looked down upon, the work not of one king nor one century, but of long ages and many generations of noble men. Belisarius concluded with an appeal to the Gothic king to consider what should be his own eternal record in history, whether he would rather be remembered as the preserver or the destroyer of the greatest city in the world.

This appeal, made by one hero to another, was successful. Totila was still bent on preventing the city from ever again becoming a stronghold of the enemy, and therefore determined to lay one-third of the walls level with the ground, but he assured the messengers of Belisarius that he would leave the great monuments of Rome untouched. Having accomplished the needed demolition of her defences, he marched forth with his army from the desolate and sepulchral city and took up a position in the Alban Mountains, which are seen by the dwellers in Rome far off on their south-eastern horizon.

When Totila withdrew Rome was left, we are told, absolutely devoid of inhabitants.[5] The senators he kept in his camp as hostages, and all the less influential citizens with their wives and children were sent away to the confines of Campania. For forty days or more the great city which had been for so long the heart of the human universe, the city which, with the million-fold tide of life throbbing in her veins,

---

5. As the passage is an important one I will give a literal translation of the words of Procopius (*De Bell. Gotthico*, iii., 22): "Of the Romans, however, he kept the members of the Senate with him, but sent away all the others with their wives and children to the regions bordering on Campania, having permitted not a single human being to remain in Rome, but having left her absolutely desolate." (ἐν Ῥώμῃ ἄνθρωπον οὐδένα ἐάσας, ἀλλ᾿ ἔρημον αὐτὴν τὸ παράπαν ἀπολιπών.) The contemporary chronicler Marcellinus Comes confirms this statement: "*Post quam devastationem XL. aut amplius dies Roma fuit ita desolata ut nemo ibi hominum nisi bestiæ morarentur.*"

had most vividly prefigured the London of our own day, remained "waste and without inhabitants," as desolate as Anderida in Kent had been left half a century before by her savage Saxon conquerors.

And then came another change—one of the most marvellous in the history of that city whose whole life has been a marvel. While Totila abode in his camp on the Alban Hills, Belisarius, rising from the bed to which fever had for so many weeks chained him, made a visit to Rome, accompanied by a thousand soldiers, that he might see with his own eyes into what depth of calamity she had fallen. At first, it would seem, mere curiosity led him to the ruined City, but when he was there, gazing on Totila's work of devastation, a brilliant thought flashed through his brain. After all the demolitions of Totila, the ruin was not irretrievable. By repairing the rents in the walls, Rome might yet be made defensible. He would reoccupy it, and the Goths should find that they had all their work to do over again.

The idea seemed at first to his counsellors like the suggestion of delirium, but as it rapidly took shape under his hands, it was recognised as being indeed a masterstroke of well-calculated audacity. Leaving a small body of men to guard his base of operations at Portus, he moved every available man to Rome, crowded them up to the gaps made by Totila, bade them build anyhow, with any sort of material—mortar was out of the question; it must be mere dry walling that they could accomplish,—only let them preserve some semblance of an upright wall, and crown the summit of it with a rampart of stakes. The deep fosse below fortunately remained as it was, not filled up.

So in five and twenty days the circuit of the walls was completed, truly in a most slovenly style of building, the marks of which we can see even to this day, but Rome was once again a "fenced city." As soon as Totila heard the unwelcome tidings, he marched with his whole army to Rome, hoping to take the city, as his soldiers said, "at the first shout." But he had Belisarius to deal with, not Bessas. There had not yet been time even to make new gates for the city instead of those which Totila had destroyed, but Belisarius planted all his bravest soldiers in the void places where the gates should be, and guarded the approach by caltrops (somewhat like those wherewith Bruce defended his line at Bannockburn), so as to make a charge of Gothic cavalry impossible.

Three long days of hard-fought battle were spent round the fateful city. In each the Goths, whatever temporary advantages they might gain, were finally repulsed, and at length Totila, who was not going to repeat the error of Witigis, marched away from the too well-known scene, amid the bitter reproaches of the Gothic nobles, who before had praised him like a god for all his valour and dexterity in war, but now, on the morrow of his first great blunder, loudly upbraided him for his imprudence, adding the obvious and easy piece of Epimethean criticism, "that the city ought either to have been utterly destroyed, or else occupied with a sufficient force." Meanwhile Belisarius at his leisure completed the repair of the walls, hung the massive gates on their hinges, had keys made to fit their locks, and sent the duplicate keys to Justinian. The Roman Empire once again had Rome.

And yet this reoccupation of the Eternal City, brilliant and striking achievement as it was, had little influence on the course of the war. Rome was now like a great stone left in an alluvial plain showing where the river had once flowed, but the currents of commerce, of politics, of war, flowed now in other channels. Belisarius, leaving a garrison in Rome, had to betake himself once more to that desultory warfare, flitting round the coast from one naval fortress to another, in which the earlier years of his second command had been passed; and at length, early in 549, only two years after his reoccupation of Rome, he obtained as a great favour, through the intercession of Antonina, permission to resign his command and return to Constantinople. It was on this occasion that Procopius passed that harsh judgment as to the inglorious character of these later operations of his in Italy, which was quoted on a previous page.

I will briefly summarise the subsequent events in the life of the old hero:

Once more, ten years after the return of Belisarius (in 559), his services were claimed by Justinian in order to repel a horde of savage Huns who had penetrated within eighteen miles of Constantinople. The work was brilliantly done, with much of the old ingenuity and fertility of resource which had marked his first campaign in Italy, and then Belisarius relapsed into inactivity. He was again accused (562), probably without justice, of abetting a conspiracy against the emperor, was disgraced and imprisoned in his own palace. After seven months he was restored to the Imperial favour, the falsity of the accusation against him having probably become apparent. He died in 565, in about the sixtieth year of his age, and only a few months before his jealous master. He had more than once had to endure the withdrawal of that master's confidence, and some portions of his vast wealth were on two occasions taken from him. But this is all that can be truly said as to the reverses of fortune undergone by the conqueror of the Vandals and the Goths. The stories of his blindness and of his beggary, of his holding forth a wooden bowl and whining out "*Date obolum Belisario,*" rest on no good foundation, and either arise from a confusion between Belisarius and another disgraced minister of Justinian, or else are simply due to the myth-making industry of the Middle Ages.

COIN OF BADUILA.
(TOTILA.)

CHAPTER 18

Narses

Soon after the return of Belisarius to Constantinople came the
Fourth Siege of Rome. Totila, who had sought the hand of a Frankish princess in marriage, received for answer from her father, "that the
man who had not been able to keep Rome when he had taken it, but
had destroyed part and abandoned the rest to the enemy, was no King
of Italy."[1]

The taunt stung Totila to the quick. We know not whether he
won his Frankish bride or no, but he was determined to win Rome.
Assault again failing, he occupied Portus and instituted a more rigor-
ous blockade than ever. But it had become a matter of some difficulty
to starve out the defenders of Rome, for there were practically no
citizens there, only a garrison, for whose food the corn grown within
the enclosure of the walls was nearly sufficient. The economic change
from the days of the Empire thus revealed to us is almost as great as
if the harvests of Hyde Park and Regent's Park sufficed to feed the
diminished population of London.

There was, however, among the Imperial soldiers in the garrison
of Rome, as elsewhere, deep discontent, amounting sometimes to mutiny, at the long withholding of their arrears of pay; and the sight of
the pomp and splendour, which surrounded the former betrayer of
Rome when they rode in the ranks with Totila, was too much for
their Isaurian countrymen. The men who kept watch by the Gate of
St. Paul (close to the Pyramid of C. Sestius, and now overlooking the
English Cemetery and Keats' grave) offered to surrender their post to
the Gothic king. To distract the attention of the garrison he sent by

---

1. Procopius, *De Bello Gotthico*, iii., 37. This is one of the passages which make me
somewhat doubtful whether we are not too confident in our denial of the title
"King of Italy" to Odovacar and Theodoric. The words are clear.

256

night a little band of soldiers on two skiffs up the Tiber as far as they could penetrate towards the heart of the city. These men blew a loud blast with their trumpets, and thereby called the bulk of the defenders down to the river-walls, while the Isaurians were opening St. Paul's Gate to the besiegers, who marched in almost unopposed. The garrison galloped off along the road to Civita Vecchia, and on their way fell into an ambush which Totila had prepared for them, whereby most of them perished (549).

Totila, now a second time master of Rome, determined to hold it securely. He restored some of the public buildings which he had previously destroyed; he adorned and beautified the city to the utmost of his power; he invited the senators and their families to return; he celebrated the equestrian games in the circus Maximus: in all things he behaved himself as much as possible like one of the old emperors of Rome.

The year 550 was the high-water mark of the success of the Gothic arms. In Italy only four cities—all on the sea-coast—were left to the emperor; these were Ravenna, Ancona, Otranto, and Crotona. In Sicily most of the cities were still Imperial, but Totila had moved freely hither and thither through the island, ravaging the villas and the farms, collecting great stores of grain and fruit, driving off horses and cattle, and generally visiting on the hapless Sicilians the treachery which in his view they had shown to the Ostrogothic dynasty by the eagerness with which, fifteen years before, they had welcomed the arms of Belisarius.

But at the end of a long and exhausting war it is often seen that victory rests with that power which has enough reserve force left to make one final effort, even though that effort in the earlier years of the war might not have been deemed a great one. So was it now with Justinian's conquest of Italy. Though he himself was utterly weary of the Sisyphean labour, he would not surrender a shred of his theoretical claims, nor would he even condescend to admit to an audience the ambassadors of Totila, who came to plead for peace and alliance between the two hostile powers.

In his perplexity as to the further conduct of the war he offered the command to his Grand Chamberlain Narses, who eagerly accepted it. The choice was indeed a strange one. Narses, an Armenian by birth, brought as an eunuch to Constantinople, and dedicated to the service of the palace, had grown grey in that service, and was now seventy-four years of age. But he was of "Illustrious" rank, he shared the most secret counsels of the emperor, he was able freely to unloose the purse-strings which had been so parsimoniously closed to Belisarius, and he had set his whole heart on succeeding where Belisarius had failed. Moreover, he was himself both wealthy and generous, and he brought with him a huge and motley host of barbarians, Huns, Lombards, Gepids, Herulians, all eager to serve under the free-handed Chamberlain, and to be enriched by him with the spoil of Italy.

In the spring of 552, the eunuch-general, with this strange multitude calling itself a Roman army, marched round the head of the Adriatic Gulf and entered the impregnable seat of Empire, Ravenna. By adroit strategy he evaded the Gothic generals who had been ordered to arrest his progress in north-eastern Italy and—probably by about midsummer—he had reached the point a little south-west of Ancona, where the Flaminian Way, the great northern road from Rome, crosses the Apennines. Here on the crest of the mountains[2] Narses encamped, and here Totila met him, eager for the fight which was to decide the future dominion of Italy.

A space of about twelve miles separated the hostile camps. Narses sent some of his most trusted counsellors to warn Totila not to continue the struggle any longer against the irresistible might of the Empire; "but if you will fight," said the messengers, "name the day." Totila indignantly spurned the proposal of surrender and named the eighth day from thence as the day of battle. Narses, however, suspecting some stratagem, bade his troops prepare for action, and it was well that he did so, for on the next day Totila with all his army was at hand.

A hill, which to some extent commanded the battlefield, was the first objective point of both generals. Narses sent fifty of his bravest men over-night to take up their position on this hill, and the Gothic troops, chiefly cavalry, which were sent to dislodge them, failed to effect their purpose, the horses being frightened by the din which the Imperial soldiers made, clashing with their spears upon their shields. Several lives were lost on this preliminary skirmish, the honours of which remained with the soldiers of Narses.

At dawn of day the troops were drawn up in order of battle, but Narses had made all his arrangements on a defensive rather than an offensive plan and Totila, who was expecting a reinforcement of two thousand Goths under his brave young lieutenant Teias, wished to

2. There is some little difference of opinion as to the site of this battle. I place it near the Roman posting station of Ad Ensem, represented by the modern village of Scheggia, in latitude 43° 25' north.

postpone the attack. Both generals harangued their armies: Totila, in words of lordly scorn for the patch-work host of various nationalities which Justinian, weary of the war, had sent against him. It was the emperor's last effort, he declared, and when this heterogeneous army was defeated, the brave Goths would be able to rest from their labours. Narses, on the other hand, congratulated his soldiers on their evident superiority in numbers to the Gothic host.

They fought too, as he reminded them, for the Roman Empire, which was in its nature, and by the will of Providence, eternal, while these little barbarian states, Vandal, Gothic, and the like, sprang up like mushrooms, lived their little day, and then vanished away, leaving no trace behind them. He had recourse also to less refined and philosophical arguments. Riding rapidly along the ranks, the Eunuch dangled before the eyes of his barbarian auxiliaries golden armlets, golden collars, golden bridles. "These," said he, "and such other ornaments as these, shall be the reward of your valour, if you fight well today."

The long morning of waiting was partly occupied by a duel between two chosen champions. A warrior, named Cocas, who had deserted from emperor to king, rode up to the Imperial army, challenging their bravest to single combat. One of Narses' lifeguards, an Armenian like his master, Anzalas by name, accepted the challenge. Cocas couched his spear and rode fiercely at his foe, thinking to pierce him in the belly. Anzalas dexterously swerved aside at the critical moment and gave a thrust with his spear at the left side of his antagonist, who fell lifeless to the ground. A mighty shout rose from the Imperial ranks at this propitious omen of the coming battle. Not yet, however, was that battle to be gained. King Totila rode forth in the open space between both armies, "that he might show the enemy what manner of man he was." His armour was lavishly adorned with gold: from the cheek-piece of his helmet, from his *pilum* and his spear hung purple pennants; his whole equipment was magnificent and kingly.

Bestriding a very tall war-horse he played the game of a military athlete with accomplished skill. He wheeled his horse first to the right, then to the left, in graceful curves; then he tossed his spear on high to the morning breezes and caught it in the middle as it descended with quivering fall; then he threw it deftly from one hand to another, he stooped low on his horse, he raised himself up again. Everything was done as artistically as the dance of a well-trained performer. All this "was beautiful to look at, but it was not war." The ugly, wrinkled old Armenian in the other camp, who probably kept his seat on horseback with difficulty, knew, one may suspect, more of the deadly science of war than the brilliant and martial Totila.

At length the long-looked-for two thousand arrived, and Totila gave the signal to charge upon the foe. It was the hour of the noontide meal, and he hoped to catch the Imperial troops in the disorder of their repast; but for this also Narses, the wary, had provided. Even the food necessary to support their strength was to be taken by the soldiers, all keeping their ranks, all armed, and all watching intently the movements of the enemy. Narses had purposely somewhat weakened his centre in order to strengthen his wings, which, as the Gothic cavalry charged, closed round them and poured a deadly shower of arrows into their flanks.

Again, as in the campaigns of Belisarius, the *Hippo-toxotai*, the "Mounted Rifles" of the Empire, decided the fate of the battle. Vain against their murderous volleys was the valour of the Gothic horseman, the thrust of the Gothic lance, the might of the tall Gothic steed. Charge upon charge of the Goths was made in vain; the cavalry could never reach the weak but distant centre of the Imperialists. At length, when the sun was declining, the horsemen came staggering back, a disorganised and beaten band. Their panic communicated itself to the infantry, who were probably the weakest section of the army; the rout was complete, and the whole of the Gothic host was seen either flying, surrendering, or dying.

As evening fell Totila, with five of his friends hastened from the lost battle-field. A young Gepid chief, named Asbad, ignorant who he was couched his lance to strike Totila in the back. A young Gothic page incautiously cried out, "Dog! would you strike your lord?" hereby revealing the rank of the fugitive and, of course, only nerving the arm of Asbad to strike a more deadly blow. Asbad was wounded in return and his companions intent on staunching his wound let the fugitives ride on, but the wound of Totila was mortal. His friends hurried him on, eight miles down the valley, to the little village of Capræ, where they alighted and strove to tend his wound. But their labour was vain; the gallant king soon drew his last breath and was hastily buried by his comrades in that obscure hamlet.

The Romans knew not what had become of their great foe till several days after, when some soldiers were riding past the village, a Gothic woman told them of the death of Totila and pointed out to them his grave. They doubted the truth of her story, but opened the grave and gazed their fill on that which was, past all dispute, the corpse of Totila. The news brought joy to the heart of Narses, who returned heartiest thanks to God and to the Virgin, his especial patroness, and then proceeded to disembarrass himself as quickly as possible of the wild barbarians, especially the Lombards, by whose aid he had won the victory which destroyed the last hopes of the Ostrogothic monarchy in Italy.[3]

(568) Not thus easily, however, was the tide of barbarian invasion to be turned. The Lombards had found their way into Italy as auxiliaries. They returned thither sixteen years after as conquerors, conquerors the most ruthless and brutal that Italy had yet groaned under. From that day for thirteen centuries the unity of Italy was a dream. First the Lombard king and the Byzantine emperor tore her in pieces. Then the Frank descended from the Alps to join in the fray. The German, the Saracen, the Norman made their appearance on the scene. Not all wished to ravage and despoil; some had high and noble purposes in their hearts, but, in fact, they all tended to divide her. The Popes even at their best, even while warring as Italian patriots against the foreign emperor, still divided their country.

Last of all came the Spaniard and the Austrian, by whom, down to our own day, Italy was looked upon as an estate, out of which kingdoms and duchies might be carved at pleasure as appanages for younger sons and compensations for lost provinces. Only at length, towards the close of the nineteenth century, has Italy regained that priceless boon of national unity, which might have been hers before it was attained by any other country in Europe, if only the ambition of emperors and the false sentiment of "Roman" patriots would have spared the goodly tree which had been planted in Italian soil by Theodoric the Ostrogoth.

COIN OF TEIAS.
(SUCCESSOR OF TOTILA.)

---

3. A gallant stand was made by Teias, who was elected king on the death of Totila, but his reign lasted only a few months. He was defeated and slain early in 553 at the Battle of Mons Lactarius, not far from Pompeii, and the little remnant of his followers, the last of the Goths, marched northward out ot Italy and disappear from history.

CHAPTER 19.[1]

The Theodoric of Saga

It is one of the most striking testimonies to the greatness of Theodoric's work and character, that his name is one of the very few which passed from history into the epic poetry of the German and Scandinavian peoples. True, there is scarcely one feature of the great Ostrogothic king preserved in the mythical portrait painted by minstrels and Sagamen; true, Theodoric of Verona would have listened in incredulous or contemptuous amazement to the romantic adventures related of Dietrich of Bern; still the fact that his name was chosen by the poets of the early Middle Ages as the string upon which the pearls of their fantastic imaginations were to be strung, shows how powerfully his career had impressed their barbaric forefathers. Theodoric's eminence in this respect, his renown in mediæval *Saga*, is shared apparently but by three other undoubtedly historic personages: his collateral ancestor, Hermanric; the great world-conqueror, Attila; and Gundahar, king of the Burgundians, about whom history really records nothing, save his defeat in battle by the Huns.

As it would be a hopeless attempt in a short chapter like the present to discuss the various allusions to Dietrich von Bern in the Teutonic and Scandinavian *Sagas*, I shall invite the reader's attention to one only, that which concerns itself most exclusively with his life, and which is generally called the *Wilkina Saga*,[2] though some German scholars

1. This chapter is based on Peringskiold's Latin translation of the *Wilkina Saga*, and on the German translation contained in F.H. von der Hagen's *Alt-deutsche und Alt-nordische Helden-Sagen*. I am also much indebted to the spirited rendering of the Sagas contributed by Madame Dahn to her husband, Professor Dahn's, volume, *Walhall*.

2. So called because it contains a large number of episodes as to King Wilkinus, his descendants, and the land known by his name, Wilkina-land (Norway and Sweden). Some suppose the name to be a corruption of Viking.

prefer to call it by the more appropriate name of *Thidreks Saga*.

The earliest manuscripts of this *Saga* at present known are attributed to the first half of the thirteenth century. There are many allusions in the work to other sources of information both written and oral, but the *Saga* itself in its present form appears to contain the story of Theodoric as current in the neighbourhood of Bremen and Münster, translated into the old Norse language, and no doubt somewhat modified by the influence of Scandinavian legends on the mind of the translator. In its present form it is not a poem but a prose work, and though the flow of the ballad and the twang of the minstrel's harp still often make themselves felt even through the dull Latin translation of Johan Peringskiold, there are many chapters of absolutely unredeemed prose, full of genealogical details and the marches of armies, as dry as any history, though purely imaginary.

I will now proceed to give the outline of the story of Theodoric as told in the *Wilkina Saga*, I shall not harass the reader by continual repetitions of the phrase "It is said," or "It is fabled," but will ask him to understand once for all that the story so circumstantially told is a mere romance, having hardly the slenderest connection with the actual history of Theodoric, or with any other event that has happened on our planet.

The Knight Samson, the grandfather of Theodoric, was a native of Salerno and served in the court of Earl Roger, the lord of that city. Tall and dark, with black brows and long, thin face, he was distinguished by great personal strength, and his ambition was equal to his prowess. Earl Roger had a most lovely daughter, Hildeswide, to whom Samson dared to raise his eyes in love. Being sent one day by her father to the tower where she dwelt, with dainty morsels from his table for her repast, he persuaded her to mount his servant's horse and ride away with him into the forest. For this Earl Roger confiscated his possessions and sought his life. Enraged at the decree of exile and death which had been passed against him, Samson issued forth from his forest to ravage Earl Roger's farms.

In his return to the forest, being intercepted by the earl and sixty of his knights, he was seized with sudden fury, and struck down the earl's standard-bearer, dealt so terrible a blow at the earl that he lopped off not only his head but that of the steed on which he rode, slew fifteen knights besides, and then galloped off, himself unwounded, to the forest where Hildeswide abode. Thus did Salerno lose her lord.

Brunstein, the brother of Earl Roger, sought to avenge his death, but after two years of desultory warfare was himself surprised in a night attack by Samson, compelled to flee, overtaken and slain. So Samson went on and increased in strength, treading down all his enemies; but not till he had persuaded the citizens of Salerno to accept him as their lord would he assume the title of king. Then did he send out messengers to announce to all the other kingdoms of the world his royal dignity. He governed long and wisely, extending his dominions to the vast regions of the west (apparently making himself lord of all Italy), and by his wife Hildeswide becoming the father of two sons, whose names were Hermanric and Dietmar.

After twenty years of wise and peaceful rule, as Samson sat feasting in his palace he began to lament the decay of energy in himself and his warriors, and to fear that his name and fame would perish after his death. He therefore resolved on war with Elsung, Earl of Verona, and to that end despatched six ambassadors with this insulting message: "Send hither thy daughter to be the concubine of my youngest son. Send sixty damsels with her, and sixty noble youths each bringing two horses and a servant. Send sixty hawks and sixty retrievers, whose collars shall be of pure gold, and let the leash with which they are bound be made of hairs out of thine own white beard. Do this, or in three months prepare for war."

This insolent demand produced the expected result. Elsung ordered the leader of the embassy to be hung. Four of his companions were beheaded. The sixth, having had his right hand lopped off, was sent back with no other answer to Salerno. When he reached that city, Samson appeared to treat the matter as of no importance and went on with his hunting and hawking and all the amusements of a peaceful court. He was, however, quietly making his preparations for war, and at the end of three months, at the head of an army of 15,000 men, commanded by three under-kings and many dukes he burst into the territories of Earl Elsung who had only 10,000 men, drawn from Hungary and elsewhere, with whom to meet his powerful foe. There was great slaughter on the battle-plain. Then the two chiefs met in single combat.

Elsung inflicted a wound on Samson, but Samson cut off Elsung's head and clutching it by the hoary locks exhibited it in triumph to his men. The utter rout of the Veronese army followed. Samson went in state to Verona, received the submission of the citizens and laid hands on the splendid treasure of Earl Elsung. He then celebrated with great pomp the marriage of Odilia, the daughter of the slain earl, to his

second son Dietmar, whom he made lord of Verona and all the territory which had been Elsung's. He marched next toward "Romaborg"
(Rome) intending to make his eldest son, Hermanric, lord of that
city, but died on the journey. Hermanric, however, after many battles
with the Romans achieved the desired conquest, and became Lord of
Romaborg and the country round it, even to the Hellespont and the
isles of Greece.

Dietmar, son of Samson, King of Verona, was brave, prudent, and
greatly loved by the folk over whom he ruled. His wife Odilia was one
of the wisest of women. Their eldest son was named Theodoric, and
he, when full grown, though not one of the race of giants, surpassed
all ordinary men in stature. His face was oval, of comely proportions;
he had gray eyes, with black brows above them; his hair was of great
beauty, long and thick and ending in ruddy curls. He never wore a
beard. His shoulders were two ells broad; his arms were as thick as the
trunk of a tree and as hard as a stone. He had strong, well-proportioned hands. The middle of his body was of a graceful tapering shape,
but his loins and hips were wondrously strong; his feet beautiful and
well-proportioned; his thighs of enormous bigness. His strength was
much beyond the ordinary strength of men.

The size of Theodoric's body was equalled by the qualities of his
mind. He was not only brave but jovial, good-tempered, liberal, magnificent, always ready to bestow gold and silver and all manner of precious things on his expectant friends. It was the saying of some that
the young warrior was like his grandfather, Samson; but others held
that there was never any one in the world to compare unto Theodoric.
When he had attained the fifteenth year of his age he was solemnly
created a knight by his father, Dietmar.

Now, while Theodoric was still a child there came to his father's
court one who was to have a great influence on his after life. This was
Hildebrand, commonly called Master Hildebrand, son of one of the
Dukes of Venice. He was a brave knight and a mighty one, and when
he had reached the age of thirty he told his father that he would fain
see more of the world than he could do by lingering all his days at
Venice. Upon which his father recommended him to try his fortune
at the court of Dietmar, king of Verona. He came therefore and was received very graciously by Dietmar, who conferred great favours upon
him and assigned to him the care of the young Theodoric then about
seven years of age. Hildebrand taught Theodoric all knightly exercises;
together they ever rode to war, and the friendship which grew up

between them was strong as that which knit the soul of David to the soul of Jonathan.

One day when Theodoric and Hildebrand were hunting in the forest, a little dwarf ran across their path, to which Theodoric gave chase. This dwarf proved to be Alpris, the most thievish little creature in the world. Theodoric was about to kill it, but Alpris said: "If you will spare my life I will get you the finest sword that ever was made, and will show you where to find more treasure than ever your father owned. They belong to a little woman called Hildur and her husband Grimur. He is so strong that he can fight twelve men at once, but she is much stronger than he, and you will need all your strength if you mean to overcome them." Having bound himself by tremendous oaths to perform these promises, the dwarf was dismissed unhurt, and the two comrades went on with their hunting. At evening they stood beside the rock where Alpris was to meet them. The dwarf brought the sword, and pointed out the entrance to a cave. The two knights gazed upon the sword with wonder, agreeing that they had never seen anything like it in the world.

And no marvel, for this was the famous sword Nagelring, the fame whereof went out afterwards into the whole world. They tied up their horses and went together into the cave. Grimur, seeing strangers, at once challenged them to fight; but looking round anxiously for Nagelring, he missed it, whereupon he cursed the knavish Alpris, who had assuredly stolen it from him. However, he snatched from the hearth the blazing trunk of a tree and therewith attacked Theodoric. Meanwhile Hildebrand, taken at unawares, was caught hold of by Hildur, who clung so tightly round his neck that he could not move. After a long struggle they both fell heavily to the ground, Hildebrand below, Hildur on top of him. She squeezed his arms so tightly that the blood came out at his finger-nails; she pressed her fist so hard on his throat and breast that he could hardly breathe. He was fain to cry for help to Theodoric, who answered that he would do all in his power to save his faithful friend and tutor from the clutches of that foul little wench. With that he swung round Nagelring and smote off the head of Grimur. Then he hastened to his foster-father's aid and cut Hildur in two, but so mighty was the power of her magic that the sundered halves of her body came together again.

Once more Theodoric clove her in twain; once more the severed parts united. Hereupon quoth Hildebrand: "Stand between the sundered limbs with your body bowed and your head averted, and the

266

monster will be overcome." So did Theodoric, once more cleaving her body in twain and then standing between the pieces.

One half died at once, but that to which the head belonged was heard to say:

If the Fates had willed that Grimur should fight Theodoric as toughly as I fought Hildebrand, the victory had been ours.

With these words the brave little woman died.

Hildebrand congratulated his pupil on his glorious victory, and they then proceeded to despoil the cave of its treasures. One of the chief of these was a helmet of wonderful strength, the like of which Theodoric had never seen before. It was made by the dwarf Malpriant, and so greatly had the strange couple prized it that they had given it their united names Hildegrimur. This helmet guarded Theodoric's head in many a fierce encounter, and by its help and that of the sword Nagelring he gained many a victory. Bright was the renown which he won from this deed of arms.

So great was the fame of the young hero that striplings from distant lands, thirsting for glory, came to Dietmar's court that they might be enrolled among the comrades of Theodoric. There were twelve of these who, when they came to manhood, were especially distinguished as the chiefs of his army, and among these Theodoric shone preeminent, even as his contemporary, Arthur, king of Bertangenland,[3] among the Knights of his Table Round.

But there were two of these comrades, friendly to Theodoric, though by no means friendly to one another, who were more renowned than any of the rest for their knightly deeds and strange adventures. These were Witig and Heime, each of whom, having first fought with Theodoric, was afterwards for many years his loyal and devoted knight.

Heime was the son of a great horse-breeder who dwelt north of the mountains, and whose name was Studas. He was short and squat of figure and square of face, but was all made for strength; and he was churlish and morose of disposition, wherefore men called him Heime (which was the name of a strong and venomous serpent), instead of Studas, which was of right his name as well as his father's. One day Heime, having mounted his famous grey horse Rispa, and girded on his good sword Blutgang, announced to his father that he would ride southward over the mountains to Verona, and there challenge Theod-

---

3. Britain.

oric to a trial of strength.

Studas tried to dissuade his son, telling him that his presumption would cost him his life; but Heime answered: "Thy life and thy calling are base and inglorious, and I would rather die than plod on in this ignoble round. But, moreover, I think not to fall by the hand of Theodoric. He is scarce twelve winters old, and I am sixteen; and where is the man with whom I need fear to fight?"

So Heime rode over the rough mountain ways, and appearing in the courtyard of the palace at Verona, challenged Theodoric to fight. Indignant at the challenge, but confident of victory, Theodoric went forth to the encounter, having donned his iron shoes, his helmet and coat of mail, and taking his great thick shield, red as blood, upon which a golden lion ramped, and above all, his good sword Nagelring.

The young heroes fought at first on horseback, and in this encounter, though Theodoric's spear pierced Heime's shield and inflicted upon him a slight wound, a stumble of his horse had nearly brought him to the ground. But then, as both spears were shivered, the combatants sprang from their horses, waved high their swords, and continued the fight on foot. At last Heime dealt Theodoric a swashing blow on his head, but the good helmet Hildegrimur was so strong that it shivered the sword Blutgang to pieces, and there stood Heime helpless, at the mercy of the boy whom he had challenged. Theodoric gladly spared his life, and received him into the number of his henchmen, and after that they were for many years sworn friends.

It was some time after this that another young man appeared at Verona and challenged Theodoric to single combat. This was Witig, the Dane, son of that mighty worker in iron, Wieland,[4] who had in his veins the blood of kings and of mysterious creatures of the deep, but who spent all his days in his smithy, forging strange weapons, and whose wrongs and terrible revenges and marvellous escapes from death are sung by all the minstrels of the north. When he was twelve years old, Witig, drawn like so many other brave youths by the renown of the young Theodoric, announced to his father that he was determined to seek glory in the land of the Amelungs.[5] Wieland would fain have had him stay in the smithy and learn his own wealth-bringing craft; but Witig swore by the honour of his mother, a king's daughter, that never should the smith's hammer and tongs come into his hand.

Thereupon Wieland gave him a coat of mail of hard steel, which

4. The Wayland Smith of English legend.
5. This was the name of Italy, Theodoric and all his house being known as Amelungs.

shone like silver, and greaves of chain-armour; a white shield, on which were painted in red the smith's hammer and tongs, telling of his father's trade, and three carbuncles, which he bore in right of the princess, his mother. On his strong steel helmet a golden dragon gleamed and seemed to spit forth venom. Into his son's right hand Wieland gave the wondrous sword Mimung, which he had fashioned for a cruel king, and which was so sharp that it cut through a flock of wool, three feet thick, when floating on the water. Witig's mother gave him three golden *marks* and her gold ring, and he kissed his father and his mother and wished them a happy life, and they wished him a prosperous journey and were sore at heart when he turned to go.

But he grasped his spear and sprang into the saddle, all armed as he was, without touching the stirrup. Then Wieland's face grew bright again, and he walked long by the side of his son's horse and gave him full knowledge of the road he must take. So they parted, father and son, and Witig rode upon his way.

Long before he reached Verona he had met with many adventures, especially one in which he overcame twelve robbers who held a strong castle by a bridge and were wont to take toll of travellers. These robbers seeing Witig draw nigh parted among them in anticipation his armour and his horse, and planned also to maim him, cutting off his right hand and right foot, but with the good sword Mimung he slew two of them and was fighting valiantly with the rest when certain knights whom he had before met on the road came to his help, and between them they slew seven of the robbers and put the others to flight. These knights were Hildebrand and Heime, and a stranger whom they were escorting to the court of Verona. Heime, who was already jealous of Witig's power and prowess, had sought to dissuade his companions from going to his help; but Hildebrand refused to do so unknightly a deed as to let their road-companion be overpowered by ruffians before their very eyes without giving him succour.

So now, the victory being won and Witig having displayed his might, they all made themselves known unto him. Hildebrand swore "brotherhood in arms" with Witig, but having heard of his determination to challenge Theodoric to single combat, secretly by night changed the sword Mimung for one less finely tempered. For he feared for his young lord's life if that sword, wielded by Witig's strong hand, should ever descend upon Theodoric's helmet.

At length the wayfarers all entered the gates of Verona. Great was Theodoric's joy to behold again the good Master Hildebrand; but

VERONA FROM PONTE VACCHIO (SITE OF PALACE OF THEODORIC IN THE DISTANCE).

great was his indignation when the young Dane, who came with Hildebrand, challenged him to single combat.

Said Theodoric: "In my father's land and mine I will establish such peace that it shall not be permitted to every rover and rascal to come into it and challenge me to the duel."

Hildebrand: "Thou sayest not rightly, my lord, nor knowest of whom thou speakest. This is no rover nor rascal, but a brave man; and in sooth I know not whether thou wilt get the victory over him."

Then interrupted Reinald, a follower of Theodoric: "That were in truth, my lord, a great offence that every upstart urchin in thine own land should come and challenge thee to the fight."

Hildebrand: "Thou shalt not assail my journey-companion with any such abusive words."

And thereat he dealt Reinald such a blow with his fist on his ear that he fell senseless to the ground. Then said Theodoric: "I see thou art determined to be this man's friend; but thou shalt see how much good that does him. This very day he shall be hung up yonder outside the gates of Verona."

Hildebrand: "If he becomes thy prisoner, after you have both tried your might, I will not complain however hard thy decision may seem to me; but he is still unbound, and I think thou hast a hard day's work before thee, ere thou becomest lord of his fate."

Theodoric in a rage called for his horse and armour and rode, followed by a long train of courtiers, to the place of tourney outside the walls of Verona, where Witig and Hildebrand, with few companions, were awaiting him. Witig sate, arrayed in full armour, on his horse, battle-ready and stately to look upon. Then Heime gave Theodoric a bowl of wine and said: "Drink, my lord, and may God give thee the victory." Theodoric drank and gave back the bowl. Likewise Hildebrand offered a bowl to Witig, who said: "Take it to Theodoric and pray him to drink to me from it."

But Theodoric in his rage refused to touch the bowl that Witig was to drink from.

Then said Hildebrand: "Thou knowest not the man with whom thou art so enraged, but thou wilt find him a true hero and not the good-for-nothing fellow thou hast called him today." Then he gave Witig the bowl and said: "Drink now, and then defend thyself with all manhood and bravery, and may God give thee his succour."

And Witig drank and gave it back to Hildebrand, and with it the gold ring of his mother, saying: "God reward thee for thy true help-bringing."

Of the fierce battle between the two heroes which now followed it were too long to tell the tale. They fought first on horseback, then they fought on foot. Witig dealt a mighty blow with his sword at Theodoric's helmet, but the helmet Hildegrimur was too strong for the sword which Hildebrand had put in the place of Mimung, and which now was shivered into two pieces.

"Ah, Wieland!" cried Witig in vexation, "God's wrath be on thee for fashioning this sword so ill! If I had had a good sword, I had this day proved myself a hero; but now shame and loss are mine and his who forged my weapon."

Then Theodoric took the sword Nagelring with both his hands and was about to cut off Witig's head. But Hildebrand stepped in between and begged Theodoric to spare Witig's life and take him for a comrade, telling of his brave deeds against the twelve robbers, and declaring that never would Theodoric have a more valiant or loyal follower than this man, who was of kingly blood on both his father's and mother's side, and was now willing to become Theodoric's man. But Theodoric, still indignant at being challenged, as he deemed, by a son of a churl, said sullenly: "No; the dog shall hang, as I said he should, before the gates of Verona."

Then Hildebrand, seeing that nought else would avail, and that Theodoric heeded not good counsel, drew Mimung from the scabbard and gave it to Witig, saying: "For the sake of the brotherhood in arms which we swore when we met upon the journey, I give thee here thy sword Mimung. Take it and defend thyself like a knight."

Then was Witig joyous as a bird at daybreak. He kissed the golden-hilted sword and said: "May God forgive me for the reproach which I hurled at my father, Wieland. See! Theodoric, noble hero! see! here is Mimung. Now am I joyous for the fight with thee as a thirsty man for drinking, or a hungry hound for feeding."

Then he rained on Theodoric blow on blow, hacking away now a piece of his coat of mail, now a splinter from his helmet. Theodoric, bleeding from five great wounds, and thinking only now of defence, never of attack, called on Master Hildebrand to end the combat; but Hildebrand, still sore at heart because Theodoric seemed to accuse him of lying when he called Witig a hero, told him that he might now expect to receive from the conqueror the same disgraceful doom which he in his arrogance and cruelty had adjudged to the conquered.

Then King Dietmar came and besought Witig to spare his son's life, offering him a castle and an earl's rank and a noble wife; but Witig spurned his gifts, and told him that it would be an unkingly deed if he, by his multitude of men-at-arms, stayed the single combat which was turning against his son. So, after these words, they renewed the fight; and now, by a mighty blow from the good sword Mimung, even the stout helmet was cloven asunder from right to left, and the golden hair of Theodoric streamed out of the fissure. With that Hildebrand relented, and springing between the twain, begged Witig, for the sake of the brotherhood that was sworn between them, to give peace to Theodoric and take him for his comrade—"And when you two shall stand side by side there will be none in the world that can stand against you."

"Though he deserves it not," said Witig, "yet since thou askest it, and for our brotherhood's sake, I grant him his life."

Then they laid their weapons aside and clasped one another's hands, and became good friends and comrades. So they rode back to Verona, and were all merry together.

Many days lay Theodoric at Verona, for his wounds in the fight were grievous. At length he rode forth on his good steed Falke, in quest of adventures, to brighten again his honour which was tarnished by the victory of Witig. After many days he reached a certain forest which was near the castle of Drachenfels. Through that forest, as he was told, there was wont to wander a knight named Ecke, who was betrothed to the chatelaine of Drachenfels, a widowed queen with nine fair daughters. Having heard of the might of the unconquered Ecke, Theodoric, who was still somewhat weakened by his wounds, thought to pass through the forest by night and so avoid an encounter. But as luck would have it, the two knights met in the thick wood where neither could see the other, and Ecke, having called upon the unseen traveller to reveal his name, and finding that it was Theodoric, tempted him to single combat by every taunt and lure that he could think of, by sneering at him for Witig's victory and by praising his own good sword Ecke-sax, made in the same smithy as Nagelring, gold-hilted and gold-inlaid, so that when you held it downwards a serpent of gold seemed to run along the blade from the handle to the point. Neither this temptation nor yet that of the twelve pounds of ruddy gold in Ecke's girdle prevailed on Theodoric, who said again and again: "I will fight thee gladly when day dawns, but not here in the darkness, where neither of us can see his foe."

But when Ecke began to boast of the stately queen, his betrothed, and of the nine princesses who had armed him for the fight, said Theodoric: "In heaven's name I will fight thee, not for gold nor for thy wondrous sword, but for glory and for the prize of those nine fair daughters of a king." Then they struck their swords against the stones in the road, and by the light of the sparks they closed on one another.

Shield was locked in shield, the weapons clashed, the roar of their battle was like the roar of a thunderstorm, but or ever either had wounded his foe, they fell to the ground, Ecke above, Theodoric below,.

"Now, if thou wouldst save thy life," said Ecke, "thou shalt let me bind thee, and take thy armour and thy steed, and thou shalt come with me to the castle, and there will I show thee bound to the princesses who equipped me for this encounter."

"Rather will I die," said Theodoric "than be made mock of by these nine princesses and their mother, and by all who shall hereafter see or hear of me."

Then he struggled, and got his hands free, and clutched Ecke round the neck, and so they wrestled to and fro upon the turf in the dark forest. But meanwhile the good steed Falke, hearing his master in distress, bit in two the bridle by which Theodoric had fastened him to a tree, and ran to where the two knights lay struggling on the earth. Stamping with his forefeet, with all his might, upon Ecke, Falke broke his spine. Then sprang Theodoric to his feet, and drawing his sword he cut off the head of his foe. Equipping himself in Ecke's arms he rode forth from the forest at daybreak, and drew near to the castle of Drachenfels. The queen, standing on the top of her tower, and seeing a man clad in Ecke's armour approach, riding a noble war-horse, called to her daughters: "Come hither and rejoice. Ecke went forth on foot, but he rides back on a noble steed. Doubtless he has slain some knight in single combat."

Then the queen and all her daughters, dressed in their goodliest raiment, went forth to meet the conqueror. But when they came nearer and saw that the arms of Ecke were borne by an unknown stranger, they read the battle more truly. Then the queen sank to the ground in a swoon, and the nine fair princesses went back to the castle and put on robes of mourning, and told the men-at-arms to ride forth and avenge their champion. So Theodoric perceived that the princesses were not for him, and rode away from the castle.

Now, Ecke had one brother named Fasold, and this man had bound himself by a vow never to smite more than one blow at any who came against him in battle. But so doughty a champion was he that this one blow had till now been sufficient for every antagonist. When Fasold saw Theodoric come riding through the wood towards him he cried out: "Art thou not my brother Ecke?"

Theodoric: "Another am I, and not thy brother."

Fasold: "Base death-dog! thou hast stolen on my brother Ecke in his sleep and murdered him; for when he was awake thou hadst never overcome that strifeful hero."

Theodoric: "Thou liest there. He forced me, to fight for honour's sake and for the sake of his betrothed and the nine fair princesses, her daughters. But a brave man truly he was, and had I known how great a warrior I would never have ventured to match myself against him."

Then Fasold rushed at Theodoric with drawn sword, and dealt a terrible blow upon his helmet, which stunned Theodoric and stretched him senseless on the ground. Remembering his vow, Fasold then turned away and rode towards the castle.

Before long, however, Theodoric's soul returned into him, and springing on his horse he rode furiously after Fasold, and with taunting words provoked him to the fight, declaring that he was a "Nithing"[7] if he would not avenge his brother. With that Fasold turned back, and the two heroes leaping from their horses began the fight on foot. It was a long and terrible combat, but it began to turn against Fasold. He had received five grievous wounds, while Theodoric had but three, and of a slighter kind.

Perceiving, therefore, that the longer the fight lasted the more certain he was to be at last slain, and as to each man his own life is most precious, this great and valiant hero begged his life of Theodoric, and offered to become his henchman. "Peace I will have with thee," said Theodoric, "but not thy service, seeing that thou art so noble a knight, and that I have slain thy brother. On this one condition will I grant thee thy life, that thou wilt clasp my hand and swear brotherhood in arms with me, that each of us shall help the other in all time of his need as if we were born brothers, and that all men shall know us for loyal comrades."

Fasold gladly took the oath, and they mounted their horses and rode together towards Verona.

On their road they met a mighty beast which is called an elephant. Theodoric, in spite of Fasold's dissuading words, persisted in attack-

7. Coward, good-for-nothing man.

ing it, but failed, even with the good sword Ecke-sax, to reach any vital part. Then was he in great danger; nor would the help which Fasold loyally rendered have availed him much, for the huge beast was trampling him under its great forefeet; but the faithful steed Falke again broke its bridle and came to the help of its master. The fierce kicks which it gave the elephant in its side called off its attention from Theodoric, who once more getting hold of Ecke-sax, stabbed the elephant in the belly, and sprang nimbly from under it before it fell down dead.

Riding some way from thence and emerging from a wood, the two comrades saw a vast dragon flying through the air at no great distance from the ground. It had long and sharp claws, a huge and terrible head, and from its mouth protruded the head and hands of an armed and still living knight whom it had half swallowed and was attempting to carry off. The unhappy victim called on them for help, and they struck the dragon with their swords, but its hide was hard, and Fasold's sword was blunt, and only Theodoric's sword availed aught against it, "Mine is sharper," cried the captive, but it is inside the creature's mouth. Use it, if you can, for my deliverance. Then the valiant Fasold rushed up and plucked the knight's sword from out of the jaws of the dragon.

"Strike carefully," said the captive, "that I be not wounded by mine own sword, for my legs are inside the creature's mouth." Even so did they. Both Fasold and Theodoric struck deft blows and soon killed the dragon, by whose dead body the three heroes stood on the green turf. They asked the liberated knight of his name and lineage, and he turned out to be Sintram, grandson of Bertram, Duke of Venice, and cousin of good Master Hildebrand, and then on his way to Verona to visit his kinsman and to take service under Theodoric.

Eleven days and eleven nights had he been riding, and at length being weary had laid him down to rest, when that foul monster stole upon him in his sleep, and first robbing him of his shield, had then opened its mouth to swallow him up and bear him away.

Then Theodoric made himself known to Sintram, who pleaded earnestly that his faithful sword might be restored to him. Great was the joy when the heroes were made known one to another. And so Sintram became one of Theodoric's henchmen, and served him long and faithfully.

Thus passed the youth of Theodoric—

When every morning brought a noble chance.
And every chance brought out a noble knight.

Ere many years were gone King Dietmar died, having scarcely reached middle age, and Theodoric succeeded him in the kingdom. And he was the most renowned amongst princes; his fame spread wide and far over the whole world, and his name will abide and never be forgotten in all the lands of the south so long as the world shall endure. After he had reigned some years, he willed to marry, and having heard of the fame of the beautiful Princess Hilda, daughter of Arthur, king of Britain, he sent his sister's son, Herbart, to ask for the maiden's hand. King Arthur liked not that Theodoric should not have come himself to urge his suit, and he would not suffer Herbart to have speech of the princess; but Herbart, who was a goodly youth and a brave knight, pleased Arthur well, and he kept him at his court and made him his *seneschal*.

Now the Lady Hilda was so closely guarded that no stranger might see her face. She never walked abroad, except when she went to the church, and then twelve counts walked on either side holding up her girdle, and twelve monks followed after, bearing her train, and twelve great earls, in coats of mail, with helmet and sword and shield, brought up the rear, and looked terrible things on any man who should be bold enough to try to speak with her. And over her head was a canopy, in which the plumes of two great peacocks shielded her beautiful face from the rays of the sun. Thus went the Lady Hilda to the place of prayer.

Now Herbart had waited many days, and had never caught sight of the princess; but at length there was a great church festival, and she went, thus magnificently attended, to perform her devotions. But neither on the road nor yet in the church could Herbart see her face. But he had prepared two mice, one adorned with gold and one with silver, and he took out first one and then the other, and they ran to where the princess was sitting. Each time she looked up to see the mouse running, and each time he saw her beautiful face, and she saw that he beheld her, and signals passed between them. Then she sent her maid to ask him of his name and parentage, and he said: "I am Herbart, nephew of Theodoric of Verona, and I crave an interview, that I may tell mine errand to thy mistress."

When they met outside the church porch, he had only time to ask the princess to arrange that he might have longer speech of her, when a monk, one of her twelve watchers, came by and asked him how he, a

277

foreigner, could be so bold as to speak with the princess. But Herbart took the monk by the beard and shook him so violently that all his teeth rattled, and told him that he would teach him once for all how to behave to strangers.

That evening the princess asked her father at the banquet to let her have whatever she should desire, and he, for his heart was merry with wine, consented to her prayer. Then she asked that Herbart, his handsome *seneschal*, might be her servant, and King Arthur, though loath to part with him, for his honour's sake granted her request. Thereupon Herbart sent back half of the knights who had accompanied him from Verona to tell Theodoric that he had seen Hilda and spoken with her, and that she was the fairest of women. Glad at heart was Theodork when he heard these tidings.

And now Herbart had speech often with his mistress, and began to tell her of his errand and to urge his uncle's suit. But she said, "What manner of man is Theodoric of Verona?"

"Greatest of all heroes," said Herbart, "and kindest and most generous of men; and if thou wilt be his wedded wife thou shalt have no lack of gold or silver or jewels."

She said, "Canst thou draw his face upon this wall?"

"Yea," answered he, "and so that every one seeing it would say, 'That is the face of King Theodoric.'" Then he drew a great, grim face on the wall, and said: "Lady, that is he; only, God help me! he is far more terrible-looking than that."

Thereupon she thought, "God cannot be so wroth with me as to destine me for that monster." And she looked up and said, "Sir! why dost thou ask for my hand for Theodoric, of Verona, and not for thyself?"

He answered: "I was bound to fulfil the message of my lord; but if thou wilt have me, who am of the seed of kings, though I am not a king myself, gladly will I be thy husband, and neither King Arthur nor King Theodoric nor all their men shall part us twain."

So the two plighted troth to one another, Herbart and Hilda: and watching their opportunity they stole away on horseback from the castle. King Arthur sent after them thirty knights and thirty squires, with orders to slay Herbart and to bring Hilda back again; but Herbart defended himself like a hero, killing twelve knights and fourteen squires: and the rest fled back to the castle. Herbart, though sore wounded, mounted his steed and escaped with his wife to the dominions of a certain king, who received him graciously, and made him duke, and gave him broad lands. And he became a great warrior and did mighty deeds.

After this Theodoric married the eldest of the nine fair princesses of Drachenfels, for the love of whom he had fought with the strong man Ecke. The name of Theodoric's wife was Gudelinda. Two of her sisters were married to two of Theodoric's men, namely, to Fasold, and the merry rogue and stout warrior, Dietleib,[8] whose laughter-moving adventures I have here no room to chronicle. And the mother, Bolfriana, who was fairest of all the race, was wooed and won by Witig. But this marriage, which Theodoric furthered with all his power, brought ill with it in the end and the separation of tried friends. For, in order to marry Bolfriana and receive the lordship of her domains, Witig was obliged to enter Hermanric's service and become his man. And though Hermanric promoted him to great honour and made him a count, this was but a poor amends for the necessity which, as you shall soon hear, lay upon Witig, to lift up his sword against his former master.

Now, Hermanric, as has been said, was sovereign lord of Rome and of many other fair lands beside: and all kings and dukes to the south of the great mountains served him, and, as it seems, even Theodoric himself owned him as over-lord, and he was by far the greatest potentate in the south of Europe. For the emperor himself then ruled only over Bulgaria and Greece, while King Hermanric's dominions included all that lay west of the Sea of Adria.

Till this time Theodoric and his uncle, Hermanric, had been good friends. The young hero had visited the older one at Romaborg, and they had fought side by side against their enemies. But now came a disastrous change, which made Theodoric a wanderer from his home for many years; and this was all the work of that false traitor, Hermanric's chief counsellor, Sibich.[9] For Sibich's honour as a husband had been stained by his lord while he himself was absent on an embassy; but instead of avenging himself with his own right hand on the adulterous king, he planned a cruel and wide-reaching scheme of vengeance which should embrace all the kindred of the wrong-doer.

Of Hermanric's three sons he caused that the eldest should be sent on an embassy to Wilkina-land[10] demanding tribute from the king of that country, and should be slain there by an accomplice; that the

---

8. Some of these adventures remind us of the story of the kitchen-knave as told in Tennyson's *Gareth and Lynette*.

9. In the Norse Siska, sometimes Bicki.

10. Norway.

second should be sent on a like embassy to England, and sailing in a leaky ship, should be swallowed up by the waves; and that the youngest should be slain by his father in a fit of rage provoked by the slanderous accusations of Sibich. Then he set Hermanric against his nephews, the Harlungs, sons of his half-brother, Aké; and these hapless young men were besieged in their Rhine-land castle, to which Hermanric set fire, and issuing forth, sword in hand, that they might not die like rats in a hole, were captured and hung by their enraged uncle on the highest tree in their own domains.

So was all the family of Hermanric destroyed except Theodoric and his young brother Diether: and against Theodoric Sibich now began to ply his engines of calumny. He represented to Hermanric that Theodoric's kingdom had for some time been growing large, while his own had been growing smaller, and hinted that soon Theodoric would openly attack his uncle. Meanwhile, and in order to test his peaceable disposition, Hermanric, by Sibich's advice, claimed that he should pay him tribute for Amalungen-land.[11] When Theodoric refused to do this Hermanric was persuaded of the truth of Sibich's words, and declared that Theodoric also should be hanged, "for right well do both he and I know which of us is the mightier."

Witig and Heime, who were now at Hermanric's court, when they heard these wrathful words, tried in vain to abate the fury of the king and to open his eyes to Sibich's falseness; but as they availed nothing, they mounted their horses and rode with all speed to Verona. At midnight they reached the city and told Theodoric the evil tidings, that on the next day Hermanric would burst upon him with over-whelming force determined to slay him. Then Theodoric went into his great hall of audience and bade the horns blow to summon all his counsellors and men of war to a meeting there in the dead of night. He told them all the tidings that Witig had brought and asked their counsel, whether it were better to stay in Verona and die fighting—for of successful resistance to such a force there was no hope—or to bow for a while to the storm and fleeing from the home-land seek shelter at some foreign court.

Master Hildebrand advised, and all were of his opinion, that it was better to flee, and that with all speed, before morning dawned. Scarcely had Hildebrand's words been spoken, when there arose a great sound of lamentation in Verona, women and children bewailing that their husbands and fathers were about to leave them, brothers

---

11. Perhaps North Italy.

parting from brothers and friends from friends. And with all this, in the streets the neighing of horses, and the clank of arms, as the warriors, hastily aroused, prepared themselves for their midnight march.

So Theodoric, with the knights his companions, rode away from Verona, which Hermanric entered next morning with five thousand men. And Theodoric rode first to Bacharach[12] on the Rhine, where dwelt the great Margrave, Rudiger, who was his trusty friend. And from thence he rode on to Susat,[13] where was the palace of Attila, King of the Huns. And when Attila heard that Theodoric was coming, he bade his men blow the great horns, and with all his chieftains he poured forth to welcome him and do him honour. So Theodoric tarried in the palace of Attila, a cherished and trusted guest, and there he abode many years.

Now King Attila had long wars to wage with his neighbours on the north and east of Hun-land. These were three brothers, mighty princes, Osantrix, king of Wilkina-land (Norway and Sweden) whose daughter Attila had married, and Waldemai, king of Russia and Poland, and Ilias, Earl of Greece, With all Attila waged war, but longest and hardest with Waldemar. And in all these encounters Theodoric and his Amalung knights were ever foremost in the fray and last to retreat, whilst Attila and his Huns fled often early from the battlefield, leaving the Amalungs surrounded by their foes. Thus, once upon a time, Theodoric and Master Hildebrand, with five hundred men, were surrounded in a fortress in the heart of Russia: and they suffered dire famine ere King Attila, earnestly entreated, came to their rescue. And Master Hildebrand said to the good knight, Rudiger, who had been foremost in pressing on to deliver them, "I am now an hundred years old and never have I been in such sore need as this day. We had five hundred men and five hundred horses, and seven only of the horses are left which we have not killed and eaten."

In this campaign Theodoric took prisoner his namesake, Theodoric, the son of Waldemar, and handed him over into the keeping of his good host and ally, King Attila. By him the captive was at first thrown into a dreary dungeon, and no care was taken of his many wounds. But Erka, the queen of the Huns, who was a cousin of Theodoric, son

---

12. Bakalar or Bechelaren.
13. Susat is identified with Soest in Westphalia, an allocation which is doubtless due to the region in which *Wilkina Saga* was committed to writing (the neighbourhood of Münster and Bremen). The geographical conditions of the story would be better suited by Buda on the Danube, which would, of course, be nearer to historical fact.

of Waldemar, besought her husband that she might be allowed to take him out of prison and bring him to the palace and heal his wounds. "If he is healed, he will certainly escape," said Attila.

"If I may only heal him," said Erka, "I will put my life on the hazard that he shall not escape."

"Be it so," said Attila, who was going on another campaign into fat Russia: "If when I return I find that the son of Waldemar has escaped, doubt not that I will strike off thy head."

Then Attila rode forth to war, and Erica commanded that Theodoric, the son of Waldemar, should be brought into the palace, and every day she had dainty dishes set before him, and provided him with warm baths, and delighted his soul with gifts of jewels. But Theodoric of Verona, who was also sore wounded, was left under the care of an ignorant and idle nurse, and his wounds were not tended, and were like to become gangrened. So before many days were passed, the son of Waldemar was again whole, and clothed him with his coat and greaves of mail and put his shining helmet on his head, and mounted his horse and rode from the palace. Queen Erka implored him to stay, saying that her head was the pledge of his abiding; but he answered that he had been all too long already in Hun-land, and would ride forth to his own country.

Then the queen, in her terror and despair, sought Theodoric of Verona, where he lay in his ungarnished chamber with his gangrened wounds; and he, though he could not forbear to reproach her for her little kindness to him, and though his wounds made riding grievous and fighting well-nigh impossible, yet yielded to her prayers and tears, and rode forth after the son of Waldemar. Striking spurs into the good steed Falke, he rode fast and far, and came up at length with the fugitive. "Return," he cried, "for the life's sake of thy cousin, Erka; and she and I together will reconcile thee to Attila, and I will give thee silver and gold." But Waldemar's son utterly refused to return and to be reconciled with either of his enemies, and scoffed at the foul wounds of his namesake. "If thou wilt not return for silver and gold, nor to save the life of thy cousin, Erka, thou shalt stay for thine own honour's sake, for I challenge thee here to combat; and never shalt thou be called aught but a 'Nithing' if thou ridest away when challenged by one wounded man."

At these words the son of Waldemar had no choice but to stay and fight. The battle was long and desperate, and once both champions, sore weary, leaned upon their shields and rested a space, while he of

Verona in vain renewed to the son of Waldemar his offers of peace and friendship; but the combat began again with fury, and at last, with one mighty sword-stroke, Theodoric of Verona struck the right side of the neck of the other Theodoric so that his head rolled off on the left side, and the victor rode back to Susat with that trophy at his saddle-bow. Queen Erka, when her cousin's head was thrown by Theodoric at her feet, wept and bitterly lamented that so many of her kindred should lose their lives for her sake.

At length, after many days, Theodoric was healed of his wounds, and went with Attila on one more expedition into Russia, in the course of which they took the cities of Smolensko and Pultowa, and Theodoric slew King Waldemar on the battlefield.

And now had Theodoric been twenty winters in Hun-land. He had fought in many great battles, and had gained broad lands for his host-friend, Attila. His young brother, Diether, who had been brought as a babe from Verona, had grown into a goodly stripling; and the two sons of Attila, Erp and Ortwin, who had grown up with him, loved him as a brother; and Erka, their mother, loved Diether as her own son. Great, too, was the reverence shown to Theodoric, who sat at the high-seat by the side of Attila, and was honoured as his chief counsellor and friend.

But Theodoric's heart pined for his home and his lost kingdom, and one day he sought the presence of Queen Erka and poured out the longings of his soul. "Good friend, Theodoric," said she, "I will be the first to aid thee in thine endeavour. I will send with thee my two sons, Erp and Ortwin, and a thousand well-armed knights. And now will I seek Attila, my lord, and adjure him to help thee." Attila at first took it ill that Theodoric came not himself to urge his suit, but when Erka had persuaded him that it was not from pride but from modesty that he made the request through her, and when she said that she was willing to send her own sons into danger for his sake, Attila gladly yielded, and bade his trusty friend Rudiger, with a body of chosen knights, accompany Theodoric and his exiled followers back to their own land.

Then Queen Erka called her two sons to her and showed them the coats of mail and the greaves of mail, bright as silver and of hardest steel, but embellished with ruddy gold, and the helmets and the thick red shields that she had prepared for their first day of battle. "Now be brave," said she, weeping, "oh, fair sons of mine, even as your arms are strong: for great as is my longing that you return in safety to my embraces, I long yet more that all men should say that you bore yourselves as brave men and heroes in the fight." And then she armed Diether in like manner, and said:

> Dear foster-son, behold here my sons Erp and Ortwin, whom I have armed for war to help thee and Theodoric in the recovery of your kingdom. You three youths, who are now here, have loved one another so dearly that never were you in any game in which you could not be on the same side and give one another help. Now you ride forth to war for the first time: keep well together and help one another in this great game on which you are now entering.

"May God help me, dear lady," said Diether, "that I may bring back both thy sons safe and sound; but if they fall in the storm of war, I will not live to tell the tale."

Of the clang of iron and steel in all the armourers' shops at Susat, of the stillness which fell upon the shouting host when Attila, from a high tower, gave his orders to the army, of the setting forth of the gallant band, ten thousand knights with many followers, it needs not to be told at length. Enough, they crossed the mountains and entered the land that had been theirs; and Theodoric, to take no unknightly advantage of his foe, sent messengers to Rome to apprise Hermanric of his coming and challenge him to battle outside the walls of Ravenna. [14]

Hermanric, too old to go forth himself to war, gave the chief command to the false counsellor, Sibich. Under him were Reinald and Witig, both of whom had been friends and comrades of Theodoric in times past, and were most unwilling to fight against him, though thirsting for battle with any number of Huns. It was appointed, therefore, that Sibich, bearing Hermanric's banner, should fight against Theodoric and his Amalungs, Reinald against the gallant Rudiger, and Witig against the two sons of Attila. The whole army of Hermanric numbered seventeen thousand men. And now were the two armies drawn up on the opposite banks of a river, and it was the night before the battle. Master Hildebrand, desiring to learn the position of the enemy, rode some way up the stream till he found a ford by which he crossed to the other side.

---

14. I here deviate from the text of the *Wilkina-Saga*, which puts the battlefield at Grönsport on the banks of the Moselle. This is evidently due to the influence of the Münster and Bremen traditions.

It was so dark that he had almost ridden up against another knight coming in the opposite direction, before either perceived the other. Dark as it was they soon recognised one another by their voices, though they had not met for twenty years. The stranger was Reinald, who had come forth on the same errand as Hildebrand. No blows were fought; only friendly words were exchanged, with lamentations over this miserable war between the brother Amalungs, and curses on the false Sibich, whose intrigues had brought it to pass. Then the moon shone forth, and Reinald showed Hildebrand from afar the great yellow tent with three golden tufts where the traitor Sibich was sleeping; and the green tent with the silver tuft in which Witig and his Amalungs were dreaming of battle with the Huns; and the black tent, then empty of its lord, that was the tent of Reinald himself.

And Hildebrand told Reinald the ordering of the troops of Theodoric, showing him Theodoric's tent with five poles and a golden tuft, and the tent of the sons of Attila, made of red silk with nine poles and nine tufts of gold; and the green tent of Margrave Rudiger. Then the two warriors kissed each other and wished one another well through the day of battle, and so they parted. And when Reinald, returning to the camp, told whom he had met, Sibich wished to send him to slay Master Hildebrand before he returned to his friends. But Reinald would in no wise permit so unknightly a deed, saying that Sibich must first slay him and all his friends ere such a thing should befall.

When day dawned Theodoric set forward his array and bade all his trumpets blow. They rode up the stream to the ford which Hildebrand had discovered the night before, and crossed thereby. And Sibich and Witig, seeing them approach, sounded their trumpets and marshalled their men. Theodoric, seeing the false Sibich's banner waving, cried to his followers:

Forward, my men! Strike this day with all your courage and knighthood. Ye have striven often against the Russians and the Wilkina-men, and have mostly gotten the victory; but now in this strife we fight for our own land and realm, and for the deathless glory that will be ours if we win our land back again.

Then he spurred his brave old steed Falke through the thickest ranks of the enemy, raising ever and *anon* his good sword Ecke-sax and letting it fall, with every blow felling a warrior or his horse to the ground. Likewise his brave standard-bearer Wildeber, who went before him, hewed down the ranks of the foe. Against him came Walter,

Sibich's standard-bearer, who rode in hero-mood towards him, and aiming the banner-staff full against his breast, pierced him through, the staff coming out through his shoulders. But Wildeber, though wounded to the death, lopped off with his sword the end of the banner-staff, and then riding fiercely at Walter struck him on his thigh so terrible a blow that the sword cut right through the coat of mail and stuck fast in the saddle below. Then did both the standard-bearers fall from their horses and lie dead on the field side by side.

When Sibich saw his standard droop and the brave knight Walter fall, he turned his horse and fled from the field, and all his division of the army with him. Theodoric and his men rode after them fast and far, and wrought dire havoc among them, but when Theodoric was miles away from the battle-plain he was overtaken by one of his men, his horse all covered with foam, who brought him evil tidings from another part of the field.

For Witig, when he saw the flight of Sibich, not terrified but all the more enraged, had ridden fiercely towards the place where the banner of Attila's sons was waving and had struck down their standard-bearer. "Seest thou," said Ortwin to Helfric, his sworn henchman, "what evil that base dog, Witig, is doing? He has slain our brave standard-bearer; let us ride up to him and stop his deadly work." So spake Ortwin, but in the fierce fray that followed both he and his good comrade Helfric, and then his brother Erp, fell dead around Witig and his standard-bearer.

Oh! then, great was the wrath of the young Diether—who meanwhile had fought and killed the standard-bearer of Witig—when he saw both of his foster-brothers slain. Eager to avenge them, he struck oft and hard at Witig's armour. "Art thou Diether, King Theodoric's brother?" cried Witig; "for his sake I am loth to do thee any hurt. Ride away and fight with some other man."

"Since my young lords Erp and Ortwin are dead, and thou, base hound, hast slain them, I care not for my life unless I can have thine." So said Diether, and struck with all his might on Witig's helmet. The helmet, of hardest steel, resisted the blow, but the sword, glancing off, descended on the neck of Witig's war-horse, Schimming, and severed its head from its body.

"God knows," cried Witig, as he sprang to earth, "that I fight now but to save mine own life." And with that he grasped the handle of his sword Mimung with both hands and struck Diether so terrible a blow that he clove his body in twain.

These were the tidings which the breathless knight brought to Theodoric and which stayed him in his pursuit of the fugitives. "Ah! how have I sinned," said he "that so evil a day should come upon me? Here am I untouched by a wound, but my dearest brother is dead and my two young lords also. Never may I now return to Hun-land, but here will I die or avenge them." And with that he turned and set spurs to Falke and rode so swiftly that none of his men could keep up with him; and so full was he of rage and fury that a hot breath, like sparks of fire, came forth from his mouth, and no living man might dare to stand before him.

And when he reached Witig, who was riding Diether's horse, his own being slain, Witig, like all others turned to flee from that terrible countenance. "Evil dog," cried Theodoric, "if thou hast any courage stand and wait till I come up to thee and avenge the death of my brother."

"I slew him against my will." said Witig, "and because I had no other way to save my life; and if I can pay forfeit for his blood with any quantity of gold and silver, that will I gladly do." But still he fled as fast as his steed could carry him, down the course of a stream to where it poured itself into a lake, and still Theodoric rode after him. But when Theodoric hurled his spear, in that very moment Witig sank beneath the waters of the lake and the spear-shaft was driven deep into the shore, and there it may be seen to this day. But some men thought that Witig was received by a mermaid and kept hidden in her cave for many days. For his grandfather had been born long ago of this mermaid, having been begotten by Wilkinus, King of Norway.

So the battle had been won by Theodoric and his allies (for in other parts of the field the Margrave Rudiger had vanquished Reinald) yet was it a bootless victory by reason of the death of Attila's sons.

And Theodoric, riding back to the battlefield, came where his brother Diether was lying; and lamented him saying: "There liest thou, my brother Diether. This is the greatest sorrow that has befallen me, that thou art thus untimely slain." And then he came to the place where lay the young princes, with their stout coats of mail and their strong helmets, which had not been able to save them from death, and he said: "Dear young lords, this is the greatest of my sorrows that I have lost you; and how shall I now return to Susat? God knows that I would gladly have many a gaping wound, if only you might be whole again."

Then he bade Rudiger lead back the army to its king, for he would neither claim his own kingdom nor return to the palace of Susat, after he had cost Attila the lives of so many brave knights and of his own sons. So Rudiger returned to the palace, but Theodoric and Master Hildebrand dwelt in a little hut in the neighbourhood of the city of Susat.

When Rudiger stood in the presence of Attila, who asked him of the welfare of Theodoric and of the host, he made answer: "King Theodoric lives, and the Huns have been conquerors in the battle, yet have we had evil fortune, since we have lost the young lords, Erp and Ortwin."

Then Queen Erka and almost all who were in the palace-hall lifted up their voices and wept. And Rudiger told Attila how Diether and many another brave knight had fallen in the battle.

But Attila answered with steadfast soul: "It has happened now as it ever does. They fall in the fight for whom it is so appointed, and neither mail nor muscle avails them anything. My sons Erp and Ortwin and their foster-brother Diether had the best arms that could be fashioned in the smithy, yet there they all lie dead." And after a space he added: "Where is my good friend, King Theodoric?"

"He and Master Hildebrand are sitting together in a mean hut, and they have laid their arms aside and dare not come into thy presence, O King! because they have lost the young lords." Then Attila sent two knights to beg Theodoric to come into his presence, but he would not for grief and shame.

Then Queen Erka rose up weeping and went with her maidens to the cottage where Theodoric abode: and when she entered it she said: "My good friend, Theodoric! how did my sons fare in the war, and fought they as good knights ere they fell?"

But Theodoric, with mournful face, answered: "Lady! they fought as good knights and parried the blows bravely, and neither of them would part from the other."

And with that she went up to him and threw her arms round his neck and said: "Good friend! King Theodoric! come now into the palace-hall to King Attila, and take thy welcome there, and be merry once more. Often before now have the brave men for whom it was appointed, fallen in the battle; and they who live still must take thought for themselves, since it profits not to be ever bewailing the dead." So Theodoric went with the queen into the palace-hall, and Attila stood up and gave him a kiss of welcome and bade him sit beside him on the high-seat. Thus he returned to Attila's palace, where he dwelt for yet many years, and all was friendship between them as before.

Two years after this Queen Erka fell sick of a grievous disease and lay at the point of death. Sending for Theodoric, she rehearsed to him how he had ever been the best friend of her husband and herself; and as it might well happen that this sickness would sever that long friendship, she desired to give him fifteen marks of red gold in a beaker and a costly purple robe, as memorials of the same, and she prayed him to take her young kinswoman, Herauda,[15] to wife. Theodoric said: "Good lady and queen! thy sickness is doubtless a dangerous one. True friendship hast thou ever shown to me and mine; and better it were for Attila to lose the half of his kingdom than to lose thee." Thereat he wept like a child and could say no more words, but went quickly forth of the chamber.

Then Erka desired to see her dear friend, Master Hildebrand, and spake to him too of the true friendship which was now about to be severed, in remembrance whereof she gave him a ring of gold. And then sending for Attila she spake to him of her coming death.

"Thus wilt thou become a widower," said she, "but so thou wilt not long remain. Choose, therefore, a good and loving wife, for if thou choosest a wicked woman she may work much harm to thee and many others beside. Good King Attila! take no wife out of Nibelungen-land, nor from the race of Aldrian, for if thou dost, thou wilt sorely repent of it, and harm unspeakable will be wrought to thee and the children whom she may bear thee."

Soon after she had spoken these words, she gave up the ghost; and great was the lamentation in all Hun-land when they heard that the good Queen Erka was no more in life.

The warning given by the dying queen was, like most such warnings, unheeded. After three years of widowerhood, Attila sent one of his nephews into Nibelungen-land[16] to ask for the hand of Chriemhild,[17] daughter of Aldrian, loveliest and wisest of the women of her time; but maddened by secret grief for the loss of her first husband, Siegfried,[18] who had been slain by her brothers, Hagen[19] and King Gunther. The suit prospered; with strange blindness of heart, King Gunther gave his consent to the union of the sister who was his deadliest enemy with

---

15. Or Herrat.
16. Burgundy.
17. In the *Wilkina-Saga*, Grimhild.
18. In the *Wilkina-Saga*, Sigurd.
19. In the *Nibelungen-lied*, Hagen is only a kinsman; in the *Wilkina-Saga*, a brother of Gunther and Chriemhild.

the mightiest king in Europe. For seven years Chriemhild waited for her revenge; then came that invitation to the Nibelungs to visit the court of Attila, which, in the infatuation of their souls, King Gunther and his brethren accepted, taking with them a chosen band of a thousand warriors.

The scheme of vengeance prepared by Chriemhild, the quarrel which she provoked at the banquet, the terrible slaughter suffered and inflicted by the Nibelungs in the palace garden, their desperate rush into the palace-hall, the stand made therein by their ever-dwindling band on the pavement which was slippery with the gore of heroes— all this has been sung by a hundred minstrels, and need not here be repeated. We have only to do with the share Theodoric and his friends took in the fatal combat. Long the Amalungs stood utterly aloof from the fray, grieving sorely that so many of their friends on both sides were falling by one another's hands. For to the Nibelungs, as well as to Attila and the Huns, were they bound by the ties of guest-friendship, and in happier days Theodoric had ridden with Gunther and with Hagen, to test the mettle of their knights against the chivalry of Britain.

So Theodoric and his men stood on the battlement of his palace, which looked down on the garden of Attila, and watched from afar the ghastly conflict. But at length they saw the good Margrave Rudiger, the ally of the Amals on so many a hard-fought battlefield, fall by the hand of his own daughter's husband, the young prince, Giselher; and then could Theodoric bear it no longer, but cried, saying: "Now is my best friend, Margrave Rudiger, dead. Take your weapons, comrades, and let us avenge his fall." He descended into the street. He forced his way into the palace-hall. Terrible was the clang of the strong sword Ecke-sax on the helmets of the Nibelungs. Many of them fell before him, but alas! many of his faithful Amals fell there also, far from their home.

At length, in all that stately palace-hall, there remained but four men still able to deal blows, and these were Theodoric and Master Hildebrand of the Amalungs, Hagen and Giselher of their foes. And Hagen stood up to fight with Theodoric, and Giselher with Hildebrand. Then, as King Attila came from his tower to watch the combat, Hagen shouted to him: "It were a knightly deed to let young Giselher go unhurt, for he is innocent of the death of Siegfried the Swift."

"Yea, truly," said Giselher; "Chriemhild, my sister, knows that I was a little child of five years old in my mother's bed when her husband was killed. I am innocent of this blood-feud, yet care I not to live now that my brethren are slain." Therewith he closed in fight with Master Hildebrand, and soon received his death-wound from the old hero.

Now there remained but one terrible encounter, that between Hagen and Theodoric. Hagen said: "It seems that here our friendship must come to an end, great as it has ever been. Let us each fight bravely for his life, and knight-like, call on no man for aid."

Theodoric answered: "Truly, I will let none meddle in this encounter, but will fight it with warlike skill and knightliness." They fought long and hard, and exchanged grievous blows, and both were weary and both were wounded. Then Theodoric waxed exceeding wroth with himself for not overcoming his foe, and said: "Truly, this is a shame for me to stand here all the day and not to be able to vanquish the elfin's son."

"Why should the elfin's son be worse than the son of the devil himself?" answered Hagen.[20]

At that Theodoric was seized with such fury that fiery breath issued from his mouth. Hagen's coat of mail was heated red-hot by this breath of fire, and he was forced to cry out: "I give myself up. Anything to end this torture and doff my red-hot armour. If I were a fish, and not a man, I should be broiled in this burning panoply." Then Theodoric sat down and began to unbrace his adversary's armour; and while he was doing this, Queen Chriemhild came into the hall with a blazing torch, which she thrust into the mouth of one after another of the prostrate warriors, her brothers, to see if they were already dead, and to slay them if they were still living.

Beholding this, Theodoric said to Attila: "See how that devil, Chriemhild, thy wife, torments her brethren, the noble heroes. See how many brave men, Huns and Amalungs and Nibelungs, have yielded up their life for her sake. And in like fashion would she bring thee and me to death, if she had the power."

"Truly, she is a devil," answered Attila. "Do thou slay her; and it had been a good deed if thou hadst done it seven nights ago. Then would many a noble knight be still living who now is dead." And with that Theodoric sprang up and clove Chriemhild in twain.

Theodoric bore the sore-wounded Hagen to his palace and bound up his wounds; but they were mortal, and in a few days Hagen died,

---

20. The myth of Hagen's being begotten by an elfin apparition while King Aldrian was absent from his realm is mentioned in the *Wilkina-Saga* (Cap. 150), but there has been no previous allusion to the alleged demonic origin of Theodoric.

having bequeathed to the woman who nursed him the secret of the great Nibelung hoard, for the sake of which he had slain Siegfried the Swift.

In the terrible encounter there had fallen one thousand Nibelungs, being all their host, and four thousand Huns and Amalungs. No battle is more celebrated in the old German Sagas than this. But Hun-land was wasted by reason of the death of so many valiant warriors, and thus had come to pass all the evil which the good Queen Erka had foretold.

And now after thirty-two years of exile, and with so many of his brave followers dead, Theodoric's heart pined more than ever for his native land, and he said to Master Hildebrand: "I would rather die in Verona than live any longer in Hun-land." To return with an army was hopeless, so scanty a remnant was left of the Amalungs. The only hope was to steal back secretly and try if it were possible to find friends enough in the old home to win back the crown.

Master Hildebrand knew of one thing which made the outlook less desperate: "I have heard that the Duke who rules over Verona is a brave knight named Alebrand; and I cannot but think that this is my son, born of my wife, Uta, shortly after I fled hither."

So they got together four horses, two for Theodoric and Hildebrand, one for the lady, Herauda, Theodoric's wife, and one to carry their raiment and store of silver and gold; and after leave taken of Attila, who wept bitterly at Theodoric's departure, and prayed him to stay till he could fit out another army for his service, they set forth from Susat and rode westward night and day, avoiding the towns and the haunts of wayfarers.

On their road they were met by a band of two and thirty knights commanded by Earl Elsung, a kinsman of that Elsung of Verona, whom Theodoric's grandfather, Samson, had slain. The blood-feud was now old, but Elsung yearned to avenge it on Theodoric. The lady Herauda wept when she saw so many well-armed knights approaching, but Theodoric bade her be of joyous heart till she saw one of her two protectors fall, and that, he deemed, would never be. And in truth, in the fight that followed, so well did the aged Hildebrand wield the sword Gram, the wondrous sword of Siegfried the Swift, and such mighty blows dealt Theodoric with Ecke-sax, that Earl Elsung himself and sixteen of his men were left dead on the field.

The rest fled, all but a nephew of Elsung, a brave young knight. Him also Hildebrand vanquished in fight, and from him, as ransom for his life, the victors received great tidings from Amalungen-land. For he told them that Hermanric was grievously sick, and that the remedies which the false Sibich had persuaded him to resort to had left him far weaker than before, and, in short, the great Hermanric was already as good as dead.

They came next in their journey to a castle which was held by Duke Lewis and his son Conrad. To them Master Hildebrand, riding forward, made himself known, and from them he received joyous welcome. They rode back with him into the forest, where Theodoric was tarrying with the Lady Herauda, and bent the knee before him. For they had heard that Hermanric was dead, and though the false Sibich aspired to be king after him, both they and all the people in those parts chose rather to obey Theodoric, and had sent a messenger into Hun-land to pray him to return. Theodoric received Duke Lewis graciously, but would not enter into his castle, for he had sworn that Verona should be the first stronghold in Amalungen-land within whose walls he would enter.

Now of Verona the lord was (as Hildebrand had heard) his son Alebrand, born after he had left the country. He was a brave knight, and a courteous, but fiery, and when the aged Hildebrand, riding towards Verona, met him in the way, the two champions rushed at one another, and fought long and desperately. The battle ceased from the mere weariness of the fighters once and again. At every pause each knight, the old and the young, asked the other of his name, and each refused to tell his name till he had heard that of his antagonist. And this, though all the time Hildebrand more than guessed that it was his own son from whom he was receiving, and to whom he was dealing, such dreadful blows.

At length, after Hildebrand had given his opponent a great gaping wound in the thigh, he fell upon him and bore him to the earth, and then with his sword at his breast said: "Tell me thy name or thou shalt die." "I care not for life," said the other, "since so old a man has vanquished me."

"If thou wilt preserve thy life, tell me straightway if thou art my son Alebrand; if so, I am thy father, Hildebrand."

"If thou art my father Hildebrand, I am thy son Alebrand," said the younger hero. And with that they both arose, threw their arms around each other's necks, and kissed one another; and both were right glad, and they mounted their horses and rode towards Verona.

From the gates the Lady Uta, Alebrand's mother, was coming forth to meet her son; but she wept and wailed when she saw his streaming wound, and said: "Oh, my son, why art thou so sore wounded, and who is that aged man that is following thee?"

Alebrand answered: "For this wound I need have no shame, sith it was given me by my father, Hildebrand, and it is he who rides behind me."

Then was the mother overjoyed, and greeted her husband lovingly, and with great gladness they entered into the city, where Hildebrand tarried for the night, and the Lady Uta bound up the wounds of Alebrand.[21]

After this Theodoric's course was easy. He was received with joyous welcome by the citizens of his native Verona, as he rode through the streets on his faithful Falke, Master Hildebrand of the long white beard holding high his banner. Alebrand handed back to his keeping Verona and all Amalungen-land, which he had received to hold from the dead Hermanric. Theodoric sat in the high-seat of the palace; the people brought him rich presents, and all the nobles took him for their rightful lord and ruler.

The false Sibich marched against him with a larger army, thirteen thousand to Theodoric's eight thousand; but Theodoric and Hildebrand rode as they pleased through the armed throng, dealing death on every side; and Duke Alebrand, engaging Sibich in single combat, after long fight, waxed exceeding wroth, and smiting a dreadful blow, clove him through from the shoulder to the saddle-bow. Then all the Romans gave up the strife, and fell at Theodoric's feet, praying him to be their lord. So was Theodoric crowned in the city of Rome; and now he was king over all the lands which had once owned the sway of Hermanric. It needs not to tell at length of the deeds of Theodoric after he had recovered his kingdom. He caused a statue to be cast in copper of himself, seated on his good steed Falke, and this statue many pilgrims to Rome have seen.[22]

Also a statue of himself, standing on a high tower, brandishing his good sword Ecke-sax towards the north; and this statue is at Verona.

---

21. The combat between Hildebrand and Alebrand, the impetuous father and the impetuous son, too proud to let words take the place of blows, is, with some variations, a favourite theme of German minstrels. In the *Hildebrands-hed* (beginning of the 9th century) the son is named Hadubrand, and he insists on the fight because he looks upon the so-called Hildebrand as an imposter (Grimm: *Deutsche Heldensage*, 25).

22. It is suggested that this is probably the equestrian statue of Marcus Aurelius on the Capitoline Hill.

In his old age he and many of his subjects turned to the Christian faith. One of those that were baptized along with him was Master Hildebrand, who died soon after his conversion, being either one hundred and eighty or two hundred years old. Theodoric's wife, Herauda, died also about this time, a good woman and much loved of the people for all her gracious deeds, even as her cousin, Erka, had been loved by the Huns. After Herauda's death Theodoric married Isold, widow of Hertnit, King of Bergara,[23] whose husband had been slain by a terrible dragon, which Theodoric vanquished. She was fair to look upon and wise of heart.

And after these things it came to pass that old King Attila died, being enticed by Aldrian, the son of Hagen, into the cave where the great Nibelung hoard lay hidden. And when he was in the recesses of the mountain, gloating over the wondrous treasure, Aldrian passed swiftly forth and closed the doors of the cave and left him to perish of hunger in the midst of the greatest treasure that was in the world. Thus Aldrian avenged the death of his father and of all the Nibelungs. But Theodoric was made king over Hun-land by the help of his friends in that realm, and thus he became the mightiest king in the world.

Of all his old warriors only Heime was left, and Heime had buried himself in a convent, where he sang psalms every day with the monks, and did penance for his sins. Theodoric, hearing that he was there, sought him out, but long time Heime denied that he was Heime. "Much snow has fallen," said Theodoric, "on my head and on thine since our steeds drank the stream dry in Friesland. Our hair was then yellow as gold, and fell in curls over our shoulders; now is it white as a dove."

And then he plied him with one memory after another of the joyous old times of the battle and the banquet, till at length Heime confessed, and said: "Good lord Theodoric, I do remember all of which thou hast spoken, and now will I go forth with thee from this place." And with that he fetched his armour from the convent-chest, and his good old steed Rispa from the convent-stable, and once more rode gladly after his lord. After doing many more brave deeds, he fell in battle with a giant, the biggest and clumsiest of his tribe. Theodoric, riding forth alone, sought out the giant's lair, and with his good sword Ecke-sax avenged the death of his friend; and that was the last battle that the son of Dietmar fought with mortal foe.

The years of Theodoric's old age were given to the chase of the

---

23. Identified by Von der Hagen with Garda; but is it not Bulgaria?

beasts of the forest, for he was still a mighty hunter when his other strength was gone.[24]

One day as he was bathing at the place which is still called "Theodoric's Bath," (as at time of first publication), a groom called out to him: "My lord! a stag has just rushed past, the greatest and the finest that ever I saw in my life." With that Theodoric wrapped a bathing-cloak round him, and calling for his horse, prepared to set off in chase of the stag. The horse was long in coming, and meanwhile a mighty steed, coal-black, suddenly appeared before him. Theodoric sprang upon the strange charger's back, and it flew off with him as swiftly as a bird. His best groom on his best horse followed vainly behind. "My lord," cried he, "when wilt thou come back, that thou ridest so fast and far." But Theodoric knew by this time that it was no earthly steed that he was bestriding, and from which he vainly tried to unclasp his legs. "I am ill-mounted," cried he to the groom. "This must be the foul fiend on which I ride. Yet will I return, if God wills and Holy Mary." With that he vanished from his servant's sight, and since then no man has seen and no man ever will see Theodoric of Verona. Yet some German minstrels say that it has been opened to them in dreams that he has found grace at last, because in his death-ride he called on the names of God and the Virgin Mary.[25]

---

24. It is probably the following legend that is commemorated on the façade of the church of S. Zenone of Verona, where Theodoric is represented as chasing a stag and met by the Devil.

25. Another version of the *Wilkina-Saga* gives a different account of the death of Theodoric. According to this, Witig, after he sank in the lake, was received by his mermaid ancestress and borne away to Zealand. Here he abode a long time, till he heard of the return and recovered might of Theodoric. Then, fearing his resentment, he betook himself to a certain island, and having made an image of Theodoric, laid a strict charge upon the boatman who ferried passengers across that he should carry over none who was like that image. Theodoric, hearing that Witig yet lived in Denmark, went thither, and, having disfigured himself so that the boatman did not recognise him, found Witig (whose sword Mimung he had hidden away), and challenged him to single combat. The battle of the boys was thus renewed between the two snow-bearded men, and was fatal to both. Witig fell down dead by his own bedside; and Theodoric, stricken with incurable wounds, journeyed through Holstein and Saxony to Swabia. Here he went to the border of a lake, and drawing the sword Mimung out of its sheath, hurled it afar into the waters, so that it should never again come into the hands of man. He then went into a little Swabian town, and the next day died there of his wounds. He strictly forbade his servants to make mention of his name or rank, and was buried in that town as a merchant. It is needless to remark on the resemblance of one part of this story to the "Passing of Arthur."

I have thus endeavoured to bring before the reader (I hope not with undue prolixity) the chief events in the life of the mythical Theodoric of the Middle Ages. Still, as late as the sixteenth century the common people loved to talk of this mighty hero. The Bavarian *Chronicle* (translated and continued about 1580) says: "Our people sing and talk much about 'Dietrich von Bern.' You would not soon find an ancient king who is so well known to the common people amongst us, or about whom they have so much to say."[26] What they had to say was, as the reader will have observed, strangely removed from the truth of history. How all this elaborate superstructure of romance could be reared on the mere name of Theodoric of Verona is almost inconceivable to us, till we call to mind that the minstrels were in truth the novelists of the Middle Ages, not pretending or desiring to instruct, but only to amuse and interest their hearers, and to beguile the tedium of existence in dull baronial castles.

Of the thousand and one details contained in the foregoing narrative, there are not more than three or four which correspond with the life of the real Theodoric, He was, as the *Saga* says, of Amal lineage. His father's name, Theudemir, is fairly enough represented by Dietmar. He was for some years of his life (but not his middle or later life) a wanderer more or less dependent on the favour of a powerful sovereign. His life during this period did get entangled with that of another Theodoric, even as the life of the hero of *Saga* becomes entangled with the life of Theodoric of Russia. After subduing all his enemies, he did eventually rule in Rome, and erect statues to himself there and at Verona. Ravenna and Verona were the places of his most frequent residence. In his mature years, when his whole soul was set on the maintenance of *civilitas*, he might very fitly have spoken such words as he is said to have used to Witig in his boyhood, "I will establish such peace in my father's realm and mine, that it shall not be in the power of every wandering adventurer to challenge me to single combat."

Moreover, throughout all the wild vagaries of the narrative, character, that mysterious and indestructible essence, is not wholly lost. No two books can be more absolutely unlike one another than the *Wilkina-Saga* and the *Various Letters of Cassiodorus*, yet the same hot-tempered, impulsive, generous man is pourtrayed to us by both.

As for the other names introduced, they are, of course, brought in at the cost of the strangest anachronisms. The cruel uncle, Hermanric, is really a remote collateral ancestor who died nearly eighty years be-

---

26. See Grimm's *Deutsche Heldensage*, 341.

fore Theodoric was born. The generous host and ally, Attila, died two years before his birth, and the especial gladness of that birth was that it occurred at the same time with a signal victory of the Amal kings over the sons of Attila. To take an illustration from modern history, the general framework of the *Wilkina-Saga* is about as accurate as a romance would be which should represent Queen Victoria as driven from her throne by the Old Pretender, remaining for thirty years an exile at the court of Napoleon, and at length recovering her kingdom on the Old Pretender's death.[27]

But, as has been often and well pointed out, the most marvellous thing in these old German *Sagas* is the utter disappearance from them of that Roman Empire which at the cost of such giant labour the Teutonic nations had overthrown. The Roman Imperator, the Roman legions, even the Catholic priests with their pious zeal against Arianism, count for nothing in the story. Just as the knightly warriors prick to and fro on their fiery steeds to the court of Arthur of Britain, with no mention of the intervening sea, so these German bards link together the days of chivalry and the old barbarian life which Tacitus paints for us in the *Germania*, without apparently any consciousness of the momentous deed which the German warriors had in the meanwhile performed, full of significance for all succeeding generations of men, the overthrow of the Empire of Rome.

COIN OF WITIGIS
WITH HEAD OF ANASTASIUS (?).

---

27. Possibly we have in the career of Witig, the craftsman's son, successively the sworn friend and the deadly foe of Theodoric and his house, some remembrance of the life of the low-born Witigis, in his youth a valiant soldier of Theodoric, in his old age the slayer of Theodahad, and the hated husband of Amalasuentha.